Seeing Home

Seeing Home

The Ed Lucas Story

*A Blind Broadcaster's Story of Overcoming
Life's Greatest Obstacles*

Ed Lucas
& Christopher Lucas

GALLERY BOOKS

JETER PUBLISHING

New York London Toronto Sydney New Delhi

JETER PUBLISHING

 Gallery Books/Jeter Publishing
An Imprint of Simon & Schuster, Inc.
1230 Avenue of the Americas
New York, NY 10020

First Gallery Books hardcover edition April 2015

GALLERY BOOKS and colophon are registered trademarks of Simon & Schuster, Inc.

For information about special discounts for bulk purchases, please contact Simon & Schuster Special Sales at 1-866-506-1949 or business@simonandschuster.com.

The Simon & Schuster Speakers Bureau can bring authors to your live event. For more information or to book an event, contact the Simon & Schuster Speakers Bureau at 1-866-248-3049 or visit our website at www.simonspeakers.com.

Interior design by Renato Stanisic

Manufactured in the United States of America

10 9 8 7 6 5 4 3 2 1

Library of Congress Cataloging-in-Publication Data

Lucas, Ed, 1939–
  Seeing home : the Ed Lucas story : a blind broadcaster's story of overcoming life's greatest obstacles / Ed Lucas & Christopher Lucas. — First Gallery Books hardcover edition.
      pages cm
1. Lucas, Ed, 1939– 2. Broadcasters—United States—Biography. 3. Sportswriters—New York (State) —New York—Biography. I. Lucas, Christopher Patrick, 1968– II. Title.
  GV742.42.L84A3 2015
  384.54092—dc23
  [B]

                                        2014044203

ISBN 978-1-4767-8583-7
ISBN 978-1-4767-8585-1 (ebook)

In memory of my parents, Edward and Rosanna.
For my beautiful bride, Allison, who is always at my side.
For my sons, Eddie and Christopher, for their love and support,
and for my grandsons: E.J., Adam, and Sean.
They have all brought me great joy.

—ED LUCAS

For E.J., Adam, Sean, Aiden, and Talon,
so that you and your children will always know that love is what
kept our family going, through all the peaks and valleys.
To the late and beloved Mrs. "Mickey" McCahill,
who helped run the office at Saint Al's.
You always took time to compliment my writing,
to encourage me, and to boost my confidence. You also asked for
the first copy of the first book I wrote. This one's for you.

—CHRISTOPHER LUCAS

Contents

Introduction: Everyone Should Be So Lucky

April 2015 marked my sixtieth straight appearance on Opening Day at Yankee Stadium covering the team. A career that I wasn't sure would ever begin has now spanned the eras from Rizzuto to Jeter. It feels odd being one of the elder statesmen, but I'm always glad to give advice to any of the new reporters, broadcasters, or bloggers who ask, though as a guy raised on typewriters and twenty-four-hour lags between composing a story and having it appear in print, I'm still amazed by the speed at which blogs get posted.

When my grandchildren, E.J., Adam, and Sean, were studying Helen Keller and Louis Braille in school, their teachers would ask me to come by to speak to the class about life as a blind person. Inevitably, the kids would ask me a lot of questions that often got right to the heart of things.

"If there was an operation now that could help you see," one of the kids would invariably ask, "would you have it?"

To their surprise, my answer would always be, "No."

At this point, I've lived six times more of my life as a blind man than as a boy with sight. It would be too much of a shock now for me to return. The only thing I say I wish is for just five minutes of sight, five minutes so I could see my sons, Eddie and Chris, my wife, Allison, and my grandsons, all for the very first time with my own eyes.

One of the kids might also ask me this: "If you weren't blind, would you still be involved in baseball?"

Surprisingly, my answer would be no to that, too.

When I put some thought into the way my life might have turned out if I didn't get hit between the eyes with a baseball in October 1951, causing me to lose my sight, I realized that I probably would have gone into some kind of science.

Baseball was definitely my career choice at twelve years old, as it is for many kids who love sports, but then life and reality set in. Like most, I'm sure I would have eventually sought a safer, more traditional profession.

The accident actually left me frozen in time. I was scared that my life was over at twelve, and baseball became an exciting escape route out of that crippling fear. I put my full focus on that, ruling out every other option. I gave myself nothing to fall back on. Happily, it all worked out.

Though I didn't realize it then, God graced me with a wonderful gift: When He took the use of my eyes away, He allowed me to gain an even better vision of the world than I might have ever known.

When you can't see, you are only able to judge people by their character and integrity, not by the color of their skin, or by how they look and dress. What's inside a person's heart became my measuring stick. I can hear their hearts in their voices. Nobody can hide that from me.

I don't ever feel pity for myself for being struck blind. I've been given an opportunity to live a life without visual prejudices and with greater empathy for the struggles of others.

This has driven me to work harder to properly honor the Good Lord, who generously chose to bless me with such an abundance of family, friends, moments, and memories. I am determined to give back, to use those same gifts and opportunities to help others overcome any obstacles in their lives, just as I learned to do.

I will cherish these gifts forever, and I am overwhelmingly grateful to God for them.

Everyone should be so lucky.

1

No Cup or Cane

Wool uniforms are extremely uncomfortable, even in cool temperatures.

When I was twelve years old, in the spring of 1951, my mother's brother Eugene gave me the wool uniform jersey he wore when he played semipro baseball in our New Jersey hometown. I remember the pride I felt as I put on the large, heavy gray shirt with the number 4 stitched on the back, and the words "Jersey City Eagles" on the front. I almost never took it off after that.

It wasn't so bad at first, but when the warm weather came, and summer started heating up, the uniform top seemed to gain fifty extra pounds from all of the sweat my slim body was pouring into it. When school let out, a typical day would go like this: I would get up in the morning, put Uncle Eugene's jersey on, match it with whatever pants I could find, and then head out to play ball with my friends. At noon I'd stop to have lunch, try to dry the shirt out a bit, then go back out to play again until I heard my mother calling me for dinner.

Baseball was my life back then. It still is.

My mother, Rosanna, knew how much I loved the game and how much the jersey meant to me. Each night as I went to bed she would lovingly take the shirt from my room and wash it. We lived in a small apartment in a public housing project, so washing machines were not readily available. Instead, she would use an old-fashioned washboard and spend an hour scrubbing out all of the sweat and grime by hand. Then she would hang the shirt up, either inside on the shower curtain or outside on a clothesline, so that it would be ready for me the next day.

My mother did all of this even though she really didn't want me to play ball at all.

It wasn't that my mother hated baseball. She regularly listened to games with me and my father, a die-hard New York Giants fan. She was just being protective of me. I was born with a medical condition that limited my sight. Even the slightest jolt might take away my vision forever. Though I could see with the help of thick glasses, I was classified as legally blind. At twelve years of age, I wasn't concerned about such things. My parents worried that their worst fear, my losing my sight completely, could happen at any moment.

My dad, Edward Joseph Lucas, Sr., was a sports fan his whole life. As a first-generation Irish-American, he lived for Notre Dame football games on the radio in the fall. His real passion, though, was baseball. No matter what time of year it was, Dad could always be counted on to talk about his beloved Giants, at that point one of the premier teams in the National League. He fell in love with them growing up in Jersey City, because their minor league club—also called the Giants—played there. I inherited my father's passion for the game.

Dad was self-educated. He had to drop out of school after the eighth grade to help support his family. Nevertheless, he was a voracious reader, always with a Bible, dictionary, or newspaper in hand. By the time he met my mom, he was working a bunch of odd jobs, including as a waiter and a dockworker constructing battleships for the U.S. Navy on the rough Jersey City waterfront.

My mother was also first-generation Irish-American. Her maiden name was Furey. She was a high school graduate and was working as a seamstress when she met my father. Back then, most ethnic and immigrant groups kept to the same close circles in the melting pot of Jersey City, just a stone's throw from New York. Therefore, she would run into him quite often when she was out and about with her sisters and brothers. A romance blossomed, and they got married in 1938.

While they didn't live in abject poverty, conditions weren't so rosy for them in the beginning. Most people in their neighborhood couldn't afford a car, so they walked and took the bus everywhere. My parents never bought a house of their own; they always lived in apartments.

Family was the key to happiness for them. Because they were all so close to each other, both emotionally and geographically, the Lucas and Furey families were there to help each other out when needed. Thanks to God and His providence, they never lacked for any of the necessities. Laughter usually filled every gathering. It was a good life.

On January 3, 1939, I was born prematurely at the Margaret Hague Hospital in Jersey City. Today, they have all sorts of technology and medicine to help "preemies," but not back then. As a result, my eyes were weakened due to an insufficient amount of oxygen provided in the premature baby tent. So as I began my life, I had to face glaucoma and cataracts and had six eye operations to try to correct things. Luckily, Jersey City had a free public hospital built during the Depression to provide aid for families like mine who couldn't afford medical care. They did their best, but they couldn't fix my eyes.

When I was two years old, knowing that my eyes were not developing right and fearing that I would go blind, my mother made an appointment with Dr. Brophy, the best ophthalmologist in the area, without telling my father. His fee was ten dollars, a fortune for her at the time, but she paid it, knowing that I would have a chance at better care. Dr. Brophy diagnosed my problem as congenital cataracts and helped fix things to the best of his ability. He saved my sight before my third birthday came along.

My father flipped out when he discovered that my mother had lied to him about Dr. Brophy and the fee. She stood her ground and told him that her baby came first. Later in life I wondered about what seemed to be an overreaction on my father's part. Why wouldn't he also want the best for his child? As I later came to understand, he was at the beginning of a problem with severe alcoholism. The stress of married life and supporting a child was driving him to the bottle.

While my father was certainly the disciplinarian in the family, he was not a mean drunk. He never laid a hand on my mother or on anyone else; he was the kind of drinker who would drown his sorrows in whiskey and beer until he couldn't function anymore. My mother prayed for his salvation, but the tension of living with a drunk who wouldn't admit that he had a serious problem was getting to her as well. She considered ending the marriage. This all came to a head shortly after that, when my dad's boss, Mr. Riley, came to the apartment and told my mother in no uncertain terms that either Dad quit drinking, or he would be fired. She delivered the ultimatum to Dad, emphasizing her own worries and fears.

Luckily for all of us, that shocking realization brought my father back from the abyss. The possibility of losing his job and losing us was his rock bottom. He started praying and going quietly to AA meetings with my mom. They would tell family members and babysitters that they were going on "a date" for the evening.

Fifteen months after I was born, my sister Maureen came along. We moved to Marion Gardens in Jersey City, another public housing development built to assist those with meager incomes. World War II was heating up, but Dad had an exemption from service because of his two children and his age at the time. He helped on the home front by working on battleships and destroyers. To supplement his income, he also decided to take a job working as a bartender, which terrified my mother. To her, it was like letting the fox directly into the henhouse. Though my father had made a vow to her, and he was keeping up with his AA meetings, she was worried that the easy temptation of alcohol might lure him back.

But Dad's newfound deep faith ensured that would never happen.

Before the crisis, my father had been a "Christmas/Easter" churchgoer. As a wise pastor I met later in life put it, Dad was the sort of person who visits church only three times in life, when they are "hatched, matched, and dispatched."

After he hit that rock bottom, my father dedicated himself to the Church, to Jesus, to the Virgin Mary, and to his special patron and middle namesake, Saint Joseph. Prayers became an important part of his life, and of ours. Sunday services were never missed. We are Catholic, so each night we would make time to say the family Rosary, putting off any other events to pray, quietly meditate on the Gospels, and spend quality time with the Lord.

With the love, strength, and compassion of the Holy Spirit filling his heart and soul, my father was able to curb his desire to consume any more alcohol.

My father never touched another drop of alcohol for the rest of his life.

When I was about five or six, we moved to another Jersey City housing project, Lafayette Gardens. My mother insisted on the relocation because this put us in the proper district for PS 22, a school that offered special classes for children with vision problems.

There were about eight to ten children in the special vision classes, many of whom—like Gene Mehl and Margie Boasci—became lifelong friends. Our books were all written in large print. We would travel from class to class, learning alongside other students. My eyes were probably the worst of all the children, so each time my desk was placed as close to the blackboard as possible.

My sister Maureen went to Assumption Catholic School, which was near PS 22. I desperately wanted to go there, too. I wanted to be like Maureen and all of the other kids, who didn't have to worry about special books or classes.

They did try letting me attend Assumption for a bit, an

experiment that ended with almost comical results. I had to use a large magnifying glass to read the books that were part of the required religious education, which were not printed with large type like the state-funded books at PS 22. One day, I was sitting by the window, intently studying one of my textbooks with the magnifying glass held up above the book. It was a bright, sunny day. The angle was just high enough for the blazing solar rays to pour through the focused glass on to the dry paper and . . .

Well, I'm sure if you've seen enough old-time comedies, you can figure out what happened next. Thank God there was an extinguisher nearby to put out the resulting fire. Nobody was harmed, but that put an end to my days at Assumption.

We had a pretty normal family life. I never felt like an outcast or that there was something wrong with me. Along with Uncle Eugene, we had my father's other brothers, Uncle George and Uncle Chris, and his sisters, Aunt Marge, Aunt Jo, and Aunt Anne, as well as my mother's family, Aunt Gerry, Uncle Vinnie, Uncle Billy, Aunt Marian, and my godmother, Aunt Jeanne, to watch us, take care of us, and to go out with us when my parents were occupied.

We couldn't afford big family vacations, so we spent summers swimming in public pools, playing in parks, and going to movies with our cousins and extended family members, like the five Dunphy kids. Their father, who was totally blind, befriended my Aunt Jeanne and her husband, Arthur, so the Dunphys spent lots of time around us. There were no fewer than three movie theaters in my neighborhood at that time. For an exotic treat, my parents would take us to the Canton Tea Gardens in Journal Square. I always felt like we were in China or on some distant

Polynesian island while consuming the pu-pu pork platters and grilled shrimp served there.

My biggest thrills, of course, were always visits to the ballpark. My dad and other neighborhood parents would take a bunch of boys on the bus down to Roosevelt Stadium on the Hackensack River to watch the Jersey City Giants play. This happened at least once a week. My pals, Joe Walsh and Eugene Turner, were Yankee fans, but our buddy Benny Darvalics supported the Dodgers—the Giants' and Yankees' biggest rivals—so we razzed him quite often. No matter what team we rooted for, the love of baseball was our bonding ritual and common ground.

I was fortunate enough, in April 1946, to witness American history in Jersey City when Jackie Robinson made his professional baseball debut at Roosevelt Stadium, breaking the color barrier in sports and paving the way for the civil rights movement. My dad, despite his flaws, was always a fair man who gave people the benefit of the doubt. He did not make assumptions based solely on skin color. Recognizing that this would be a special moment, Dad kept me out of school that day to go to the game. I'm eternally grateful that he did.

Years later, I shared with Jackie my story of seeing him play in his first professional game. He expressed his deep appreciation for the way the fans in my hometown treated him that day. Robinson remembered the fifty-two thousand Jersey City rooters giving him a standing ovation, even though he was a member of the opposing team and actually went four for five with a home run to help beat our home team.

In 1947, I paid my first visit to Yankee Stadium. I don't remember who took us or how we got there—all I vividly recall is the explosion of color that greeted me when I entered the Cathedral of Baseball: From the bright green grass, the sepia-tinged dirt, and the green-gray of the signature copper awning framed by the clear blue skies, this was definitely a special place.

I don't remember much from my sighted life, but I remember Yankee Stadium. I knew, even then, that I wanted to spend my lifetime there.

The one image from that day that remains sharpest in my mind is that of Yankee catcher Yogi Berra crouched behind the plate with his crisp white pinstripe uniform and the number 8 stitched across its back. The number was partly obscured by the brown leather straps and buckles that kept his protective equipment strapped to his body.

That's what a Yankee looked like to me. It still is.

I've told that story to Yogi many times. Shortly after the opening of the Yogi Berra Museum on the campus of Montclair State in New Jersey in 1998, Berra took me behind the scenes of one of the exhibits to let me feel the very same equipment that I remembered from that day fifty-one years earlier. That was quite a treat.

Baseball was my passion. Even with my limited abilities, I absolutely *had* to play the game, despite my mother's worries and fears. One particular day, Wednesday, October 3, 1951, was the perfect day for a game.

I had no idea that it would alter the course of my life.

THE 1951 BASEBALL season was a wild one in the National League. While the Yankees were cruising to their customary World Series spot as the representative of the American League, the senior circuit—the National League—saw a nail-biting finish. The Brooklyn Dodgers, led by Jackie Robinson, had all but sewn up the spot at the top of the standings in late summer. At one point they led the second-place New York Giants by a margin of fourteen games. The season doesn't end in late summer, though. The Giants pulled off an incredible series of winning stands, while the Dodgers hit a slump. As a result, the teams were tied when the season ended, and they went to a three-game playoff series to decide who would go on to face the Yankees for the title.

The first two games were split between the teams. This led to a decisive showdown at the Giants' home park, the Polo Grounds, on 155th Street in Manhattan. I would have given anything to be at that game. Unfortunately, it was on a Wednesday, a school day, and they were not yet playing nighttime playoff games.

Like the rest of the Dodgers and Giants fans in school, I was on pins and needles wondering what was happening in the game, which began shortly after 1:00 p.m. The end-of-day school bell couldn't come fast enough. As soon as we were dismissed, I raced home five blocks and noisily entered the living room just as the game was reaching the last three innings. Bad news: the Giants were losing four to one.

My father, who at the time was working a night job as a pressman for the *New York Times* while my mother worked the day shift at the A&P, was sitting on his favorite chair, rosary beads in hand, praying for a miracle while he watched the game on our small black-and-white twelve-inch Philco TV. I remember snapping and cracking a piece of chewing gum as my father snarled at me to be quiet in a tone that would scare away the devil himself. This was serious business for my father. The Giants could not come this far only to lose to the hated Dodgers.

Dad's prayers were answered in the bottom of the ninth when one of my boyhood heroes, Bobby Thomson, stepped to the plate with men on base and hit a walk-off home run that catapulted the Giants to the World Series. We were watching the game on TV, the first nationally televised game, and the legendary Ernie Harwell was announcing. I don't remember at all what he said to close the game. What sticks in my head, and in most people's minds, is the frantic radio call made by Russ Hodges. In what is perhaps the most famous baseball radio moment of all time, Hodges screamed over and over again into the microphone: "The Giants win the pennant! The Giants win the pennant!"

I never heard that call live, and even if we had had the radio on, I wouldn't have heard it, as my father was doing his own screaming. He was so elated with the victory that Dad opened all of the windows and started yelling at the top of his lungs. I happened to be setting the dinner table and was so startled by Dad's cheering that I dropped the stack of dishes I was holding. They went crashing to the floor. At that moment, I could have smashed all of my parents' good china and my father wouldn't have cared. Bobby Thomson's home run had given me temporary immunity from all parental rules.

I seized upon this unique opportunity to ask Dad if it was okay to go outside and play ball. If my mother had been home, the request would have been denied even before I finished asking. My father was on a cloud of happiness. He may not have even been listening to what I said. In any case he gave me the green light. I was off and running. I quickly changed into my trusty wool uniform shirt and a pair of jeans and headed down to meet the other neighborhood boys at our local baseball spot.

Since we were living in a public housing project, the government wasn't going to spend extra money on amenities like proper baseball fields for the kids. We had to make do with what was available. In this case, we played at what was affectionately called the "skating rink." Basically, it was a run-down old fenced-in blacktop area. I wasn't quite sure whether it was a former parking lot, a storage space, or actually a place for skating. Nevertheless, it was perfect for baseball.

At this point, most of the people in the neighborhood were outside, either commiserating with each other if they were Dodgers fans, or slapping each other on the back if they were Giants rooters. The few Yankee fans around just said, "See you in the Series next week." Some older boys had a bat, and we chose sides. Most of the time, we played with a pink rubber "spaldeen" ball. The unusual name came from the way residents of the New York area pronounced the actual brand name written on the ball, "Spalding." It was the unofficial city kid's choice, because it was cheaper than a real ball.

But this day was special, and someone had brought along a major league ball for us to play with. They'd caught it in the stands at the Polo Grounds a few weeks before. For the first time in years, we'd be using the genuine article. We also didn't have the required eighteen players that the big leagues had, maybe only ten, so there were five guys on each side, with the rules decided at the beginning of the game. We were still playing baseball, but had to adapt it as the situations dictated.

We played for as long as we could. As the October sky started to get darker, some of the kids headed home and we had to make do with fewer players. This meant switching positions. I was catching, but now they wanted me to pitch. This was a great opportunity for me. Because of my glasses and limited sight, I was never asked to pitch. They didn't even have time to finish the question before I ran to the mound and grabbed the ball. The first thing I did was to take off my glasses. I laid them carefully on the ground next to me.

In retrospect, that might seem like a foolish thing to do, but it made sense to me at the time. None of my favorite big league pitchers wore glasses on the mound, and I was sure some of them had trouble seeing the catcher. If they could do it, I could, too.

As the first batter approached the plate, the excitement was building inside me. Flush with the thrill of the Giants' win and the opportunity to emulate the fireballers I'd seen on TV, I reached back and used all of the strength in me to throw a pitch right down the middle.

I was hoping for a swing and a miss, an easy strikeout and glory. What actually happened was that the batter connected perfectly with the ball, and it made a rapid approach straight back to the mound. Physics tells us that when a ball is hit, no matter how fast the pitch comes in, the velocity and force will increase as it is batted back.

It was on a crash course for my face.

I'll never know whether I would have had enough time to react if I'd kept my glasses on and the daylight on the skating rink had not been waning. Before I knew what happened, the ball smacked me right between the eyes with a force so great that it knocked me to the ground. Luckily, I never lost consciousness, but I knew immediately that I was in deep trouble.

The twilight of an October afternoon on a makeshift baseball diamond as a white horsehide sphere shattered my fragile vision was the last clear thing I ever saw.

The pain was overwhelming as I stood up. Bright flashes obscured my sight. I couldn't focus properly. I put my glasses back on and tried to act casual, but I was terrified. The other boys were concerned, and offered to help. I refused them and walked carefully back home all by myself, aided largely by memory and reflex.

I tried to avoid my parents when I got home. I didn't want to spoil my dad's joyous celebration of the Giants' victory, and definitely didn't want my mother to know that I had disobeyed her orders and played baseball. I also didn't want to admit that she was right about how dangerous it could be for me.

My mother had scheduled a routine eye exam months before for October 8, the following Monday. I'd completely forgotten that. I could fool my parents, family, and friends into thinking everything was okay, but how in the world was I going to put one over on my doctor? During the weekend, as I continued to pretend to be able to see, I came up with the perfect scheme.

The Jersey City Free Eye Clinic, where I was a patient, was made up of little examination cubicles and a big eye chart on the wall for everyone's use. The waiting room, cubicles, and exam room were all in one open area. You could hear everything that went on. While I was waiting for my turn, I listened carefully to the other patients as they recited the lines on the chart for the doctors. After about a half hour, I had the exam sequence down cold: top line, "EFPTO-ZL6EC," middle line, "FEL3CQZPD2," and so on. The smallest line on the bottom, the one nobody ever gets right? No problem, I figured it out just by listening to the mistakes and corrections. By the time I was called in, I was good to go.

As expected, I was able to breeze right through each question the doctor asked me. My answers were so on the money that even my mother was amazed at how much my vision was improving. Things were going great, I'd be out of there soon, and nobody would be the wiser. Surely the pain in my eyes would go away by itself in just a few days.

There's a problem with a foolproof plan like mine. Fools are making them.

My doctor, who had the degree and years of experience, was able to see right through my scheme. He said, "That was very good, Ed. Now let's start again. This time I'm going to put a pencil next to a random letter on the chart, and you tell me what it is."

Final score: Eye Doctor, one. Ed Lucas, zero.

As soon as it was confirmed that I couldn't make out even the largest letters on the chart, my doctor went into full crisis mode. Something was terribly wrong with my vision. I tearfully confessed what had happened. It was quickly diagnosed that the blow to my eyes had detached my retinas and caused the possibility of blood clots. I might lose my sight completely if nothing was done about it. He sent me home with drops and medicine and scheduled a major operation to possibly salvage what sight was left.

At just twelve years of age, thanks to fate, genetics, and a poor decision, I was facing a life of darkness.

The thought terrified me.

. . . .

Years before, I had been walking through New York City with my mother, father, and sister, and we came across a blind man standing outside the Port Authority Bus Terminal, on the corner of Forty-Second Street and Eighth Avenue. He wore dark sunglasses and ragged clothes. In his left hand was a tin cup, which was apparently full of coins, judging by the rattle that it emitted when he shook it. In the other hand he held a cane. In front of him was a sign saying PLEASE HELP ME. I'M BLIND.

To me, this was the only fate for a person who couldn't see, standing on a corner with a cup and a cane, helplessly begging for coins. Even the Bible was filled with stories of blind men, lepers, and cripples, alone in the streets, scorned and pitied by society.

The moment I left that eye clinic, my world started to crumble around me, and I slipped into a deep depression. Was I about to spend the rest of my life begging on a street corner?

Not if my parents had anything to say about it.

They were determined that there would be absolutely no cup or cane in my future.

2

Not a Handicap, Just an Inconvenience

There are many places that a twelve-year-old boy longs to be. Lying in a hospital bed in total darkness is not one of them.

From the time of my accident in October 1951 until late December of that year, I was in and out of the hospital. The doctors were trying everything medically available at the time to restore at least part of my vision.

Compared with today's twenty-first-century technology and treatments, the methods of the 1940s and 1950s seem practically barbaric. Their intentions were good, but the applications, and their results, could be absolutely frightening.

Dr. Brophy, my original physician, had been trying to strengthen my eyes for years, but it was not working very well. His successor, Dr. Saraydarian, was convinced that he could help bring about a miracle, something my family and friends were praying hard for.

Doctor Saraydarian was a unique and quirky guy. I can still vividly recall his trademark. He incessantly chewed gum. It struck me as an odd habit for a doctor, but at least he wasn't a dentist. His brand of choice was a bold one, Beech-Nut Gum. A spin-off from their successful chewing tobacco brand, Beech-Nut Gum came in a bright yellow wrapper that shined like gold, so I could spot it from a distance even when I had limited sight. It also had quite a powerful fragrance. I knew that Dr. Saraydarian was coming moments before he entered the room. The sweet, distinctive Beech-Nut smell and the snapping and cracking of the gum in his mouth were a dead giveaway.

My doctor's first choice of treatment was to operate on my eyes, with the hope of putting the retinas back in their proper place, assisting them in functioning again. The operation went well, but they wouldn't know whether it was a complete success until two weeks later, when the muscles and tendons had a chance to settle. The slightest jolt or movement, even a cough, could jar the retinas and undo the hours spent in the operating room. The remedy for that was to completely immobilize me, ensuring that I wouldn't unwittingly do more damage to myself.

How do you keep a young boy from moving, or from scratching his nose? The answer was to keep me strapped down, with sandbags piled high on both sides of my head, blocking me from turning in either direction. I was to be kept as still as a statue for two weeks.

For the next fourteen days, I was forced to eat my meals through a straw. All necessary bodily functions had to be done from my bed as I lay there. It was a helpless feeling, extremely boring and monotonous. I held still, hoping against hope that when it was done, I'd be able to have full vision, strong eyes, and the ability to live a normal life, like other kids my age.

Unfortunately, that was not in God's will. The operation was a failure.

The ball's hitting me between the eyes had done too much damage to be reversed by a scalpel. Dr. Saraydarian did not give up. He decided that the next best course of treatment was to fill my bloodstream with what was known as "foreign protein."

Developed in 1893, foreign protein injections were the predecessors to early versions of vaccine shots. In my case, they were hoping to use these foreign antibodies to dry up the blood in selected spots of my veins and arteries to help sweat and filter out any blood clots forming near my eyes. It was a long shot, but worth the effort, according to the medical community.

I was given these series of foreign protein shots every other day. They were extremely painful, almost unbearable. Minutes after the needle went in, my legs began to tighten up, making it hard to walk. Once again, I put up with the discomfort in the hope that it would bring a cure. As was the case with the previous operation, the injections proved to be a failure, too.

As much of a letdown as these ineffective treatments were for me, they were a thousand times worse for my parents. My mother and father both ached for a sign that I might have even a glimmer of eyesight left. It seemed like a lost cause.

In a last-ditch effort, my parents went to see Dr. Saraydarian to offer up one of their eyes as a transplant for me, so that my vision could be restored. They were each prepared to go through life with only one eye, so that I might be able to see from both of mine.

Whenever I stop to think about that for a moment, I am moved to tears. What great courage it must have taken on the part of my mother and father to make such a request. As a parent, I can now understand the unconditional love that one feels for one's children, and how one would sacrifice anything to make sure that they were safe and secure, but their act went above and beyond that.

Unfortunately, it would not have been of any use.

Doctor Saraydarian was sympathetic to their plea, but he gently explained that such a transplant was the stuff of theory in 1951. Plenty of medical journals at the time were discussing the idea, but there was no possible way to achieve it with the tools and data known then. The doctor promised to keep my parents updated as progress was made, and also to put me at the top of the list for any procedures that might become available.

With no medical solution seemingly possible, my parents continued with the only thing they were confident would help give me my former life back: prayer.

Their faith had been a comfort to them throughout their lives. My parents had seen miracles great and small. Because of this, no matter their situation or circumstances, they were always able to feel joy and to count their many blessings. Mom and Dad believed in giving thanks in prayer to the Lord. This would be the biggest request they would ever make of Him.

As Catholics, my mother and father were also used to calling on saints and angels for help.

They were not using the saints as a replacement or substitute for God, or as idols; they were relying on them as intermediaries. The belief behind this is that saints are closer to God than we are, so that if we ask them for assistance in prayer, they can presumably bring our requests to Him on our behalf. It's the same as if you asked a friend to pray for and with you. These friends just happen to be departed holy men and women. It is still His will ultimately that prevails.

Every saint has a special cause. Saint Lucy is the patron saint of the blind, so of course my parents sought her intercession on my behalf. In addition, they asked for the help of Saint Jude, Saint Rita, and Saint Anthony, all three of whom are especially known as the patron saints of impossible causes. Mine was as impossible as you could get.

My father's most passionate requests were directed to our family's patron, Saint Joseph.

As the man who protected, loved, and adopted Mary's newborn son, Jesus, teaching him his faith and the values of hard work, Saint Joseph is uniquely honored as the patron saint of fathers, workers, and families. Dad turned to him more than any other, in the hope that Saint Joseph would whisper my family's prayers for me into the ear of Jesus. They sought a miracle that would fit the Lord's will, helping me to live a productive and fruitful life.

I was finally released from the hospital a few weeks after the accident.

When I got back to daily life in the projects, it was odd at first. Doctor Saraydarian gave orders that I was not allowed to go to school. He wanted me to rest, at least until the summer. There was also the possibility that I might be called back into the hospital for follow-up operations and procedures. My routine was disrupted. I was now homebound, and my mother was being even more careful than ever.

Staying confined to a hospital bed was bad enough, but being at home all day felt like being trapped in a cage. I was in my own bed, yes, and extremely grateful for that, but I missed doing the things that most people take for granted.

My mobility was limited. I knew the layout of our apartment by heart but was still scared of tripping over something or bumping into and breaking objects as I walked around. I usually needed an escort, and that was extremely frustrating.

Telling time was another normality that disappeared with the accident. Always good at math, I was one of the first kids in the neighborhood to figure out how to decipher the numbers on a clock, and the "big hand, little hand" stuff. It became very easy. I treasured the first watch I ever wore, happily telling anyone who asked, and even some who didn't, what time it was. It made me sad to realize that from now on I would have to ask others for the time. I wouldn't be able to look at a clock or watch again to do it for myself.

Reading was also a special pleasure taken from me by my accident. The school used to provide me with oversized books. I read all of them. From Tom Sawyer to Robin Hood, I would get lost in worlds that I could only dream of. Without sight, those stories would remain the stuff of dreams. I was entirely dependent on someone reading to me. It made me quite upset.

My father knew that I missed reading the sports pages. In the New York metro area where we lived, there were dozens of morning, afternoon, and evening papers, all with award-winning sports columnists. Each morning, Dad would come home from his night shift with a stack of newspapers in hand. I knew that he must have been dead tired from his work as a pressman, but he never failed to take at least a half hour to sit there with me and read each and every article about baseball, sometimes twice for good measure. We'd sit at the kitchen table and talk about sports for another thirty minutes or so, before he went off to bed to rest for work later that night.

In an effort to keep me occupied, and from being a shut-in, my mother bought a long extension cord. She plugged our radio into it. There were no small portable radios back then, or at least ones we could afford, so this was a makeshift option. On nice weather days, Mom would run that cord out of the front window and drag the radio outside. I would sit by the porch listening to it as the world passed by.

I was never a big fan of music before the accident. Sports was more my thing. Since baseball season was over, there weren't many sporting events to listen to on the radio as I sat there, so—out of sheer necessity—I tuned in several of the local New York area music stations.

Rock and roll hadn't really made a splash yet. The pop musicians of the day were people like Perry Como, Bing Crosby, Patti Page, Kay Starr, Nat King Cole, and, of course, Frank Sinatra. The "Chairman of the Board," Sinatra, was a local boy. His hometown, Hoboken, was right next to Jersey City and there were many people in my neighborhood who knew him and his family. Years later, I would get to know them, too, but for now I was just a fan.

I loved all of the singers, but was most captivated by the teen idol of the day, Johnnie Ray. He was the Donnie Osmond, New Kids on the Block, *NSYNC, Justin Bieber, and One Direction of 1951, all wrapped up into one. Ray's two biggest songs that year were melancholy ballads called "Cry" and "The Little White Cloud That Cried." He and his band, the Four Lads, were very theatrical and gained large audiences with their swerving and swaying. A young Elvis Presley copied Ray to a certain extent. Johnnie Ray was known as "The Prince of Wails." I was a big admirer.

Luckily, despite the fears my parents had of shunning and isolation, the neighbors and their children responded to me and my situation with love, concern, and care. Our bell rang nightly as people came by to check on me, and to ask my parents if there was any way they could help.

The boys and girls I played and hung out with also made every effort to welcome me back and to act like nothing was different.

My sister Maureen, who despite being younger was extremely protective of me and was pretty tough on anyone who got in her way or mine, often walked me over to the "rink" when the other kids were playing their sandlot and pickup games. While I couldn't actually play ball with them, I was made their manager or coach during games. They let me call plays, pick teams, make substitutions, and generally stay involved. It was very therapeutic.

One of my best neighborhood friends was a boy named Louis Schuman, who also happened to be blind. I actually got to know Louis before my accident, when he was a student at PS 22. His parents owned a clothing store not far from our home. We became close buddies. Despite his disability, Louis was an amazing piano player. I was fascinated by that. Something else that captivated me was his ability to easily read Braille.

Braille is a series of raised dots on heavy paper that was devised by a young boy in France and introduced in 1839, one hundred years before I was born. It quickly became the standard method for blind people to read and write. My friend Louis was proficient at it. Whenever I held the Braille cards and books he carried and felt the funny little bumps on them, I figured it was impossible to learn unless you'd been doing it since you were little, as he had.

Louis was also a big baseball fan. We used to spend hours talking about our favorite players and teams. It really kept my mind off of things. I did have moments of depression, though, especially when Louis and the other kids were in school.

In early December, Doctor Saraydarian had some bad news for me and my parents. I was to be admitted back into the hospital for more foreign protein injections and further testing. There was no determination of how long I'd be in there. I was crushed.

My dad, God bless him, took out our enormous reel-to-reel tape recorder and continued to read all of the newspaper articles on tape so that I wouldn't miss a beat. Each day, he would deliver the messages to the hospital to keep me company while I recuperated. Mom would say a few words to me at the end of each tape. Listening to these recordings was incredibly comforting. My parents were there with me, even when they weren't.

I had a radio in my room, so that occupied me, too, but there were no 24/7 sports talk stations back then like we have today. The closest thing we had to a Chris "Mad Dog" Russo, Tony Kornheiser, Mike Francesa, or Colin Cowherd was a guy named Stan Lomax, who did a fifteen-minute sports wrap-up show each night on WOR. I couldn't wait to hear his show.

The big topic of conversation the week that I was readmitted was that the Yankees superstar center fielder, Joe DiMaggio, was retiring after a thirteen-year Hall of Fame career. It was huge news. I remember the doctors, orderlies, and nurses buzzing about it in the hallway. They were doubtful that his replacement, some fresh-faced kid from Oklahoma named Mickey Mantle, would ever be able to fill the shoes of, or live up to, the departing legend.

Years later I spoke to both DiMaggio and Mantle about their "changing of the Yankee guard." Joe said that he was mournful about having to end his career and stop playing the game he loved, but the well wishes he'd gotten from fans all over the world since that day made him feel better. Mickey told me that he was terrified that his time as a Yankee was over before it even began. In the second game of the 1951 World Series, Mantle, the right fielder that day, was chasing down a fly ball when DiMaggio called him off. Mickey slowed up and caught his spikes in a drainpipe on the field. His knee blew out and he had to be carted off the field. The damage limited his mobility from that day on. Mantle spent the rest of his stellar career in and out of surgery. Like me, he never enjoyed being in a hospital bed.

The thing that hurt the most about this December admission was the timing. Christmas was just a few weeks away, and they couldn't give me any guarantees that I'd be home before then. Going through this ordeal was bad enough, but having to spend the holidays in confinement was almost too much to bear.

Early on the morning of December 24, Doctor Saraydarian came into my room. There might have been cheerful Christmas carols playing in the background, but I tuned them out. The merriest sound I heard was my doctor saying, "Ed, you are cleared to go home." I nearly leaped out of the bed to hug him.

Since it was Christmas Eve and the hospital was understaffed, it took a while for them to get in touch with my parents to let them know they could pick me up, and to get the paperwork processed for my discharge. Late in the afternoon, I left the Jersey City Medical Center, after what was to be my last extended stay. I was happy, but couldn't go without leaving a little Christmas present behind for Dr. Saraydarian.

While I didn't have any frankincense or myrrh to give, I'm sure the good doctor appreciated my gift of gold—well, a pack of Beech-Nut Gum with its shiny golden wrappers, anyway.

I settled back in at home and opened presents with my sister. The first thing that our family did on Christmas Day was go to church to thank God for all of the blessings He had given to us and continued to give, no matter what trials we faced.

As usual, the Christmas Day service was completely packed. It was standing room only at the Church of the Assumption. Back then, before the rules were changed, there was only one way to receive communion. There was no walking up the aisle and putting your palms out for a minister to place the Host in your hands to be immediately consumed. It was a truly communal experience, with the entire congregation kneeling along a railing at the front of the church. The priest would then walk along the railing distributing communion. When he approached you, the requirement was to stick out your tongue so that the Eucharist could be placed there and you could head back to your pew to pray.

When it came time for communion, I asked my sister Maureen to walk me up and to kneel next to me. Since it was crowded and the music was loud, I wasn't able to hear the priest, or the accompanying altar boy who held a small plate under your chin to catch any crumbs that might accidentally drop, as they made their way down along the railing. To remedy this, I told my sister to give me a little nudge or tap when the pastor was close, so that I could stick my tongue out. Maureen, ever the practical joker, decided to trick me. She bumped me with her elbow while the priest was still about eighty feet away.

There I kneeled, for what seemed like an eternity, with my tongue sticking out, for God and everyone else in the church to see, until they reached me minutes later. My mouth was as dry as the Sahara by the time the sacred bread was placed in it. I was pretty steamed at Maureen, but eventually we had a good laugh about it.

A little over a week after I was released from the hospital, on January 3, 1952, I officially became a teenager.

Turning thirteen was exciting, but I was still filled with dread. I wouldn't be going back to the hospital, but I also wouldn't be regaining my sight.

That night, my Uncle Eugene stopped by to wish me a happy birthday. He brought a present with him, one that definitely topped his baseball jersey from a year before.

"Unc," as I called him, handed me a small box. As soon as I opened it, I could feel the familiar contours and shape of a watch and band. This confused me. Why would my uncle give me a watch? He knew that I loved telling time, but he surely also had to know that I wouldn't be able to see the dial. Any watches that I wore would be purely for decoration.

Sensing my puzzlement, Uncle Eugene took the watch from me. I heard him do something to it before handing it back. When I held it again, I noticed that the glass face on the watch, which was normally used to protect the hands and mechanism, was open. This was new. I'd never felt a timepiece like this before.

Uncle Eugene had given me a Braille watch.

Specially made for blind people to tell time, Braille watches are ingenious. They look identical to other watches, except that the protective crystal part can be flipped up by pressing a button on the side, allowing its wearer to feel the hands, as well as raised bumps next to the numbers. It was, and still is, a terrific innovation. I've worn a Braille watch ever since my thirteenth birthday.

Once again, time was on my side.

A Braille watch was a nice diversion. I thanked Uncle Eugene for it, but I was still a little gloomy. My dad sensed this, and came into my room to chat with me before heading off to work. "What's wrong, pal?" he said with concern. I opened up to him, shouting "I'm thirteen and my life is over!" He assured me that wasn't the case, that I had a lot going for me. I knew that he was trying his best to help, but I lashed out with the only thing I could think of to say, "I'm handicapped! I can't do anything without someone else! What am I going to do now with my life?"

I didn't mean to hurt my father. I realized that by raising my voice to him, I might have gone over the line a bit. It certainly wasn't his fault; I was just confused and scared. Despite this, Dad left in good spirits, after assuring me that with God's help, everything would be okay.

When Dad got to work, with our conversation fresh in his mind, he happened to mention to some of his coworkers that it was my birthday and how low I was feeling. These were crusty, tough Hudson County union guys, straight out of central casting. They all worked the night shift for a company called ALCO Gravure, on the Hoboken waterfront, in a drafty 130,000-square-foot warehouse. Their job, as pressmen, was to do the tedious heavy lifting and labor required to put out daily and weekend editions of papers like the *New York Times*, as well as catalogs and inserts for stores like Macy's, Sears & Roebuck, and Montgomery Ward.

As flinty as they seemed on the outside, they were all family men and big teddy bears at heart. They took up a collection for me and gave my father money to buy a special birthday gift.

The next morning, I went food shopping with my mother and sister before my dad got home. When we returned, I entered our apartment to the sounds of Kay Starr's "Wheel of Fortune" filling the tiny front room. As I listened to Ms. Starr's angelic voice singing about fate smiling on her, I noticed something. This wasn't the radio. The sound was full of scratches and hisses, not the clear music I was accustomed to coming in over the airwaves.

My father called me from a corner of the room. "Come over here, Ed, I want you to feel something." I followed the sounds of the music to him. When I got to the source, Dad took my hand and put it on an unfamiliar object. Within seconds, I recognized it as an RCA Victrola–style record player. These were very expensive machines, designed to look like pieces of furniture, where the turntable itself is seamlessly blended inside so as not to be noticed. I was stunned. I'd been hoping to get one of those for years, but there was no way we could ever afford one.

My father's coworkers had chipped in to buy me a Victrola, so that I could listen to my favorite songs and artists whenever I wanted!

Not only that, they gave him extra money to buy a stack of records. Dad told me to be very careful as he handed me the latest vinyl albums from all of my favorite singers. There were 78 rpm ones, 33⅓ ones, and even some of the fancy new 45 rpm singles, which had just been introduced two years before. Those felt very tiny in my hands.

I was ecstatic. I listened to the albums over and over again that whole day. I resolved that any extra money I earned or got as a gift from then on would go toward buying new albums, not baseball cards, which was where I'd usually spent my discretionary bucks.

My father came into my room to have a chat with me that night, just as he'd done the night before. He almost began it the same way, too: "How you doing, buddy? I hope you like the selection of records we picked out." I wanted to make up for our previous conversation, so I cheerfully told him that I loved every one of them. This was, in fact, true. He'd managed to buy almost every album I would have picked out for myself. Dad's next question caught me completely off guard. "Is the big hit guy in there, the one the girls scream about, you know, the guy that cries?" I said, "You mean Johnnie Ray? Sure, he's in here. I think he's terrific." Dad replied, "You know, one of the guys at the plant told me something interesting about Johnnie Ray last night."

Hmmm, union guys were talking about a teen pop idol? Okay, now Dad had my attention.

"Did you know that this Johnnie Ray is deaf?" Dad said, nonchalantly.

I responded with disbelief. My father went on to tell me the story of how Johnnie Ray had been in an accident at age thirteen that cost him his hearing. Noting the parallels in our stories, Dad explained that the singer had not let the inevitable depression get to him. Instead, he fought to carve out a successful career in music, despite an injury that could have ended it all.

"Yesterday you told me that your life was over because you were handicapped, that you had no idea what you would do," Dad said. "You are my son, and I know that God gave you special talents, a passion for sports, and a gift for using words and phrases that make people take notice."

I was moved by my father's pride in me, and he continued: "Johnnie Ray was given a gift for music. He could have also walked away from them like you seem to be doing with yours."

Now I felt bad, but Dad lifted me even higher: "Johnnie Ray honored God by finding a way to use his talents despite the setbacks. He never let his accident stop him. In fact, he used it to bring him to greater places. You can do that, too, Ed."

Dad's next words changed my outlook on life forever. "Never forget, son, you might be blind, but you are still alive. God has a plan for you, even without your sight. You have to trust Him and have faith in Him. Look at your blindness this way: It's not a handicap, it's an inconvenience."

That's been my credo ever since.

A FEW WEEKS later, we had an unseasonably warm early spring day. Dad took me for a walk around town while my sister was in school and my mother was at work. We stopped at our church for morning services and then just ambled from there. We saw some familiar faces along the way and got some good exercise as we chatted and bonded. At one point we found ourselves in front of the Jersey City Printing Company, a big brick building that stretched for a block.

There was a nun sitting outside the building with a basket collecting donations for charity. My father, as was his custom, went over to put a few dollars in the container. I remember the nun saying "God bless you" in a heavy Scottish accent. The events that followed were nothing short of miraculous.

As Dad and I walked in the opposite direction from the building, we were startled as the nun shouted after us, "Sir! Excuse me, sir! Can I speak to you for a moment?" At first, we thought we must have misheard her, or that she was calling for someone else.

We were the only ones around.

Once again, she yelled, "You, sir, with the boy, I'd like to speak to you, please."

For Catholics like me and my dad, the rule is pretty simple: When a nun gives you directions, you follow them. We walked over, confused and nervous about what she had to say.

"I'd like to know, sir," said the mysterious nun, as she stood to face us, "why isn't your son in school today?" My dad sheepishly replied, "This is my son, Ed. He's blind, Sister, so his doctor doesn't want him going to school." The nun's volume got louder. "I can see that he's blind, sir. That's no excuse, doctor or not, to keep him from getting a proper education!"

My dad gently protested, "But, Sister, he's blind, they don't think he's ready for school yet." The nun's tone softened as she properly introduced herself. "I'm Sister Hugh," she said in her Highlands burr, "my order runs the Holy Family School for the Blind here in

Hudson County. If you send Ed to our school, I can promise you that we will give him a good education and help him to have full confidence and independence going forward in life."

While I listened in stunned silence, the two of them spoke for a few more minutes about the details and what it would take for me to start in the fall.

Dad had been made aware of Holy Family even before my accident, but he didn't know if I was ready for enrollment. With Sister Hugh's assurance that I was, he was excited to go home to tell my mother that he'd found the perfect school environment for me.

As we walked away, my father turned to ask Sister Hugh about the one thing she had yet to mention. Exactly which order was she and the other nuns at the school members of?

"The Sisters of Saint Joseph of Peace," she replied. "We are dedicated to Saint Joseph. He is our special patron. The school is named in honor of his place as the protector of Mary and Jesus and of families everywhere."

I couldn't see my dad's face, of course, but I could tell by his grip and the happy bounce in his step that he knew his prayers for my life had been answered.

It would turn out just fine. What I had was not a handicap, it was an inconvenience.

3

Pick Up Your Oar and Start Rowing!

Dad and I rushed to tell my mother the good news about the Sisters of Saint Joseph of Peace and Holy Family School, which was just a few blocks from our home. As expected, Mom was a bit skeptical. Her initial response was, "I'll think about it."

She was just as excited at the prospect of continuing my education as my dad was, but my mother also had lingering fears. Dr. Saraydarian hadn't yet cleared me for school. My activities were still limited and restricted. Because the doctor was worried that I might do even more damage to the ligaments in my eyes, or cause deadly blood clots that could travel to other parts of my bloodstream or my brain, causing a stroke, I was not allowed to lower my head for any reason. Something as simple as a haircut became an ordeal. Not bending my head made it difficult for my barber to get to the hair in the back and at the nape of my neck to give me a proper, clean cut. Sounds minor, I know, compared to more serious problems, but when you are thirteen and don't want to be even more out of fashion with your fellow teens than you already are, that's a very big deal. The restrictions also kept me from doing other fun things that might expose me to sudden bumps or jolts, like riding on a bike, or using playground equipment.

My father suggested a visit to the doctor's office to discuss the plans for enrolling me in a new school, so off we went. Fortunately, Dr. Saraydarian determined that enough time had passed since my accident and that I could resume many normal activities, including going to school.

I was elated.

The first order of business, according to my mother, was to take a tour of Holy Family. While she was pleased that the school was run by a religious order, free of charge for students, and supported financially by parishes, churchgoers, and donations from the community, she still needed to see the place in person.

Just a few weeks after our fateful meeting with Sister Hugh, my parents and I got an escorted visit of the school. The building itself was an imposing six-story-high brick structure in the Jersey City heights, perched on a cliff overlooking the Journal Square train yards. My father told me that it also had an amazing view of the Statue of Liberty and New York Harbor. It sat adjacent to a home for blind senior citizens, run by the same order of nuns. Sister Hugh actually worked there.

Our tour was personally conducted by Sister Gregory, the principal of the school. She acted as the mother superior for the nuns who lived and taught there. Though she seemed to be a naturally stern woman, Sister Gregory did have a softer side, which came through as she patiently addressed all of my mother's concerns.

Since Holy Family was essentially a boarding school, and I'd have to stay there from Sunday night until Friday afternoon each week, my mom was worried. I'd never been away from home or from my parents for any length of time. She feared that I wouldn't be able to handle myself, and questioned Sister Gregory about how I could possibly learn independent living skills in a school populated almost exclusively with other blind children.

These were normal fears, but they were fueled even more by the reaction of my mother's and father's families when they heard that my parents were considering enrolling me at a boarding school for the blind. My aunts and uncles couldn't quite understand that I needed to be taught new learning and living methods in an environment created to help me succeed. To them, I was just being institutionalized and cast aside by my parents. It took a while before they realized and accepted that my parents had my best interests at heart, and that Holy Family was the ideal place for me.

Before even setting foot on the second floor, my mother had made up her mind and was all for letting me enroll. What moved her most was not anything that Sister Gregory said or did, or the fact that the building seemed to be spotless from top to bottom, though those things were helpful. It was the sight of one of the nuns, Sister Rose Magdalene, lying down on the floor with a small blind girl, gently playing with dolls and singing the alphabet song together.

Today, many nuns have stopped wearing the traditional habits, so it's not unusual to see them roll up their sleeves and get dirty in service of their causes. Back in 1952, however, it was shocking for my mother to see a nun in full habit and dress (think *The Sound of Music*) lying on the floor, whether it was clean or not.

The sight of this nun humbling herself by getting down to the level of a blind child, in order to make a connection and to help that child learn, was startling, yet heartwarming. It showed my mother and father just how much the sisters of Saint Joseph of Peace cared, that they weren't just there to babysit blind children, they genuinely wanted students like me to succeed and to live out our dreams and to reach our goals and be productive.

My parents both felt that God had directed us to just the right place and to just the right teachers.

I was to be enrolled for the school year beginning in September 1952, just a few months away. I also took an academic evaluation test after the tour was done. It was determined by Sister Gregory that I would be taking classes on a seventh- and eighth-grade level. Just before we left, Sister Gregory suggested that my parents register me with the New Jersey Commission for the Blind to help me prepare for life at the school, as the commission offered several free programs and services for blind children, including a summer camp.

I was thrilled to be going back to school in the fall after almost a year away, but—like every other kid—I wanted to enjoy the summer first. For a city boy like me, that usually consisted of lazy days spent on sweltering asphalt streets with the occasional spray from open fire hydrants to cool us off.

Thanks to the New Jersey Commission for the Blind, however, I'd be spending the few months before I entered the school for the blind having fun in the country.

Camp Marcella, originally known as the New Jersey Camp for Blind Children, was opened in 1947 and covered two hundred acres in Rockaway, New Jersey, roughly twenty-five miles north of Jersey City. It was just like every other summer camp in the United States, except that it was designed specifically with blind children in mind.

Thanks to the New Jersey Commission for the Blind, and the generosity of the public, and service organizations like the Lions Club, Camp Marcella was absolutely free, and provided an opportunity for blind children to experience the same rite of passage that thousands of others have, the summer sleepaway camp.

I arrived in Rockaway in July 1952 for an eight-week stay. This was the very first time that my parents had loosened the reins a bit and allowed me to explore or to be independent. I was both frightened and thrilled at the same time. As I settled in and unpacked my bags in the wood cabin, it was a bit overwhelming. I became lost in the smell of clean, fresh country air, and the sounds of the crickets and wildlife, such as I'd never experienced before.

Luckily, there was some familiarity there, too. My Jersey City pal Louis Schuman was one of my fellow campers, so I wasn't completely alone. I was also introduced on that first day to my bunkmate for the summer, a guy my age named Eddie Reis, who was both blind and deaf.

Eddie was a student at Perkins School for the Blind in Watertown, Massachusetts, the same school that graduated Helen Keller. People communicated with Eddie in the same way they did with Helen Keller, by writing words in the palm of his hand. It was difficult for me to do at first, but once I got the hang of it, we became inseparable. Eddie never let his disabilities get in his way. He was an accomplished wrestler and in great physical shape. Like me, he also had a passion for baseball, especially for the New York Giants and Yankees, so we bonded over that. We even got to play some real live baseball games.

Camp Marcella had a baseball diamond set up in the open area between cabins with markers for blind children to feel where the bases and lines were. They used a special ball with a bell inside to make batting and pitching easier for the campers. Eddie and I organized a league that would play at night, after dinner. We didn't need lights, of course. I helped Eddie at bat, and he, in turn, gave me pointers on pitching. The other campers relished this chance to play baseball without restrictions. The counselors had a blast watching our games and cheering us on.

There was a cook at camp named Oda Hardy. She was a wonderful woman. Everybody loved Oda, and she loved baseball, so Eddie and I named her the commissioner of our league. Oda was a die-hard Dodgers fan, but we didn't hold that against her. She never missed one of our games, and allowed me and Eddie to sneak into the kitchen during the day to listen to ballgames on her transistor radio. I would "call" the game for Eddie by writing the play by play out in his palm.

It was great to be playing baseball again, but I knew that I probably wouldn't be able to do so when I got back home, without the luxury of a special ball or diamond. I still had a desire to be involved in baseball for a living. Calling the games for Eddie gave me the idea of being a broadcaster like my heroes, Russ Hodges, Ernie Harwell, Red Barber, and Mel Allen, but that dream seemed impossible, since I didn't know Braille and couldn't get around on my own.

Since my parents didn't own a car and couldn't drive, Uncle Eugene and his wife, Jeannie, volunteered to bring them up to the camp on the visitors' weekends. It was a real treat. They were delighted watching me having fun again as I played with my newfound friends, but my father almost had a heart attack when he saw me run off a diving board and take a giant leap into the camp's lake.

It wasn't so much my jump that bothered Dad; it was my landing in the water. He wasn't that confident in my swimming ability. A few years earlier, there was an incident in a similar lake where I almost drowned. We'd all gone to a big Lucas/Furey family picnic at an upstate resort not too far from the camp. I was fooling around in the water with my sister Maureen. We were tossing each other back and forth when I slipped and became disoriented. When I came back up to the surface, I tried to focus on the shore. Unfortunately, I wasn't wearing my glasses. Using my limited sight, I thought that I spotted my parents and began swimming toward them. It turned out that I was going in the opposite direction. Within seconds I found myself in water deeper than I'd ever been in before. Panic set in and I went under, heading for the bottom. Luckily, there was a lifeguard nearby who saw my situation and rescued me.

I wasn't allowed to go swimming much after that.

The lake at camp was roped off and the counselors were carefully monitoring us, so there was no danger of slipping out to deeper water. This gave me the confidence to become a stronger swimmer, and I never missed a day in the lake. That put my parents at ease.

The summer at Camp Marcella was a great experience, and a natural bridge from my life of being confined to my house to the independence and mobility challenges that lay ahead as I prepared to enter my new school.

Despite the fact that I'd spent the whole summer on my own at camp, there were plenty of tears when my parents dropped me off at Holy Family that first Sunday night. They were wiped away quickly as Sister Gregory introduced me to what would be my home for the next two years.

The boys' dormitory, where I lived, was on the fourth floor. There were girls at the school, too, but their dorms were on the level below us. Each floor in the school had a specific purpose. The ground floor had an auditorium and the main entrance. There were classrooms on the second level, as well as a TV room that doubled as our typing room. In addition to beds for the girls, the third floor had classrooms for the younger children. The radio and game room was on the fourth floor with our beds (twelve bunks in all), and our dining room and gym was a level above that. There was a fenced-in playground on the roof, which was a great way to spend recess and free time on nice weather days. We even had an indoor swimming pool in the basement.

A bedroom on each floor was reserved for the nuns who lived and taught at the school, and they kept watch on us 24/7. In addition to Sister Gregory and Sister Rose Magdalene (the nun who impressed my mother by getting on the floor) there was Sister Rafael, who was extremely hard of hearing, Sister Thomas Ann, who never said a bad word to or about anyone, Sister Madeline, who was barely out of her teens herself, and Sister Fabian, who was from Ireland and had a brogue as thick as they come.

The nun who made the biggest impression on me, however, was

also the one who would go on to become one of the guiding lights in my life: Sister Anthony Marie.

MY FIRST ENCOUNTER with Sister Anthony Marie was a memorable one. It was my first night at Holy Family and I was given some free time to explore and to get my bearings. I immediately headed over to the staircase to make my way down from the dormitory floor to the main level. As I walked down the stairs, I stretched my right hand out to feel the wall, which was my habit, so that I'd know where I was going. I barely had time to move a step or two down when my hand was swatted away from the wall.

I was shocked by the sudden correction, but before I could even ask who had done that to me, I heard a small yet powerful voice bellow: "Eddie Lucas, this is Sister Anthony Marie. What are you doing?" Still stunned, I managed to blurt out, "Sister, I'm just feeling the walls so that I'll know where I'm going." Her response was crisp. "At this school, we don't put our hands out to feel the walls. We keep them by our sides." I protested immediately, "Sister, I'm blind, and I'm new here. If I don't put my hands out, I won't be able to figure out where I'm going!"

Her answer seemed harsh to me at the time, but now I can see that it was filled with volumes of wisdom. "Isn't that a shame, Mr. Lucas?" she said in a commanding tone. "You're not the only disabled person in the world. All of us have challenges to overcome in life, and places to go. We are all in the same boat together. I suggest that you pick up your oar and start rowing!"

. . . .

EACH MORNING, A different nun would come into our dorm at 5:00 a.m. to wake us up. We washed and got dressed, then formed a line for inspection. While we didn't have official uniforms like other parochial schools, the boys were all required to wear a clean shirt, jacket, and tie every day. All twelve of us had individual lockers, and the nuns taught us a system of organizing our clothes so that we would know which ones matched and which didn't. With a little assistance from the sisters in the beginning, we would hang up and separate the outfits by color, and then coordinate appropriately. It's a method I still use to this day.

Once we passed inspection, we would meet up with the girls and head next door to a small chapel in the home for the blind for morning church services before eating breakfast and starting classes at 8:00 a.m. Sister Gregory taught the seventh- and eighth-grade students, so I was with her all day. She covered every subject, from geography (we had a special globe that featured raised areas to indicate boundaries between countries and natural features) to typing (we actually learned on classic Underwood typewriters using the "QWERTY" system).

Those typing lessons proved helpful to me years later, and I became surprisingly proficient at it.

In math class, we were asked to use a strange board with holes and pegs designed to be a counting system for the blind. It's hard to describe it, other than to say it was close to the weirdest abacus you'll ever see. I never quite got the hang of that one, but I was good enough at math that I could just do the calculations and work out the problems easily in my head.

Sister Gregory saw that I wasn't using the peg board, yet was still acing all of my exams, so she became suspicious. "Eddie Lucas, are you cheating and copying off of others?" she asked. "Sister," I replied impertinently, "how could I copy from the person next to me? It's not like I can peek at their papers or anything."

Her curiosity grew as she continued to question me. "Then how in the world are you getting all of these answers right, Eddie?" When I explained that I was really good at math, Sister Gregory challenged me to stand up in front of the room as she rapidly fired off question after question. From multiplication to division, fractions, and beyond, I was able to answer them all without stumbling. It worked. I never used that crazy peg board again.

One subject that Sister Gregory definitely spent extra time on with me was Braille.

Since my accident occurred a little bit later into my childhood, I wasn't as skilled at Braille as some of my classmates, who had been exposed to it since preschool. I always thought that learning Braille would be a difficult task given my age, until I discovered that its namesake and inventor, the young French boy Louis Braille, devised and learned his new system at just about the same age. The ironic part is that Louis Braille was accidentally blinded when he was struck in the eyes with an awl, the very same tool that he used to create his system of raised dots on heavy paper.

If he could do it, so could I. Sister Gregory assured me that I was up to the task.

I began simply, by punching out easy words like "cat," "dog," and "ball" on paper using a specially designed awl and stylus, until I became more comfortable with the system and its vocabulary. To save time, and paper, words weren't always spelled out completely. You could even say that my friends and I were sending our versions of abbreviated text messages like "LOL," "BTW," and "TTYL" long before today's teenagers caught on to it.

Each day, Sister Gregory gave me Braille homework. I got stronger at it, able to put together and read whole sentences. It was almost like a new language. Time and constant exposure to Braille as well as immersion in it gave me the ability to advance. I got so strong, in fact, that it was sometimes used in my discipline at the school.

The nuns were kind, but knew how to correct us firmly but lovingly when necessary, and they were pretty clever about it. They often did it in ways that aided our education. I found this out when I misbehaved in front of good old Sister Anthony Marie.

I wasn't reaching out to feel the walls anymore; I'd grown too comfortable and confident for that. This time, it was the opposite action that got me in trouble. I was racing up the stairs at top speed without a care when I heard Sister Anthony Marie's familiar voice call out: "Eddie Lucas, are we supposed to be running up and down the stairs in this school?" "No, Sister," I replied sheepishly. "Then you know that you were breaking the rules. For your punishment, I want you to write I WILL NOT RUN UP AND DOWN THE STAIRS five hundred times in Braille. Have it to me by tomorrow morning."

Facing an assignment like that is bad enough when you are sighted and are writing it out by hand, but when you have to meticulously punch those words out over and over again with a tiny awl, well, let's just say that I didn't get much sleep that night.

Dormitory life was fun. We had an interesting mix of students at Holy Family, every race, religion, and creed, not all of whom were from New Jersey. Rafael Redding, who was enrolled in the seventh- and eighth-grade classes with me, was from Mexico City. Like my friend Louis Schuman, Rafael was a great piano player. He also played the violin. Rafael spoke English, but we had students from Guatemala and Mexico who had to learn the language. Other kids at the school hailed from New York, the South, and the Midwest. The most interesting story was that of Billy Joe Carter, who'd been left on the steps of Holy Family as a baby. The Sisters of Saint Joseph of Peace raised him, and our dorm was the only home he'd ever known.

Billy Joe and the boys from far away had to live in the school for the entire week, but I was fortunate enough to be able to go home on Friday afternoon to be with my family for the weekend. My father was usually the one who came to pick me up on Fridays, and it was generally an easy process. It was on one of these afternoons that Sister Rose Magdalene taught Dad and me a lesson we'd never forget.

There happened to be a big snowstorm on this particular January Friday, so my father brought along a pair of galoshes to make it a bit easier on me as we walked home. Snow is like fog to the blind. It covers and erases all natural landmarks, like curbs and steps, making it extremely difficult to get bearings. Dad saw how I was struggling to figure out the buckles on the boots, so he kneeled down to help, when—out of nowhere—Sister Rose Magdalene raced over and demanded to know what my father was doing. Dad cheerily replied, "Oh, good afternoon, Sister. I'm not sure if you've seen the weather, but there's a lot of snow outside, so I'm putting these boots on Eddie." She was having none of that. "Mister Lucas, your son is just blind; he's not handicapped. He can put these boots on all by himself, and when he does, you can both leave."

An hour and a half later, we left.

I DIDN'T GO home every weekend. There were occasional special events where the nuns asked us to stay over for field trips and parties.

Generally, our daily entertainment at the school was limited to the television room on the second floor or listening to the radio on the fourth floor after our classes were over at three in the afternoon and we had our daily snack. Some nights the older kids were invited next door to the home for the blind to watch a movie with the residents or to see an entertainer or celebrity who dropped by to visit. But the weekend excursions were something different.

Groups like the Lions Club and the Holy Name Society would sponsor trips for us to visit places like Palisades Park, the popular theme park that sat on the New Jersey Palisades cliffs on the Hudson River, which overlooked New York City. The tiny amusement area was later immortalized in a 1962 rock and roll song called "Palisades Park," by Freddy "Boom Boom" Cannon.

Many of us had never been to an amusement park like this before. It was quite a thrill to be able to ride the carousel, Ferris wheel, and roller coaster without a care, just like all of the other kids. It was the perfect way to relax, and it seemed like the sisters were having just as much fun as we were. There was one ride that I wasn't particularly fond of, however.

The Hurricane ride was set up like a series of bobsleds all connected in a row. It spun round and round at various speeds and sometimes even backward. I wasn't a fan of spinning, but Rafael and the other boys convinced me to go on with them. The ride was disorienting enough, but what made the experience even worse for me was the ride operator, who kept shouting into the microphone, "One more time and even faster for all the kids from the school for the blind!"

My stomach still hasn't recovered.

One of the biggest supporters of Holy Family was a fellow named Charlie Summers. He was a vice president with the Port Authority of New York and New Jersey, which controlled the airports. Mr. Summers was close friends with the legendary World War I flying ace Captain Eddie Rickenbacker, who owned Eastern Airlines. Summers spoke to Rickenbacker about the school and, in a wonderful act of generosity, the world-famous captain arranged a special flight in one of his planes for all of the students and the nuns.

Many of us had never been on an airplane before, and some wouldn't ever be again. This was a rare chance for us to experience the feeling of liftoff and soaring thousands of feet in the air. The plane left Newark Airport and circled the skies of New York, New Jersey, and Pennsylvania for an hour as the crew described what we were flying over. Unlike the Hurricane, this was one ride that I did want to experience again and again.

Perhaps the most special trip for me in the two years I was at Holy Family was an overnight camping trip with the Scouts. The reason it meant so much was that I was the one who brought scouting to the school for the first time. Before my accident, I'd been active in the Cub Scouts and really enjoyed it. I missed that feeling, so I made inquiries with my old scoutmasters, Joe Flanagan and Arthur Whalen. They got the approval for me to establish Scout Troop Number 78, the first troop for blind children in the state of New Jersey. It got a lot of attention, and even made the newspapers.

As an added bonus, the article was read by my old friend Louis Schuman's father. Mr. Schuman got in touch with me and asked if Louis could join our troop even though he didn't go to Holy Family. Sister Gregory agreed, and Louis became a member of Troop 78. His dad was thrilled when Louis got to march in a big parade with us, something he thought his boy would never be able to do.

We got a lot of cheers from the people of Jersey City when we marched through the streets in the parade, but that wasn't surprising. The community always showed a lot of support for the Sisters of Saint Joseph of Peace and for Holy Family. My mother talked about the school with everyone she met. Duke Reagan, whose daughter worked with Mom at the A&P, was especially interested. Mr. Reagan offered to go around to all of the saloons, restaurants, and pubs in the twelve towns in Hudson County and put collection boxes for the school in them.

Once a month, on a Saturday when I was home from school, I would visit each and every one of these locations with Mr. Reagan and my mom to pick up the boxes full of money. Not only was it a way to gain exposure and raise thousands of dollars for my school, it was also a way for me to get to know people and places in the New York metro area, well beyond the few blocks I was used to traveling at the time.

This familiarity would come in handy later on in my life.

In June 1954, my time at Holy Family School for the Blind was drawing to a close. I'd completed all of the required seventh- and eighth-grade courses and was ready to enter high school. My initial choice was Saint Peter's Preparatory in downtown Jersey City, which is still one of the most prestigious private schools in the United States. I aced the entrance exam and would have had no problem with the academic levels required.

Sister Gregory was proud of me for being capable enough to make the cut at Saint Peter's, but was still worried about my mastery of Braille. Two years of working hard at it had made me more confident and fluent than I was before I got to Holy Family, but not quite to the point where I'd be able to enter classes and keep up with sighted students. For my own good, Sister suggested that my parents enroll me at the New York Institute for the Blind in the Bronx, which was the best high school in the area designed for nonsighted students. I was disappointed at not being able to attend St. Peter's but understood the reasoning.

There was still one last big milestone to go: graduation.

My graduating class was small, just me and Rafael, but the nuns made a big deal out of our final day. In addition to the traditional cap and gown, we marched down the aisle to Sir Edward Elgar's "Pomp and Circumstance" and even had a choir made up of our fellow students. Rafael's parents couldn't come from Mexico, so my mother and father stood in for them. Diplomas were given to us, both in print and in Braille. Sister Gregory and the rest of the nuns included a pair of rosary beads, a Braille Bible, and other small gifts as a nice surprise. It was quite a day.

As it came to a close and we were getting ready to leave, my parents stood outside chatting with the local pastor, who had come over for the ceremony. I started making my way down the stairs one last time, when I felt compelled to do something.

I couldn't exit without touching the building that had been my home, as a way of saying good-bye. Call it sentimental or superstitious, but I just had to reach out and feel it, so that I'd have that sense memory forever. The moment my fingers glanced the wall, I heard the footsteps of Sister Anthony Marie right behind me.

I was embarrassed. I immediately turned around to offer my apologies for breaking the rule that she had given me on my very first day, when Sister Anthony Marie interrupted me, quietly saying "Don't worry about that, Eddie." I could hear her voice breaking as she continued, "We're going to miss you around here, young man. You are very special indeed."

I started crying. As she put her hand on my shoulder, she said, "From now on, don't worry about walls. If you have any in front of you, just knock them down. Whatever you want to do or accomplish, you can, Eddie Lucas, don't let anyone or anything ever stand in your way!"

I was stunned by her kindness, and mumbled a thank-you. She gave me a quick hug and said, "God bless you, Eddie, please don't forget us."

With that, she was off to attend to the other students, and I made my way to my parents.

Thanks to the dedication, kindness, patience, persistence, generosity, and—yes—even tough love of Sister Anthony Marie, Sister Gregory, and all of the other teachers at Holy Family, I was ready to move on to a life less scary than I'd imagined just a few years before, and to a dream that now seemed quite possible to reach.

4

Baseball Took My Sight and Gave Me My Life

Just after my accident, as I recovered from the surgery in my hospital bed, my mother sat next to me listening to the 1951 World Series on the radio, when a thought struck her.

I was still very depressed, which caused me to zone in and out on the play by play. My mother noticed, however, that I perked up whenever my favorite Giants players like Bobby Thomson, Willie Mays, Alvin Dark, or Monte Irvin came to bat. The gloom that hovered over me when I thought about my future as a blind person seemed to lift when baseball was the focus. The nurses told my mother that it was a shame that the games couldn't last all year.

My mother agreed, and then she was inspired.

If the players could no longer come to me, via radio or television, since the season was ending, why not bring me to the players? Mom started a letter-writing campaign to the stars, coaches, and broadcasters from all three local New York baseball clubs, the Yankees,

Dodgers, and Giants. She would tell them about my accident, explain how passionate I was about the game, and ask if they could somehow find time to meet with me, perhaps to offer a few words of encouragement.

Mom was a habitual letter writer. Her penmanship was impeccable, the result of years of Palmer Method training in grammar school and high school. I'd often find her on quiet mornings sitting at the kitchen table practicing the loops and swirls required for cursive writing as she sipped her coffee. My mother understood the power that letters can hold, especially notes written from the heart. Many of our family members still have letters from her that they've kept and cherished.

I had no idea that she was writing these letters to the ballplayers, nor did my father, so it was a great surprise when we began hearing back from some of my idols.

The first was Giants broadcaster Ernie Harwell. Later known for his forty-year Hall of Fame announcing stint with the Detroit Tigers, Harwell began his career in New York. His was the voice I imitated as a boy when I narrated sandlot games for my friends. Within days of receiving Mom's letter, Harwell was on the phone with her. Since the baseball season was over, he would be heading home to Georgia for the winter, but made arrangements for my mother to bring me to the broadcast booth during the 1952 season to sit in on a game with him.

Shortly after that exciting call, Mom got a letter from the Brooklyn Dodgers. They extended a very gracious invitation for me and my family to come to their home park, Ebbets Field, in the spring to be the personal guests of Happy Felton, the popular host of the Dodgers pregame show called *The Knot Hole Gang*.

Even though I was a Giants fan, I loved tuning into WOR, Channel 9 on TV, to watch the Dodgers pregame with Happy Felton. The format was simple. Three youngsters from the New York/New Jersey area would be chosen by Felton for each game and they would be given a mock tryout for the team. A Dodger player would be their instructor, selecting a winner at the conclusion of each of the live half-hour telecasts. The lucky kid would get a certificate, a signed Dodger cap, and box seats to a future game. Because of my disability, I couldn't be one of the three contestants on *The Knot Hole Gang*, but the Dodgers wanted me to spend time with Felton and the players anyway.

But the most amazing reply came from Giants manager Leo Durocher. Known to many as "Leo the Lip," Durocher had a fiery temper and was considered a gruff hothead by players, fans, and reporters alike. Underneath all of that bluster, though, Leo Durocher had quite a heart of gold. Leo's volcanic personality stemmed from his intense love for and devotion to the game of baseball. It helped to drive him to great heights. After reading my mother's letter, Leo sensed that same kind of passion in me.

Like Ernie Harwell, Durocher was away from New York for the winter, but he invited my mother to bring me as his personal guest to the Polo Grounds sometime during the 1952 season. Imagine that! The personal guest of Mr. Leo Durocher!

Mom was excited to plan these surprise excursions to the ballpark for the following year, but was even more eager to have me talk to a ballplayer as soon as possible, and it was the New York Yankees who helped her out with that.

IN RESPONSE TO her letter, the reigning World Series champions let my mother know that several of their star players would be staying in the New York area during the off-season and could be found working as celebrity greeters at American Clothing Shop in Newark, New Jersey, just a few miles from our home.

In 1951, baseball players, even superstars who had just won the World Series, did not make nearly as much money as they do today. As a result, many had to take second jobs in the winter to make ends meet. The owner of American Clothing Shop was very clever. He realized that if he hired famous players to be greeters for his store, fans would flock to his business and profits would triple, which they did.

Can you imagine someone like the Angels' Mike Trout or the Dodgers' Clayton Kershaw working during the off-season as, say, Wal-Mart greeters today?

When my mother discovered that Yankee shortstop and MVP Phil Rizzuto would be working at American Shop in November 1951, she made arrangements for us to visit as a family, under the guise of buying new clothes for school.

Though we'd heard stories of major league players working at the store, my father and I had no idea going into that day that we'd be meeting one of the biggest stars in baseball. Within moments of walking through the door, we were greeted by one of the tiniest salesmen we'd ever met with a hearty, "Hey, folks, welcome to American Clothing Shop!" Dad brushed past him, on the way to the boys' suits section, when he stopped to comment on something he'd observed about this overly cheery employee. "You know," my father said, "you look an awful lot like Rizzuto, the guy that hit a home run against my Giants in the World Series. Anyone ever tell you that?"

"They should," the salesman replied, "because I cash his checks all the time."

It suddenly dawned on me who we were talking to. "Wait a minute, you mean to tell me that you are *the* Phil Rizzuto?" I squealed. "I have your baseball card at home!"

"That's great," he answered. "Too bad you didn't bring it, kid, I would have signed it for you. I can autograph something else for you if you want."

As he drew closer to shake my hand, Rizzuto suddenly noticed the damage to my eyes. He glanced at my mother, who silently acknowledged what he'd just realized. She motioned for him to come over so that she could speak to him in private.

"Holy cow!" Rizzuto said to me as he walked toward my mom, "will you look at that, I forgot about these customers that I have to say good-bye to. Let me walk these huckleberries out and thank them for buying our suits. I'll be right back, I promise." My mother took Phil to the other side of the store and explained the whole story to him, making sure to point out the huge grin that I was wearing as I stood in the same room as a real live major league player.

She told him that smiles like that hadn't been seen too often on me since my accident.

Moved by my story, Rizzuto hurried back over and threw his arm around my shoulder as he warmly said, "Sorry I took so long, kid. What's your name, anyway?"

Still a bit starstruck, I managed to get out a quiet, "My name is Eddie, Mr. Rizzuto."

I could hear the exuberance in his voice as he quickly answered, "Please call me Scooter. All of my friends and teammates call me that, and now you're my newest friend, Eddie." I couldn't believe what I was hearing, let alone what came next. As he placed a small card in my hand, Rizzuto said, "This is my business card, Eddie. I signed it for you, and I also wrote my private home phone number on it. Any time you want to call and talk baseball, you do that, okay?"

"Wow, thanks . . . Scooter!" I said in disbelief. "Do you really mean that? Can I really call you anytime?"

Without a beat, he replied, "You bet, Eddie. I'd like to call you sometime, too, when I feel like talking baseball. Is that okay, or is your home number unlisted?"

We all laughed, and then my mother reminded us that we were also here to buy clothes. My new friend Scooter directed us to the best tailor in the place, where Dad and I were promptly fitted for new suits. On our way out, I said one last good-bye to Mr. Rizzuto and promised to stay in touch.

Thus began a close relationship that lasted for over fifty years. From that moment on, Phil Rizzuto took me under his wing and became a mentor to me.

PHIL RIZZUTO'S JOURNEY in baseball was a most unlikely one. Born in Brooklyn, he dreamed of playing for one of the three big league clubs in his hometown of New York City. Nobody gave him a chance. Generously listed as a mere five feet five inches tall, Phil was tiny by any standard in sports. Still, the passion for baseball burned inside him and he pursued his goal with vigor. After being passed over by the Dodgers, Giants, and every other team in baseball, his persistence earned him an amateur tryout with the powerhouse Yankees in 1937. Rizzuto dazzled the skeptics and won a spot on the big league club. He eventually became the Yankees All Star shortstop and was the heart of a squad that won seven World Series titles. Red Sox Hall of Famer Ted Williams once said that if they had Rizzuto on their team all of those years, it would have been Boston, not New York, that became a dynasty. That's high praise, indeed.

Still, Rizzuto's small size made him the butt of jokes. It was one of the reasons he was given the nickname Scooter, which he grew to love. I guess this made Phil more sensitive to the underdogs of the world, because he always seemed to try his best to encourage others. At any rate, that is exactly what he started doing with me.

True to his word, Scooter called me even before I got up the nerve to dial his number.

Just a few days after my visit to his store, Mr. Rizzuto phoned to ask my parents if it would be okay if he and his wife, Cora, picked me up to take me out to dinner. Mom and Dad, of course, agreed.

I had a marvelous time and was thrilled to be hearing stories about the glory days of baseball from a superstar of the game. I was a Giants fan, but Rizzuto's charisma and "local boy made good" story crossed all lines of team affiliations. Even those who hated the Yankees respected and admired the Scooter. He was never full of himself. He had a kind word for everyone.

I was also lucky enough at that early age to get a glimpse of what life with a celebrity is like. Scooter would pick me up and take me to appearances and dinners all over the New Jersey/New York area. I would listen as toll collectors, restaurant owners, parking lot attendants, store clerks, and others would regularly refuse to take any money from Mr. Rizzuto, no matter how much he protested. They were so happy to have a Yankee in their midst that they would comp him for everything. Phil never abused this honor. He would take the money intended for the services that he got for free and donate it to local charities and causes.

In addition to his work at the store, Rizzuto made some extra money in the off-season by operating a bowling alley in Clifton, New Jersey, with fellow Yankee legend Yogi Berra. On our visits there, I got to know many of their All Star teammates. These guys would often unwind by popping in to bowl a few games and to mingle with their fans.

As the spring drew close, Scooter had to get himself prepared for the upcoming baseball season, so our visits and excursions became less frequent, but he did stay in touch by phone and promised to get me tickets any time I wanted to come to a game at Yankee Stadium.

A few weeks after that, the 1952 baseball season finally arrived. I couldn't wait.

May 22 was a date I was especially looking forward to. It happened to be Ascension Thursday, a rare midweek day off for other kids in the neighborhood, allowing them to be able to come over to play, but that's not what I was so happy about. May 22 was also the date that the Dodgers had selected for me to visit Ebbets Field.

My mother had to work that day, so Dad took my sister and me over to New York by subway. It wasn't an easy trip. We had to get on the New Jersey tube trains in Journal Square, switch to a crosstown train on Thirty-Third Street in Manhattan, and then connect to a Brooklyn-bound train to arrive in Flatbush, home to Ebbets Field. This long, winding journey might explain why I'd never been to this particular ballpark before, though I could describe every inch of it from what I heard on the radio and got to see on TV before losing my sight.

We arrived early at the press gate and were greeted warmly by a Dodger representative, who gave us our passes. Mr. Felton hadn't gotten there yet, so the head of security at the gate, Joe Brown, took us to the side and told us to wait there. Within minutes, some of the Dodger players began to enter the gate on their way to the clubhouse. Mr. Brown made certain that each one of the players came over to say hello before going past.

I couldn't believe that big-name Dodgers stars like Pee Wee Reese, Gil Hodges, Ralph Branca, and Carl Erskine were making time to have conversations with me. I conveniently left out the fact that, as a Giants fan, I had rooted against them in the playoffs the year before. Today, at least temporarily, my blood was Dodger blue. It was a little harder for my dad to switch allegiances for the day, but even he did, considering how kindly the Dodgers were treating us, and the fact that they happened to be playing the Reds, not the Giants.

The nicest moment at the gate that morning was when Jackie Robinson greeted me warmly, as if we'd been friends for years. He opened up to me and gave me special encouragement, instructing me to never lose my passion for baseball, no matter how many obstacles got in my way. Advice like that from Robinson, who faced barrier after barrier in his own life, yet pushed through them all with grace and dignity, meant a lot and had a powerful, lasting impact on me.

Soon, the time came for us to join Happy Felton himself for the pregame festivities. I'd been to plenty of professional baseball games before, but this would be the first time I'd actually be stepping out onto the playing field itself. Dad took me by the arm and escorted me from the inner press gate area toward the dirt track area surrounding home plate, where we were to observe the *Knot Hole Gang* show. As I walked up the steps leading to the field, I immediately felt the warm May sun on my face. As the base path clay crunched under my feet and I smelled the freshly cut grass just inches away, I could instantly envision all of the unique features and quirky details of the rustic old red-brick-walled Ebbets Field that I'd seen in photos and onscreen. It was magical, a feeling that I wanted to get used to.

Mr. Felton was cordial as he chatted with us before going on air, while players from both the Reds and Dodgers took batting practice inches away. My father was even lucky enough to catch a foul ball, something that had never happened to him at a Giants game. When the pregame ended, we were shown to our seats, prime spots just behind the Dodgers dugout. This team really knew how to treat their guests right.

It turned out to be an exciting game. Brooklyn was losing 7–3 in the bottom of the eighth when Pee Wee Reese and Jackie Robinson both singled. Reese advanced to third as Robinson stole second base, which he'd also done earlier in the game. Catcher Roy Campanella smashed a three-run homer to tie the contest. Gil

Hodges followed that with a score of his own to take the lead. Joe Black, the Dodger pitcher, shut Cincinnati down in the top of the eighth and did the same in the ninth to win the game. I couldn't have scripted a better finish.

As we headed back to Jersey City after a long day, I was grateful for the experience the Dodgers had given me, and for the memories that I made, but I was already looking forward to Saturday, June 14.

That was the day that my mother had set up with Leo Durocher for me to go on the field at the Polo Grounds to stand alongside my beloved heroes, the New York Giants.

In 1949, Mom bought me a paperback called *Bat Boy of the Giants,* a first-person account by Garth Garreau of his days as a teenager assisting the players in the Polo Grounds clubhouse and on the field. Before I lost my sight, I'd devoured all 206 pages of that book from cover to cover numerous times. I still have the book. It's dog-eared and tattered, but a nice reminder of my boyhood days.

My goal was to be a batboy like Garth, or at least to be able to throw out the first pitch at a Giants game, like they let him do a few times. After my accident, I knew that those things were never going to happen. Thanks to my mother and her letters, however, something even better and wilder than anything I read in that paperback was about to occur.

Due to the recommendation of Sister Gregory on the tour of the school a few weeks before, I'd be heading to Camp Marcella in July, and would be starting at Holy Family in September. Mom didn't want me getting too distracted late in the summer, so she purposely scheduled an early June date with Mr. Durocher and the Giants, hoping for nice weather. My father was called in to work an extra shift that day, so he couldn't go with us to the game. My sister Maureen also had something to do, so Mom and I went to the game alone.

The home park for the Giants was a little easier for us to get to than Ebbets Field. Situated under a bluff overlooking the Harlem River on 155th Street in Manhattan's Harlem section, the Polo Grounds sat almost directly opposite Yankee Stadium, which was over on 161st Street in the Bronx. There were several trains that were easy to get to from our house that would take us to a stop just one block from the ballpark.

The Polo Grounds was no tiny field like the Dodgers' home. Originally built for polo matches in the early 1900s, as the name implies, the stadium was immense. It had a weird horseshoe shape, with home plate situated at the curved part of the shoe. The center-field wall was almost five hundred feet away from home, an impossible distance for most batters to reach. As a result, to save space and to add more seats, the Giants placed their clubhouse right above the outfield, as opposed to in the customary area behind the dugouts. This meant that players had to walk back and forth to center field and then up a flight of stairs to get showered and dressed before and after games.

When Mom and I arrived at the Polo Grounds, we were met by Tom O'Brien, the longtime Giants front gate attendant. He let us in and called someone to escort us right onto the field. Visiting Brooklyn was great, but this time I was even more ecstatic. I was walking on the same ground as men who were giants, in both senses of the word, to me. The stroll from home plate to the center-field steps seemed to take forever. I soaked up every minute. We made the climb up to the clubhouse door. Mom promptly introduced herself to the guard, Barney O'Toole.

A large, barrel-chested, ruddy-faced Irishman, O'Toole was an imposing figure. He loved to joke, and was pleasant enough, but he was also responsible for making sure that nobody was admitted into the Giants' inner sanctum without permission. Unfortunately for my mother, that list, in 1952, did not include any women.

While Leo Durocher had extended the invitation to both my mother and me to visit, even he could not bend the rules when it came to the long-standing ban against females entering major league clubhouses. As a result, she had to sit on the sun porch outside the clubhouse door while Mr. O'Toole allowed me to enter by myself. Mom was disappointed, but she was also delighted that I'd be getting the chance to meet my heroes.

A clubhouse attendant took my arm after Barney let me in. I was escorted directly to the manager's office. Mr. Durocher wasn't there, so the attendant had me sit in the skipper's chair, behind the desk where all of the important decisions about the Giants were made.

I thought to myself, Can it get any better than this?

I got my answer as soon as Leo the Lip burst through the door.

"Eddie Lucas, it's so great to finally meet you!" Durocher bellowed, as he strode across the room.

"Thank you for having me here, Mr. Durocher," I said, hardly believing that I was in a place I'd dreamed of being for years, "I'm a big fan of the Giants and I can't wait to go out on to the field to meet the players."

There was silence for a moment, and then Leo gruffly said, "No, sir! I'm afraid that won't be happening today." My heart dropped. I was barely holding back my tears of disappointment when Mr. Durocher continued, "You are my personal guest, Eddie, and these players take their orders from me. You don't have to go out to meet them; they have to come in here to meet you. If they don't, then they'll hear from me!" With that, Leo opened the door, whispered something to the attendant, and the parade began.

One by one, all of the Giants players filed into the manager's office to spend a few minutes with me, guys like Bobby Thomson, Don Mueller, Sal Maglie, Whitey Lockman, and Sal Yvars, my heroes. I'd enjoyed my drives and chats with Mr. Rizzuto, and the passing moments with the Dodgers a few weeks before, but this was something completely different. I had the entire roster of my favorite team coming in to sit at their manager's desk to spend a few minutes shooting the breeze with me, a thirteen-year-old fan. Not one of them mentioned my blindness or acted like they were forced to be there, and each took a genuine interest in what I had to say and complimented me on my knowledge of the game.

The funniest part was that they all seemed to think they needed to bring a gift along to the meeting. I'm not sure if Durocher told them to do it, but most of them concluded that a bottle of Coca-Cola would be fitting for a thirteen-year-old. Before I knew it, there were about twenty Cokes lined up on Leo's desk, all for me.

Bobby Thomson asked me to get up from Leo's chair and come over to him. As I stood there, the pennant-winning hero from the previous October took my arms and showed me exactly how low the ball that was pitched to him by Ralph Branca came in, the one that he hit for his miracle home run. I'd replayed that moment many times on my own; now the man himself was showing me how it was done.

One of the biggest surprises that day was the appearance of Monte Irvin, who went on from the Jersey City Giants to have a Hall of Fame career with the big league club. I knew that Irvin had broken his leg sliding into a base in spring training and was on the disabled list, so I wasn't expecting him to come through Leo's doors on crutches just to see me. "Hey, kid," Irvin said with a grin as he hobbled gingerly into the room, "I heard you had a pretty bad accident a while ago. I did, too. It's not going to stop me. I'll be back in action soon, and so will you, Eddie. I promise." If I needed any more motivation to pursue my dream, Irvin had just given it to me.

Since the game started about thirty minutes after my arrival, I knew that the chats couldn't have been that long, but it felt like I had been in there for hours. I was now a member of the Giants' "in crowd."

The one player I didn't get to meet was my newest idol, Willie Mays. The Rookie of the Year winner in 1951, Mays made quite a splash and was on his way to being the biggest star the Giants would ever have. Like many young men of that era, he'd just been called up in the military draft for the Korean War. He had to miss the 1952 and 1953 seasons while he served his time in the army.

The game was about to begin, so the players left to head out to the dugout. Mr. Durocher came to say good-bye. As he walked me out the clubhouse door to the porch where my mother was patiently waiting for me, he gave one last order, this time to Barney O'Toole. "This is my pal Eddie Lucas," Leo barked. "Any time he wants to come by to meet the players, Barney, you let him in, even if I'm not here. Eddie is part of the Giants now!" Durocher spotted my mom, gave her a hug, and thanked her for bringing me. As he walked off to deliver the lineup card to the umpires, we made our way to our seats.

"I'm so happy for you, Ed," Mom said with great pride. "I'm glad that you got to do this, and I hope it cheered you up."

"Thanks, Ma," I said. "It was incredible; you won't believe what those guys said to me. I feel like a million bucks. I'm just sorry that you couldn't be in there with me, but I remembered it all and I'll tell you whatever you want to know."

"Just one question," came her quick reply. "Why are you carrying so many bottles of Coke?"

Just before the 1952 season ended, my father took me to the Polo Grounds for my promised visit with announcer Ernie Harwell. Thanks to Barney O'Toole, Dad and I got to say hi to Mr. Durocher and to some of my newfound friends on the team before heading up to the press box for the start of the game. Mr. Harwell was just as friendly as Durocher was. He gave me a book about baseball as a souvenir of my visit and bestowed some great advice.

Harwell shared his on-air duties with Russ Hodges, the man who'd made the famous "The Giants win the pennant!" call on the radio the previous October. I was introduced to Mr. Hodges, and we had an instant rapport. Hodges, like Rizzuto and Harwell, became a lifelong friend. The Giants were playing the Cardinals that day and their biggest star, Hall of Famer Stan "The Man" Musial, stopped by to say hello to Ernie. Mr. Harwell told Musial all about me and about my mother's letter. Stan shook my hand and made me promise to meet him after the game any time I was at the Polo

Grounds when the Cardinals were playing. I did just that, and Mr. Musial always gave me a ride home so that we could talk baseball and he could make sure I got home safe.

The Giants games were broadcast on WMCA on the radio and WPIX, Channel 11, on the TV. Mr. Harwell and Mr. Hodges alternated innings on both mediums. They told my story to listeners and viewers during the game that day.

If my friends didn't believe me about all of the good baseball fortune I'd had that year, they did by then. I was almost famous.

LIFE GOT BACK to normal after the 1952 season was over, and the ballpark visits stopped. I got into the routine at Holy Family as baseball gave way to schoolwork. The game was never too far from my mind, though. Mr. Rizzuto would drop by our apartment on weekends occasionally to check in. He and his wife, Cora, even visited the school, to see me and my fellow students.

Scooter Rizzuto went above and beyond for me. The first time that I was told about Holy Family's annual student trip on an airplane, I was excited, but also very nervous. Like my father, I had a fear of heights and I wasn't sure if I'd be able to manage the sensation of being thousands of feet in the air. I gave Mr. Rizzuto a call at home because I figured that he must have been on many planes as he traveled across the country. He told me not to be nervous, that planes were very safe and that Captain Rickenbacker and his Eastern Airlines pilots were the best in the business. That put me at ease.

The morning of the flight, all of the students and nuns were on the plane safely buckled up and awaiting takeoff when I heard the cabin door open. There was some laughter coming from the front when suddenly a familiar voice came over the speakers. "Holy cow, were you huckleberries going to take off without me?" It was Mr. Rizzuto. He'd secretly arranged with Sister Gregory to be a guest on the flight, to help narrate the trip. Everyone, including me, had a ball, as Scooter made us laugh from takeoff until landing. It was the perfect way to fly, and helped to settle our nerves. He saved the day!

Years later, I found out from Mrs. Rizzuto that Phil was terrified of airplanes in the early 1950s. He tried to avoid flying whenever he could. Since most baseball teams were still east of the Mississippi, the Yankees, like other clubs, were still traveling everywhere by train. Scooter actually put aside his own nerves and fears to ensure that we would all have a pleasant flight.

What a remarkable man he was.

In the summers that followed, on my breaks from school and Camp Marcella, I visited the Polo Grounds often, getting to know players from the Giants and visiting teams. That was when Yankee Stadium started to become a second home to me. Just as Mr. Durocher had done with Barney and the Giants, Mr. Rizzuto introduced me to someone who would allow me and a guide access to Yankee Stadium any time that I wanted.

Jackie Farrell was a Jersey City native. He loved baseball and dreamed of being a player, but had a hereditary condition that stunted his growth. Just shy of five feet tall, he pursued a career in the front office instead. By 1952, Farrell was head of the Yankees' publicity, media relations, and promotions department, but liked to bill himself as "Vice President in Charge of Handling Kids Who Want to Shake Hands with Yogi Berra and Mickey Mantle."

Farrell was smaller in size than Phil Rizzuto, but had a charitable nature that was just as big. As soon as Scooter introduced me to Jackie, we clicked. It was thanks to Farrell and Rizzuto that I was able to get my first brushes with Yankee greatness.

The Yankees invented the idea of Old-Timers Day, following the gathering of pinstriped legends that came to say good-bye to Lou Gehrig in 1939, the day he made his famous "I'm the luckiest man on the face of the Earth" speech. Bringing alumni back became an annual tradition, and I was blessed to be part of these reunions, starting in 1953.

Born too late to have known Babe Ruth or Lou Gehrig, I did get to hang around at these Old-Timers events and listen to stories from their teammates from the 1920s and 1930s like Bill Dickey, Tony Lazzeri, Lefty Gomez, and Frank Crosetti. I also formed a special bond with Mr. Rizzuto's best friend, the man whose December 1951 retirement announcement I'd heard when I was in the hospital, Joe DiMaggio.

DiMaggio was on baseball's Mount Olympus, right up there with Ruth, Gehrig, Cy Young, Ty Cobb, and other immortals of the game. He was bigger than life, and everyone wanted to be his pal. Mr. DiMaggio could also be very aloof. He guarded his privacy and free time diligently. Very few people were allowed into his inner circle. Scooter was one of them. He and DiMaggio were roommates on the road and were inseparable while they played together, so Mr. Rizzuto had access to "Joltin' Joe" that almost nobody else did.

I was, understandably, quite nervous when Mr. Rizzuto brought me into a private room at the Stadium where Mr. DiMaggio and his good friends were gathered. It was like meeting the pope. Phil told him a little about me, and how the two of us had grown close. To break the ice, Joe opened up with, "So, Eddie, nice to meet you. Tell me, what's your favorite Italian dish?"

That threw me. I was expecting to talk baseball, not high cuisine. At a loss for words, I said the first thing that popped into my head, regretting it the instant it left my mouth. "Well, let's see, every Tuesday my mom usually opens up a can or two of Chef Boyardee. I like that." I heard an audible groan from the men in the room, all of whom doted on DiMaggio and knew that as he was the first-generation American son of Italian immigrants, my answer was probably quite offensive to him.

After what seemed like an eternity, the great man laughed, slapped me on the back, and said, "Somebody get this skinny Irish kid a bowl of pasta e fagioli, and fast!"

Joe then relaxed and started telling me tales of the glory days of the game. I was in! From that meeting on, Mr. DiMaggio treated me as a confidant. I had joined his exclusive club, and I wasn't even a bit Italian.

IN AUGUST 1954, Jackie Farrell helped me to arrange a special moment for a friend, my buddy from Camp Marcella, Eddie Reis.

I explained to Jackie that Eddie was blind and deaf, and that he was a huge Yankee fan, though he'd never actually been to Yankee Stadium. Eddie's favorite player was Mickey Mantle. He told me once that it was his dream to be able to meet Mantle in person. As soon as I mentioned that to Jackie he said, "Pick a day."

I arranged for a day pass from camp for Eddie and me. One of the counselors agreed to take us to Yankee Stadium. Mr. Farrell met us and took us right down to the tunnel underneath the ballpark that stretched between the dugout and clubhouse. We waited for Mickey, who was taking batting practice, to finish his daily reps. Mantle had inherited center field from DiMaggio in 1952, and was the new face of the Yankees. With his boyish charm, blond hair, chiseled features, and God-given gift to hit baseballs a mile, he was a natural matinee idol.

Soon, we heard the click, click, click of hard metal spikes on the concrete surface of the runway. They had an odd cadence compared to the other times I'd heard the same sound. The rhythm was almost a half-step off. I realized that it must be Mickey. The accident he suffered two years earlier made him walk with a slight limp and a crooked gait.

Mantle was complaining about being tired and sore when he got to where we were standing, but still took a moment to say hello. I'd met Mickey a few times before, so he was familiar with me. Mr. Farrell pointed out Eddie Reis to him, as I wrote "Mickey's here!" in my friend's palm.

Mantle was fascinated with this method of communication and when I told him that he was Eddie's favorite player, he asked how he was able to follow the games if he couldn't see or hear. I showed Mickey how I described the play by play in Eddie's hand. The Yankee superstar walked over to Eddie and shook his hand, while saying in that famously slow Oklahoma drawl of his, "Nice to meet you. Thanks for being a fan." Of course Eddie had no way of hearing this. I quickly translated to Eddie what Mantle had said to him. In return, Eddie spelled out something for me. "What's he writing to you?" said Mickey.

It took me a moment to say the words out loud. I had to be sure that I was getting the message correct. Eddie's request was an unusual one. He told me to ask Mickey if it was okay to feel his muscles.

Mantle didn't hesitate. He pulled Eddie toward him and flexed his biceps a bit so that my friend could touch and experience up close the powerful arms, shoulders, and chest that had won over so many admirers and helped to propel baseballs far over the fence. This wasn't vanity on Mantle's part, just a quiet moment between a player and a fan, away from any cameras or spotlights.

Eddie turned back to me and grabbed my hand, writing the same thing over and over again while making squealing noises with his mouth. "What's he saying now?" Mickey asked.

"Just one word," I replied, "your name, over and over again. He's chanting Mickey! Mickey! Mickey!"

With that, Mantle abruptly said, "Um, I've gotta go, guys, it was nice meeting you!" and hurried off. I was confused by the rush, until Jackie Farrell told me what had actually happened.

The young slugger was so moved by the excitement on Eddie's face that he could barely compose himself emotionally enough to stay in that spot to continue chatting. Eddie's visit, and the subsequent reaction to it, had touched him so much that Mickey Mantle, hero to millions, was sitting alone in a corner of the clubhouse, reduced to uncontrollable sobs.

. . . .

In 1954, Willie Mays returned from the army to the Giants. He had an amazing season, leading his team to a shocking World Series upset victory, including one of the greatest catches ever, over the Cleveland Indians. Unfortunately, I never got to meet him that year, or to get to a Series game, because I'd just graduated Holy Family and had begun classes at my high school, the New York Institute for the Blind, on Pelham Parkway in the Bronx. My school schedule would mostly keep me from visiting the ballparks for a few years.

The New York Institute was a boarding school, like Holy Family. It was not, however, within walking distance of my house. The school was thirty miles round trip from Jersey City, hardly accessible by train or bus. My father decided it was in our best interests to buy our first-ever family car. Of course we couldn't afford a new model automobile, so Dad searched high and low for a bargain until he found a 1944 army surplus Chevy sedan at a price low enough for our meager budget. It was a little scuffed up and needed some paint, but it was safe and ran great and that's all he cared about.

This school was quite different from my last. Braille was heavily emphasized, of course, and we had some talking books. The biggest change, though, was the amount of freedom that students were allowed. At Holy Family, the nuns kept us pretty sheltered, on a rigid schedule. The institute recognized that we were maturing teenagers. They gave us more flexibility, so it was almost like living on a college campus.

Most of the institute's students were from the New York area.

Many had been blind since birth. We even had a few teachers who were blind. One of my favorites was Mr. Whitstock, who used a Seeing Eye dog named Kelly to get around school. I was fascinated by that. Orientation and mobility was something we really never focused on at Holy Family, but it was stressed at the institute.

During junior and senior years, we were taught the best methods of navigating the world as a blind person. Special training was given, focusing primarily on the use of canes. At first, that horrified me. I still had memories of that guy on the street corner begging with the cup and the cane. I soon came to realize that canes were not just objects meant to evoke pity for blind people, but useful tools to help us explore and expand our horizons. The cane soon became an extension of my arm. By tapping it back and forth in a sweeping motion, I could sense and avoid any objects or pitfalls that might present a danger to me. After a while, I was comfortable enough to walk without a sighted guide.

One thing bothered me the most about the New York Institute. Many of the students led very sheltered lives. We were given the freedom to roam off campus, but my classmates still stayed in. They had become used to living in isolation and had no social circles outside of the school. Extracurricular activities barely existed. I wanted to change that.

I was able to convince the administration to allow us to take longer field trips to places like Philadelphia, to eat meals out at New York restaurants, and even to create after-school social clubs and organizations. We also set up the institute's first-ever formal senior prom, just like all of my friends back home were having at their schools. You know, normal teenage stuff.

The most exciting accomplishment for me was a club that I established with my fellow baseball lovers at the school, which we proudly christened "The Diamond Dusters."

There were many fans of our national pastime at the institute. We all enjoyed talking about the game for hours on end. We'd come up with lists of great players and moments in the sport. The idea of our new club was to formally organize these debates, keeping up with all of the latest news. One of our teachers, Mr. Meyers, was the moderator. He would read us the baseball news and columns from the local papers, just as my father had done years before. We also decided, as a club, to select a "Diamond Dusters' Player of the Week" during the baseball season.

Each week, we would choose a player that we thought did a great job and send him a Diamond Dusters certificate in Braille, congratulating him on the honor. Mrs. Kearney, our English teacher, would helpfully write the words in print underneath the dots on the page, so that the recipients could read along. The players really got a kick out of it.

Inspired by my mother, I decided to start sending letters to the most famous baseball players from each of the American and National League teams, as well as some retired ones, asking them if they would come by to talk to the students.

Jackie Robinson was one of the first to respond.

IN EARLY 1956, Jackie Robinson was traded from his beloved Dodgers to their hated rival, the Giants. This was just one year after he had led Brooklyn to its first and only World Series title. There was no such thing as free agency back then. A player who was traded basically had two options. He could either go wherever the club sent him, or simply retire from the game. Robinson bravely chose the latter. At the peak of his talents, he walked away from baseball rather than disappoint his fans by playing for another team. He was immediately offered the plum job of vice president of corporate relations for Chock Full O'Nuts Coffee, which he accepted. By doing so, he broke yet another barrier, becoming the first African-American vice president of a major U.S. corporation.

I contacted Mr. Robinson at Chock Full O'Nuts. Two weeks later I received a wonderful reply accepting the offer to speak at the school. Our principal, Mr. Frampton, and his assistant, Mr. Mitchell, hastily set up an assembly. Jackie had requested no media presence, so it was a quiet gathering of just the 150 students at the school, and the teachers. Robinson thrilled us all with stories of his days with the Dodgers. He spoke about overcoming obstacles and prejudice with grace and humility. I then led a Q&A session with our guest, and we followed with a small reception so the students could meet him up close.

It was an incredible afternoon, the perfect way to kick off what became a regular series of speakers. Russ Hodges of the Giants, Gil McDougald of the Yankees, and, of course, Scooter were among those who came out over the next two years to support the Diamond Dusters by spending the day at the school. I kept inviting Willie Mays, but for some reason or another, he couldn't make it. I was disappointed, because he was the one player I had yet to meet, and I really wanted to talk baseball with him.

One of the best speakers the Diamond Dusters ever had wasn't even on the original guest list.

Shortstop Alvin Dark was one of my buddies on the New York Giants. In June 1956 he was traded to the St. Louis Cardinals. I wrote to him in early 1957 and invited him to speak at the institute when the Cardinals came to town. He got back to me and said to call him at the hotel on the off day between games and that he'd be happy to come by to meet the students.

When the morning arrived, I phoned, as promised, and got some disappointing news. Dark was being admitted for emergency dental surgery and couldn't make it. He apologized, but suggested that I call the room of outfielder Wally Moon, who would happily sub for him. When I was connected to Moon's room, I was crushed to hear another voice say, "Sorry, Wally is out for the day and won't be back until later." This was quite a blow, as the assembly had already been set up, and everyone was waiting for a player to appear. I said, "Okay, thanks anyway."

I was about to hang up when the guy on the other line sensed the disappointment in my voice and said, "Did you need Wally for something special?" I told the whole story to this mystery gentleman, and he finally identified himself. "I'm not Alvin or Wally, of course, my name is Lindy McDaniel. I pitch for the Cardinals. If you'd like, I can come by today." This was amazing news! I immediately answered, "Of course I know who you are, Mr. McDaniel. The Diamond Dusters would love to have you as our guest today!" "Outstanding," replied the young pitcher, "just tell me how to get there and I'll see you at one-thirty."

Lindy McDaniel did a wonderful job stepping in to take over, which is not surprising since he was one of the best relief pitchers ever. He and I remain close friends to this day.

As I ENTERED my senior year in September 1957, I started to seriously think about what my career path would be. I wanted to be a baseball broadcaster and writer, but still wasn't sure if I was good enough for it, or up to the task. I mentioned this to Scooter and he said, "Let's go for a ride, Lucas!" By then, Mr. Rizzuto had retired as a player and was a broadcaster himself. He formed an unusual habit of referring to everyone by their last names only, as a sign of affection. I was not exempt from it.

Phil picked me up at the institute, and we just drove around talking about baseball, and life in general. He surprised me by saying, "You know, Lucas, you are amazing. When I first met you, I saw this scared little nervous kid that thought his life was over because of some accident with a baseball, and now I see you running all over the place impressing everyone you meet with your knowledge of the game. I wish I had half the energy and memory that you do." I was quite touched by this. Scooter was a lighthearted guy, so it was rare to hear him get this deep. He then followed by asking, "What made the difference? Was it the school, your parents, the nuns, Cora and me, all these Italian meals?"

I chuckled at the last remark and then quietly responded with one word: "Baseball."

Phil was confused as he repeated my answer, "Baseball?"

I continued, "All of those other things are great, and you all helped me come back in so many ways, but it's baseball that makes me feel alive. I love the game. I think about it all day, and then I dream about it at night. I wish I could still play, but that's okay, too, because I can always listen and be a part of it."

Phil asked if I regretted playing on the day of the accident. I boldly said, "I wouldn't change a thing about it. What happened was God's plan, and this is where He wants me to be. Look at it this way: without that, I wouldn't have met you and Mrs. Rizzuto, or have done any of these other amazing things. I just have to have faith that things will work out."

My heart was pounding as I suddenly realized something and said it out loud for the first time. "I know for sure now that I want to spend every minute I can around this game. I love it more than almost anything else. Baseball took my sight, but it also gave me back my life!"

Phil said, "Good for you, Lucas, good for you!" We then spent the rest of the trip talking about the best colleges to get a degree in journalism and broadcasting as we made our way back to the institute.

Baseball in New York changed forever in 1957 when the Dodgers and Giants announced that they were leaving the area after the season was over to move to new homes in Los Angeles and San Francisco, respectively. The Yankees would then be the only team in town.

Games at the Polo Grounds in 1957 took on a funereal atmosphere as they inevitably led to the final home match on Sunday,

September 29. My father was too heartbroken to go, so Uncle Eugene volunteered to take Maureen and me over. As soon as we were done with church, still dressed in our Sunday best—suits, ties, and all—we packed up the car and drove over to Harlem.

To save a fee, my uncle parked at the top of Coogan's Bluff, above the stadium, which meant that we had to walk down an immense flight of stairs to get to the park. The descent wouldn't have been so bad, except for the fact that Uncle Eugene had allowed me to bring my tape recorder to the game with me. In the late 1950s, recorders were not compact and portable the way they are today. The model I happened to be using was a Pentron T-90, which was a monster. It was almost as big as a suitcase and weighed over fifty pounds. The whole thing came in a thick metal carrying case that had to be plugged into an outlet while you were recording. You had to stay in one spot as you were taping and couldn't really walk around with it. Uncle Eugene, God bless him, never complained once about having to carry the load for me as my sister and I walked gingerly toward the Polo Grounds, down the dangerously steep incline with the steps carved directly in the face of a cliff.

Leo Durocher had been dismissed as the Giants manager two years before, but Barney O'Toole was still there. Barney continued to honor the former skipper's instructions to allow me access to the field and clubhouse and to the players. I was going to use this last opportunity at the Polo Grounds to practice my broadcast and interview skills on tape. It was a big day, as the Giants brought back some of their all-time greats for one last good-bye. Barney greeted me with a big hug that was also a bit melancholy, as it would likely be the last time we'd ever see each other.

Thanks to Barney's assistance, Uncle Eugene and I were able to set up and plug in the recorder at the corner of the bench in the dugout while Maureen went up to our seats in the stands. I spoke to some old friends and recorded my memories of the Polo Grounds on the massive reel-to-reel tapes as I waited for the signal from the guards to leave the dugout area so that the players could prepare for the game.

I checked my Braille watch and realized that there were only a few minutes left until game time, so I started to pack up. Then I heard Barney bellow, "Hang on, Eddie, I've got someone else for you to talk to." I thought it might be an official from the club, or an old-timer, when suddenly Uncle Eugene blurted out, "Son of a gun! It's Willie Mays!"

Barney knew how much I wanted to meet Mays, and how we kept missing each other, so he arranged this meeting on the final day of Willie's tenure in New York. Barney had told the Giants superstar center fielder that I was going to begin a career as a broadcaster soon and that I wanted him to be my first official interview guest.

"Say hey, man!" came the familiar greeting from Mays, who was commonly known as the "Say Hey Kid" because of it. I scrambled to get my little square Pentax microphone back out and come up with questions for him in my head. "So, what do you have for me today, Eddie?" said Mays, putting me right at ease. We then spent the next fifteen minutes talking about his life and career.

Uncle Eugene brought his little Brownie camera to the game. I heard him clicking away, taking photos as Willie and I sat there talking. Mays switched between pensive and cheerful moods as he reflected on his time in New York and gave his thoughts on the move to the West Coast. I was just stunned that my goal of interviewing a big league star, the biggest one in baseball, was now a reality.

There was another strange sound happening while I was doing the interview. I identified it as feet pacing and tapping on the wooden floor of the dugout. What I couldn't see was that while I was talking to Willie, several people, including Giants publicity men and an impatient reporter from the Associated Press, were standing there waving at Mays in an effort to get him to end the interview and clear the dugout. He steadfastly refused, giving me his full attention. Willie waited until I had asked all the questions I wanted.

As we wrapped up our chat, Mays put his arm around me and said, "Those were great questions for a first interview, Eddie. You're pretty good at this. Keep it up, man. I'll see you next year."

I almost cried. That was just what I needed to hear.

With those words of encouragement from my idol ringing in my ears, as well as the constant boosts from Scooter, I began the process of applying to colleges and universities. I was more certain than ever what the future held for me. I was determined to be a broadcaster and writer, covering baseball for a living.

The next step was finding just the right school.

5

Hey, Buddy, Is That One of Those Sight-Seeing Dogs?

Seton Hall University was completely covered in snow the first time that I visited its campus, in December 1957.

I'd narrowed my choice of colleges down to just a few. While schools like Syracuse, Temple, and Columbia University all had world-class journalism and broadcasting programs, there was no way my parents could afford to send me to those places. In addition, I would have had to live in dormitories if I went to another state. After six years of basically living away for most of the week, I wanted to stay home and to commute.

Hudson County may be tiny, but it has two excellent schools. Saint Peter's College and Jersey City State College are both located right on the main boulevard that runs fifteen miles through my home county. They would have been easy for me to get to, but neither had a strong enough communications department at the time.

This led me to select a school that was actually three bus rides away in South Orange, New Jersey.

Choosing Seton Hall turned out to be one of the best decisions I ever made.

Founded as a private school in 1856 by Archbishop James Bayley, Seton Hall was named for his aunt, Elizabeth Ann Seton, the first American-born saint. They had a well-respected school of divinity and theology. Seton Hall's law school was also ranked just below Princeton's as one of the best on the East Coast. What really attracted me, though, was their radio station.

WSOU is a twenty-four-hundred-watt campus studio at Seton Hall that began broadcasting in 1949. Originating in the small town of South Orange, the transmitter was powerful enough for its signal to be carried all over the New York/New Jersey area. We used to listen to WSOU at the institute. They played mostly music, with a few chat shows. Other than coverage of Seton Hall basketball games, however, there was a definite lack of sports talk. I sensed an opportunity.

When Mom found out that I wanted to apply to Seton Hall, she reserved a date for us to tour the campus together. Mid-December was the only time available. Unfortunately, there had been a major storm two days before. We had to step around and through gigantic mounds of snow. My mother did not want to cancel our appointment, so we made the long three-bus trek out to South Orange. Dad was working an extra shift and couldn't come. I'd fill him in later.

We were met at the gates by Father Shea, the head of the admissions department. Because of the weather conditions, we pretty much had a private tour. It was a great tour, even better than the one we'd taken at Holy Family five years before. The thing that impressed me the most was how Father Shea took an interest in me but never once mentioned or reacted to my blindness. To him, I was just another prospective student whom he was hoping to recruit.

Before we left, I filled out the application for admission and paid the fee. I would later submit forms to Saint Peter's and to another college, only because my parents urged me to have a "safety" school in case I didn't make the cut at Seton Hall.

I wasn't worried. My nightly prayers were to be a Seton Hall student and for God to allow me to use the gifts He gave me to develop my broadcasting talents on WSOU. If it was in His will, I knew that He would make it happen.

I even asked Saint Joseph, my patron, to intercede on my behalf.

By that time, my family had moved out of the Jersey City projects. My mother was tired of living in meager, hardscrabble conditions. The main reason we moved to Lafayette Gardens in the first place was that that particular public housing complex was close to PS 22. It was also not too far from Holy Family. Once I was done with those two schools, there was no need to live there anymore, so my parents began sacrificing, saving their money and working extra shifts.

They still couldn't afford to buy a house. My mother began looking in local papers, like the *Jersey Journal* and *Hudson Dispatch*, for nice furnished apartments to rent. She finally found one, in Weehawken, which was about five miles or so from Jersey City.

The owners of this particular apartment weren't asking for prospective tenants to come see the place in person. Instead, they requested a written essay to be sent, which would describe why yours would be the perfect family to live there. It had to be mailed to a PO box.

Write a persuasive letter to rent this apartment? My mother had already proven that she was the master at that particular skill. Once Mom put that essay in the mailbox, everyone else should have just thrown in the towel.

As expected, my mother's note was the winning entry.

Our new landlords, the Hanks family, were terrific people. They were an older couple, named Frances and George, with two sons. We were welcomed warmly. The boys, Georgie and Buddy, were a few years younger than me but were both big baseball fans. The Hanks family became like close relatives to us. In fact, they introduced my sister Maureen to one of their cousins, Jimmy Hanks. A few years later, she married him.

We lived on the lower level of the house, with five spacious rooms, a big bathroom, and heat and hot water included. George and Frances were not typical landlords. On our first day, they told my mother and father to pick out any wallpaper, furniture, paint, or appliances that they wanted, which would be provided at no extra charge. George's father, George Sr., lived across the street and was always at their house, helping with repairs and mainte- nance. George Sr. loved taking breaks on the porch to recount tales of his glory days riding alongside Teddy Roosevelt and his Rough Riders during the Spanish-American War. The front porch was semicovered, perfect for conversations or for listening to a game on the radio. The Hanks family even put rocking chairs out there in the warm-weather months.

The house was located on Fiftieth Street in Weehawken, in St. Joseph's parish, just off of Boulevard East. Weehawken is a Native American word meaning "city built on cliffs that look like big trees." They weren't kidding.

Just across the east side of the main boulevard from Fiftieth Street was a little park encompassed by a large iron fence. The fence was there to prevent anybody from getting too close to the edge of the Palisades cliffs, on which Weehawken stood. They were steep and massive. Venture past the barrier, and you'd find yourself dropping over the cliffs, 560 feet down to the Hudson River.

The bright side to having the Hudson River below was that the New York skyline was directly across. I didn't get to enjoy the view, of course, but people came from all over to sit on the Hankses' porch to take in the dazzling scene of the Empire State Building, Chrysler Building, George Washington Bridge, and other famous landmarks. This million-dollar sweeping vista made our area of Weehawken a very desirable place to live. Hollywood legend Fred Astaire, famed choreographer Jerome Robbins, and jazz great Thelonious Monk were a few of the luminaries who had lived just blocks away from us. I never got to meet them. The Weehawken resident I was most excited about living near was my best friend from PS 22, Gene Mehl.

Once I started boarding for the week at Holy Family and the New York Institute, the days of daily play with my childhood friends came to a halt. I especially missed Gene, who lived on Fifty-Fourth Street in Weehawken and would travel by school bus to PS 22 in Jersey City. Since I wasn't enrolled there anymore, I didn't get to hang out with him as much as I used to. Occasionally, my parents would bring me to see him, but those visits were few and far between. Now that we lived in Weehawken, I could spend time with my best friend whenever I wanted.

Gene wasn't a big baseball fan, but he was an excellent musician.

I was a Sinatra and big band enthusiast; "Young At Heart" was my favorite song at the time. Gene loved rock and roll. He would keep me up to date on all of the latest pop music stars and songs. He was also very active, full of energy. Gene made it his mission to get me out of the house as much as he could. We'd walk the streets of Wee-hawken as he described my new hometown.

I also kept pestering Gene to let me ride his bicycle. It had been years since I'd done that. My mother was, as always, overly cautious. She would not even hear my arguments about why I should have a bike. I had to find another solution.

After months of pressure from me to use his bicycle, Gene finally gave in. He agreed, with one condition. He wanted to ride with me. Gene would pedal the bike and I would steer, according to his directions. I happily agreed to this bit of teamwork.

It was a thrill for me to be in control of a bicycle again. The freedom was indescribable. Gene was enjoying it, too. He even suggested that we head east on Fiftieth Street, downhill, to pick up more speed. I loved the idea. I'd also completely forgotten that Fiftieth Street abruptly ended with the safety fence and the cliff.

As the bike made its way across the boulevard, rapidly approaching the precipice, Gene began to panic and shouted, "Turn! Turn! Turn!" Instead of complying, I shouted "Which way?" as the bike continued on a crash course toward the barrier. Luckily, Gene had enough sense to grab me by the collar and to pull me off the speeding bicycle just before it slammed into the iron bars, smashing it to bits. Gene and I rolled safely to the ground just inches from the fence, as I heard the seat of the bicycle fly over the gate and smack into the side of the rocky Palisades cliff over and over again, making its way fifty-six stories down to the river.

With my heart beating rapidly, body drenched in sweat, I thanked Gene for having the presence of mind to save us at the last minute.

I also had one request: "Let's not tell my mom about this, okay?"

By this time, I was mostly using my cane to get around. The training they'd given me at the institute had made me more confident than ever. I enjoyed showing my parents and others how independent I'd become.

My mother wasn't so sure.

One day, I decided to take a walk around Weehawken by myself. My ultimate destination was a candy store on the corner of Fiftieth and Park, not that far away. I said good-bye to Mom and Dad and headed off. The trip was uneventful. Once I got there, I enjoyed a chocolate malt as a small reward for my show of independence. The way back was mostly uphill. I was able to do it just as easily. As I got close to home, I noticed that the footsteps I'd heard a few times on my trip were still there in the background, as if someone was shadowing me. It took a moment for the identity of the mystery person to dawn on me. I spun around and called out, "Mom?"

My mother, who had been trailing me the entire time, confessed. I shouted at her, "Why would you do that?" With a trace of hurt and anger in my voice that was typical of a frustrated teen, I continued, "I can take care of myself now. I don't need you to follow me!" With that, my mother began to cry, and said, through her tears, "I'm sorry, Eddie. I worry about you, and I just want to make sure that you are safe. I'm not trying to make you feel helpless. I'm your mother and I'm always going to worry." I immediately felt foolish for snapping at her. I apologized, and my own tears began flowing.

Mom and I hugged and headed home. We'd both gotten our points across and felt much better.

A few weeks later, on Wednesday, March 19, 1958, the Feast of Saint Joseph, I was in my dorm at the institute when I received a very happy call from my mother. The letter that we'd both been waiting for had arrived at my home that morning. Seton Hall University approved my application! I'd be starting there in the fall. Once again, my mother and I were in tears, but this time they were joyous ones. I celebrated with my classmates after hanging up with Mom. We would have gone out to mark the occasion, but in a serendipitous twist, our area was covered in snow, just as it was on the day of my campus tour. The Saint Joseph's Day 1958 blizzard was one of the worst ever, dropping almost two feet of snow. The party would have to wait.

I was excited to be attending Seton Hall. This time my father was the one who was worried. His concern was my commute. I'd be living at home and "day hopping" back and forth to campus. Dad wondered how I'd manage the trip all the way to South Orange, even if I was proficient with the cane. My mother, who'd witnessed how well I was getting around by myself, was firmly in my corner. This still didn't sway Dad. To make his point, my father took me on the ride I'd have to make for the next four years. He didn't use the car. My father wanted to simulate the bus trip to Seton Hall exactly the way that I'd have to make it.

. . . .

ON THE DAY of our trial run, Dad and I got up at 4:30 a.m. We had breakfast, got dressed, and were out the door an hour later. Our first step was to take a bus from Weehawken through the Lincoln Tunnel into the Port Authority Bus Terminal on Forty-Second Street in Manhattan. As crazy as that sounds, we had to cross state lines in order to get a bus back to New Jersey and the general area of Seton Hall. There were no direct buses to South Orange originating in Hudson County. From New York, we boarded the number 118 to Newark. The trip, during morning rush, took almost an hour. Once in Newark, we got off at the corner of Raymond Boulevard, only to have to walk four long blocks to Broad and Market. It was there that we caught the 31 South Orange bus to the campus of Seton Hall, arriving just before 9:00 a.m.

Dad's point was made. As stubbornly independent as I was, there was no way I'd be able to make the voyage to Seton Hall and back each day without a partner. I needed a teammate. The problem was finding one. I had many friends at the time, and I even knew a few people who were going to Seton Hall. None of them would be able to escort me on a three-bus trip each day. I was frustrated at being so close to my goal, but at an impasse. Then I remembered my teacher, Mr. Whitstock, and his amazing guide dog.

The thing that struck me the most about Mr. Whitstock's dog, Kelly, was that she was all business. Unlike other canines, where petting was encouraged, this dog was always on duty as a guide and we had to treat her as such. While he was pleasant about it, we were told by Mr. Whitstock that as long as the harness was on his dog, we could not pet or play with Kelly. This wasn't some arbitrary rule set by him. This was part of the extensive training given to dogs by the Seeing Eye.

A few years earlier, our English teacher, Mrs. Kearney, had given me a Braille book about the Seeing Eye written by Peter Putnam. I read it several times and took extensive notes. The Seeing Eye was based in New Jersey, so I was somewhat aware of it. Thanks to Mr. Putnam's book, I learned even more about this innovative facility for training guide dogs, including the fascinating story of its co-founder, Morris Frank.

Mr. Frank was the very first person in the United States to have a guide dog. Blinded as a teenager due to an accident while he was boxing with a friend, he read about blind World War I veterans who were being paired with trained dogs in Europe. He wrote a letter to the founder of that school and was invited to join them. After returning to the United States with his new dog, Frank asked the founder of the European school to establish one in the States. She agreed. They christened it the Seeing Eye in 1929. A facility was opened in Whippany, New Jersey, two years later. Mr. Frank then began a successful crusade to change laws, allowing guide dogs to enter buildings and places that pets were normally not permitted. He was an inspiration to me.

After serious deliberation, I proposed my idea of getting a Seeing Eye dog to my father. He was surprisingly open to it. I submitted my application in the spring of 1958, in order to be part of the July class that year. It would take four weeks to go through the training at the Seeing Eye, living in their Whippany dorms to grow accustomed to my new dog. I'd already registered for pre-semester August classes at Seton Hall to ensure enough time to familiarize myself with the campus, so I needed my four-legged "eyes" by then.

The admission process for the Seeing Eye was no breeze. I was subjected to a series of physical and mental evaluations so that they could be sure that I was mature enough to be able to handle life with a dog as my guide.

My friends who were being drafted into the army at the time underwent easier exams than this.

Thanks to God's grace, I passed. I'd soon be living life with a Seeing Eye dog at my side.

I was excited as I arrived in Whippany in July 1958 for my training. For the fourth time in less than six years, I'd be boarding someplace new with a roommate. This time it was Richard McStraw, a twenty-year-old chess master and massage therapist from Erie, Pennsylvania. He was getting his first dog, too. There were eight people in our class. They came from all over the world. The Seeing Eye paid for transportation to and from New Jersey, but applicants had to pay the $150 fee for the room, board, and dog themselves. They were pretty firm about that.

The Seeing Eye believed that if they or some service club like the Lions paid the fees for you to get your dog, the sense of partnership wouldn't be as great. They wanted you to have a stake in the well-being of your new companion. If the fee came out of your own pocket, the chances were likely that you wouldn't see it as charity, maintaining your dignity and valuing the experience even more. To this day, the Seeing Eye's fee remains $150. If your dog passes away or is unable to guide anymore, then the fee drops to just $50 for any successive stays for training with a new dog. It's a lifetime commitment on their part.

This was no vacation. We were worked hard for twenty-eight days straight. On our very first day, we were asked to go to the courtyard outside. Our trainers, Fred Kreitzer and Roger Taylor, divided us into two groups of four. They led us around by a special harness, patented by the Seeing Eye. The trainers, who had already spent weeks with our group of dogs, would use this time to assess our pace and level of fitness. They would then have the information needed to pair us up with just the right dog.

The next day, we were brought into the common room to meet the animals that would be part of our lives for years to come. Mr. Kreitzer, who was assigned to be my trainer, came into the room and said, in his thick German accent, "Mr. Lucas, I'd like to introduce you to your new partner. Her name is Kay." He continued, describing her to me in great detail. "Kay is a twenty-two-month-old German shepherd. She is tan with black spots and is as gentle as they come." I was eager to get to know Kay, so Mr. Kreitzer allowed me to go back to the room to bond with her for the rest of the day before the real training began the following morning.

There are guide dogs all over the world, but Seeing Eye dogs are a special breed. Their training and commands are unique to the New Jersey facility. They are born and raised to be guides. The dogs are taught from an early age to be aware of their surroundings, beyond the normal range of most canines. Kay had to be my eyes, so she needed to look to her sides, front, back, and even above while walking with me. If there was an awning or low-hanging branch, she had to see that and to steer me away from the danger.

I'm left-handed, but Seeing Eye dogs always walk to the left side of their partner, since this is basically a right-handed world and it's easier to go through doorways and to navigate things like staircases with your right hand free. That took some getting used to.

Kay wore the special Seeing Eye harness, as well as a small leash and chain. The most important part of the training was actually for me, not for Kay. I had to learn to trust myself enough to direct her, not the other way around. She was watching out for me and keeping me safe as we walked, but ultimately I was the one who had to know where we were heading so that we would wind up in the correct place. I used commands like "left," "right," "forward," "hop up," and "phooey" for navigation and correction. They were simple, yet effective. I was also told to shower her with praise whenever she did the right thing, as positive reinforcement.

Rather than try to simulate real-life traffic conditions, the Seeing Eye brought us from Whippany to the nearby village of Morristown. While it wasn't exactly Jersey City or New York, Morristown had a population of seventeen thousand and was busy enough to suit our purposes. The town had everything we needed, a main square with several big intersections, tree-lined streets with obstacles above and below, and a large department store with escalators, so we could train inside.

Mr. Kreitzer was a step behind me and Kay as we made our way toward Morristown's South Street, which had lots of traffic. While stopped at the corner for the light, my trainer's instructions to me were simple. "When I tap you on the shoulder," Kreitzer said, "tell Kay to go forward." A moment later, I heard the rumbling of a giant truck coming toward us. I felt a tap on my shoulder. Thinking that I was imagining it, that my trainer couldn't possibly want me to step in front of an oncoming truck, I remained silent. As the large vehicle drew closer, I felt the tap again. This time, Kreitzer was yelling at me, "Mr. Lucas, why are you not giving your dog the command to cross?"

"Are you crazy?" I shouted back. "We'll be squashed by that truck!" My trainer was insistent. He implored me to trust Kay and to let her decide whether it was safe to cross. I finally gave in. The moment the truck was just a few feet away from us, I gave Kay the order to go forward, ready to pull her back before she got us both killed.

Kay never moved.

What I'd just experienced was something called intelligent disobedience, which was something they stressed at the Seeing Eye. Dogs were trained early on to ignore the commands of their partners when following them meant putting us in danger.

By the time I left the Seeing Eye, Kay and I were an inseparable team. At times it felt like boot camp, but the four weeks of intense work paid off as my confidence level rose dramatically thanks to my new canine sidekick. I could go anywhere from now on, without relying on another person to accompany me. Kay filled that job nicely.

My mother and father adored Kay. I had to be careful that Mom didn't indulge and overfeed her. She was a working dog, after all, not just a pet. Kay and I used the training we'd acquired on the streets of Morristown to help us get around Weehawken. Most shop owners were gracious to us. They never prohibited Kay from entering their stores, despite the fact that Seeing Eye dogs were still a rarity in the late 1950s.

Kay often brought out the strangest responses from passers-by.

Children were the most curious about my dog. She was quite friendly, and loved to be showered with affection, but when we were walking around, Kay had a job to do. Like Mr. Whitstock, I had to gently remind the children that they couldn't pet her while she was in the harness because Kay needed to be free of distractions. They usually understood. Adults were the ones who seemed to be a little more confused.

As I walked along Park Avenue with Kay one day, a woman stopped me and said, "Excuse me, sir, is that dog real?"

I stifled my laughter as I responded, "No, ma'am. I just push a bunch of buttons on the harness and it makes the dog move." A typical wiseguy Jersey response, yes, but I couldn't help myself. Another time, as I made my way down Boulevard East, a cab driver rolled down his window and yelled out to me, "Hey, buddy, is that one of those sight-seeing dogs?"

I nodded, then silently chuckled as I pictured Kay with binoculars and a tourist map at the top of the Empire State Building, wearing a little Statue of Liberty crown.

The next test for Kay would be our bus rides to and from Seton Hall.

ONE OF THE most important parts of our daily training in Morristown was the visits we made to the local train and bus depot. Since these dogs were to be used primarily for blind people who needed the freedom and mobility to travel back and forth to work, they had to be comfortable using public transportation. We worked repeatedly on the proper way for our guide dogs to board and lie by our feet quietly, especially when the vehicle was crowded. Kay excelled at this.

Even if there was another animal in the area, our dogs had to be silent and not react. One of the ways the Seeing Eye accomplished this was to set up the dining hall so that the tables of six allowed our dogs to stay motionless underneath, facing each other while we ate. It was remarkable how much Kay acted like a human being while she was doing her job guiding me.

We arrived on campus with no problems and went to see Mr. Flood, one of Seton Hall's course counselors. It was his suggestion that I take the late-summer classes to get my feet wet before the rush of students came back in September. As we sat planning my schedule for the fall, Mr. Flood had a slew of questions for me, most concerning Kay. He wondered how she would react to other students in the halls, whether she would bark during class, or even if she would try to grab everyone's food or rummage through the garbage in the cafeteria. I assured Mr. Flood that none of these things would happen.

I was also introduced to Father James Kerry for the first time. He would be my professor for the religious education and Bible study courses on my schedule. This lively priest had an excellent sense of humor and was an avid baseball fan, so we bonded immediately. Every morning for the next four years, with just a few exceptions, Father Kerry would greet me and Kay upon our arrival. We'd then have a cup of coffee together before classes began.

In 1958, Seton Hall still had an all-male student body. Kay would be the first exception to that. We were required to wear jackets and ties to class. Kay was an exception to that rule, too. The administration and my classmates made every effort to help me fit in. I never felt like I was being treated as anything less than the typical student. I appreciated that.

There were, of course, some concessions made to help me adjust.

At the beginning of each semester, the counselors at Seton Hall would look at my schedule and determine which books I would need for those classes. They would then have those books pressed on special flexible disks. I was given a talking book machine to play back those disks. It made things much easier. When it was time for midterm and final exams, I was brought out into the hallway or into a private room, to take them orally. We never missed a beat.

I couldn't take notes during class, even with Braille. Professors spoke too fast for me to be able to punch out what they were saying in time to keep up. The solution was for one of my fellow students to use carbon paper underneath his notebooks while he wrote. He would then provide me with a copy of the notes so that someone could help me to review them later.

Father Kerry had the great idea to put up a flyer outside the divinity school department asking for volunteers to help me with my studies. He was looking specifically for students who lived near Weehawken who could come by my house at night to read and review the carbon-copied notes with me. The response was overwhelming.

Rocky Provenzano, who later became a priest, was the first to respond. He was from Hudson County, so Rocky took it upon himself to broaden the search for readers beyond Seton Hall. He went to the local CYO asking for volunteers. Two of them, Marilyn Dundero and Claire Derasmo, became dear friends. Another was the home economics teacher from Weehawken High School, who stopped by once a week. Quite often, it was just a group of my classmates sitting around in my home discussing what we'd heard that day in class, while my mother spoiled us with food.

A guy who was in more than a few classes with me was George Franconero. George, who was studying to be a lawyer at Seton Hall, was the first-generation American son of an Italian candy store owner from Bloomfield. He introduced himself to me during the first week of school, and we hit it off.

A few years before, George's family had moved from Bloomfield to Essex Fells, a wealthy suburb not too far from campus. He would occasionally drive me to his home for lunch. This was no ordinary house, it was a mansion. The Franconero kitchen alone was as large as my family's apartment. It was also my first experience with an island in the middle of a kitchen. The backyard was massive, too. I'd been to other New Jersey houses with swimming pools, but none with a series of cabanas like the ones that dotted George's poolside area.

The first time I visited his house, we walked through the many hedges and flowers that wrapped around the front as we made our way in. George brought over an older gentleman who was wearing gloves and pruning the roses. When he removed his glove to shake my hand, George introduced the man as "our little Italian gardener." When they both started to laugh, I realized that it was actually George's dad. He invited us inside. Mrs. Franconero was waiting there with plate after plate of fruit and homemade dishes. Even if I was completely full, there was no way George's mother, Ida, would let me leave the house without eating something. George's older sister, Concetta, was usually away from home, so I never got to meet her.

One day, George said to me, "Ed, I'm not going to be in school for the next week. Can you get the notes and assignments for me?" I replied, "Sure, George. Is everything okay?" He smiled as he said, "Oh, it's nothing big, just that I have to go to California with my parents to be on Ralph Edwards's TV show."

He was referring to *This Is Your Life,* a wildly popular program on NBC on which Mr. Edwards would bring celebrities in on a ruse, surprising them with visits from friends and family in front of a live audience. George had me curious. I said, "Why do they want you on that show?" George nonchalantly answered, "Ralph Edwards is surprising my sister on the show, so they are flying us out." I was confused. "Why," I asked, "are they interested in Concetta?" George finally let me in on the secret he'd kept all along. "Her real name is Concetta Franconero," he said with a laugh, "but most people know her better as Connie Francis."

My best friend in college turned out to be the brother of one of the biggest pop music stars in the world. His sister's records, like "Who's Sorry Now?" "Where the Boys Are," and "Stupid Cupid," were all smash hits and he never mentioned it once. George wanted to be his own man.

Like Gene, George didn't really follow baseball, he loved the movies. I did, however, meet two huge Giants fans at Seton Hall. They also happened to be brothers studying to be priests.

John and Drew Bauman were seminary students at Seton Hall's divinity school. By that time, the Giants and Dodgers had moved out of New York City, so there were no National League teams around. On our days off, Drew, John, and I used to make the drive ninety miles south to Philadelphia to see our favorite squads play, talking baseball all the way.

Yankee Stadium was never too far. Thanks to Mr. Rizzuto and Jackie Farrell, I had an open invitation to the House That Ruth Built. Scooter kept up with me during my time at Seton Hall, praising me when I hit high marks with my grades and giving me a boost when I got a bit low. It was Phil who encouraged me to approach the head of programming at WSOU in my freshman year.

Al Close was the manager at the campus radio station in 1958. This was a part-time duty, which he balanced with his official job as a professor teaching classes in communications, public relations, voice, and diction. I met with Professor Close and pitched an idea for a weekly baseball show called *Around the Bases*.

Most of the students who had programs airing on WSOU lived on campus. If not, they stayed long into the evening to learn the technical ins and outs of running a sound board and equipment. That was a requirement that I could not fulfill because of my dependence on the bus schedule, so it was already a strike against me. Professor Close was skeptical about my hosting a program, and was about to deny my request when I made one last attempt to convince him. I mentioned my connection with Phil Rizzuto, the Yankees, and some of the other friends I had made in baseball. I promised to get at least one interview per show with a professional ballplayer.

That did the trick. Close agreed to give me a shot. *Around the Bases with Ed Lucas* would debut on WSOU in the spring of 1959.

. . . .

OPENING DAY AT Yankee Stadium was, and still is, a big day. It's especially exciting when the Yankees are returning as World Series champions, as they were in 1959. Jackie Farrell had arranged for media passes for me and John Bauman at the '59 opener to interview players on the field and in the clubhouse. This would be my fourth straight opener. I was using a much smaller tape recorder by then. We took the afternoon off from school and headed over in John's car to the Bronx. I also brought Kay, to get her used to walking around a ballpark.

The Yankees happened to be playing the Red Sox. My old hero from the Giants, Bobby Thomson, was in the waning days of his career and was at the Stadium that day. He greeted me with a hearty, "Hey, Eddie, how have you been?" We caught up for a bit, I introduced him to John and Kay, and then Thomson said casually, "Have you ever met Ted Williams?"

I was stunned. Ted Williams was like the John Wayne of baseball. He was a stoic, masculine, quiet man, and a true legend. I'd never met him, but I was eager to. Thomson walked me over to Williams's locker. As we approached, Ted called out, "Hey there, fella, what's your name?"

I cheerily replied, "I'm Ed Lucas, Mr. Williams, it's an honor to meet you."

He interrupted me with a curt, "Not you!"

I quickly realized that Williams, an avid bird hunter and noted curmudgeon, was addressing my dog, not me. I quietly corrected myself by whispering, "Kay, her name is Kay. She's female."

Williams spent the better part of the next ten minutes fawning all over Kay, grilling me about the relationship between Seeing Eye dogs and their masters. It was not exactly the conversation that I'd imagined with the man many still call the greatest hitter who ever lived.

When Ted was done talking, I began to walk away. He called after me, saying, "I see that you have a recorder there. I can't do it today, but any time I'm in town and you want an interview, Eddie, let me know. Just make sure that you bring sweet little Kay with you!"

Ted Williams didn't go on the record with me that day, but Joe DiMaggio's younger brother Dom, who was a former All Star player with the Red Sox, just happened to be in the clubhouse. I interviewed him for thirty minutes about his career. That became the highlight of my first *Around the Bases* show. I'm pretty sure that Dom's elder sibling had spoken to him about me, because the last thing Boston's DiMaggio said as we concluded our chat was, "I hope you're laying off that Chef Boyardee stuff, Eddie."

THE NEXT MORNING, as usual, I had my coffee with Father Kerry. He asked me why I'd been absent the day before. I could have come up with some contrived excuse, but decided to be honest. I told him that John and I had played hooky to go to Opening Day. "Yes, Eddie, I know all about it," he said. I was puzzled as I asked, "How in the world could you know that, Father?" He replied with a grin, "The whole world knew you were there, Eddie."

I had no idea that while John and I were standing on the field, the Yankees' TV announcer, Mel Allen, had the cameramen take shots of me and Kay. He then spoke on air for about five minutes

about the historic moment of having a guide dog on the field at
Yankee Stadium for the first time. Father Kerry, and many others
at Seton Hall, just happened to be watching.

Between the on-air mentions during Yankee games and my
Around the Bases spots, my profile was growing on campus. I'd
gotten several great reviews for my work. My fellow students
would give me compliments whenever they spotted me and Kay
in the halls. One of the biggest tributes I got from the students at
Seton Hall didn't even involve baseball. It actually occurred at a
basketball game.

In 1960, the Seton Hall Pirates men's basketball team had a new
coach, Richie Regan. He would go on to lead them to several winning seasons. In his first year, the team was invited to play in a tournament at New York City's historic Madison Square Garden. The
whole student body was excited. Plans were made for groups of us
to travel over by subway to fill the stands and to root on our team.
As a commuting student, this was an excellent opportunity for me
to experience another part of campus life, the traditional cheering
section at a big game.

When I arrived at the entrance gate, ticket in hand, I was held
back by a security guard before I could go through the turnstile. "Is
there a problem?" I asked. The reply was immediate. "Yeah, there's
a problem," the guard rudely said, "you're trying to bring a dog
into my building." I patiently explained to him that Kay was my
guide dog and, as such, legally allowed to escort me anywhere. He
was having none of it. "The only dogs allowed in Madison Square
Garden," he screamed at me, "are the ones from the Westminster
Dog Show, and yours ain't no top breed!"

My blood started boiling, but before I could even do anything, one of the other students in line—I still have no idea who it was—said, "Well, if Eddie's dog isn't allowed in, then nobody is going in!" He then organized a formal blockade, with hundreds of Seton Hall students lining up in solidarity, blocking every gate to prevent anybody from entering the arena. I was worried that a riot would start, but once the other ticketholders heard about how my guide dog was being barred, they joined in the protest.

None of this moved the obstinate security guard. He still wouldn't let me pass.

Finally, after forty-five minutes and a little intervention from the NYPD, the top brass at the Garden allowed Kay in and I took my seat. A cheer went up from the crowd, which by then numbered in the thousands. Our miniprotest had been successful.

I never got an apology from Madison Square Garden, not even a dog biscuit for Kay. They did, however, change their policy on guide dogs shortly after that.

Kay and the WSOU baseball show were my two calling cards on campus. They both served as icebreakers to put people who were nervous about discussing my blindness at ease. Monsignor Walter Jarvais, the spiritual director of Seton Hall, was escorting the archbishop of Newark on a VIP tour one day when they ran into me. The monsignor introduced me to His Eminence and then quickly pointed at Kay, saying proudly, "And here is my best girl Kay, she's the queen of our campus!"

Just a few months shy of graduation, in 1962, I was summoned to the office of Monsignor John McNulty, who'd served for over a decade as the president of Seton Hall. I'd never met him before.

Most students weren't called in to him directly, so I was quite interested in discovering what this mystery meeting was all about.

The first thing Monsignor McNulty said when I entered his office was, "I'd like to ask you a few questions about your dog, Mr. Lucas." By now I was used to people inquiring about Kay and the Seeing Eye, but I never expected it from him. The monsignor continued, "We're thinking of hiring our first blind teacher here at the Hall. Like you, he has a guide dog, and I want to be sure that they will be able to handle getting around." I reassured him by sharing stories of how well Kay had behaved in my four years there. I told him that I thought it would be a fantastic idea to add this man to the faculty. As I stood up to leave, Monsignor McNulty came out from behind his desk, put his arm around my shoulder, and said, "I'm glad that we were able to get the Ed Lucas seal of approval for this. We're proud of you, young man. You've been a real groundbreaker. God bless you in all that you do."

I just wish that my mother and father could have been there to hear the monsignor's kind words.

Seton Hall's Career Day 1962 was going to be an exciting one for me. Most of the seniors had already sent in resumes and applications to the large corporations and firms that would be represented. This would be followed by personal interviews, which would, we hoped, lead to the promise of a job after graduation.

I was told by Mr. Close that several radio stations and newspapers would be in attendance for Career Day, so I sent them samples of my radio interviews and articles. My grades were very high, and my professors gave me glowing recommendations. I got calls from more than a few of them, saying they'd be excited to meet me when they came to campus.

As the appointed day arrived, I dressed in my finest suit and set off earlier than usual with Kay to be sure I'd get to South Orange long before my first meeting. There were knots in my stomach when my name was called to go in, but I was also full of confidence that I'd walk out with a new employer.

Those dreams were shattered as soon as they saw Kay.

One by one, I heard audible sighs of disappointment once I stepped into the rooms and the hiring managers and representatives realized that I was blind.

There was no reason for me to indicate that fact on my resume, or on the forms provided by them, so I didn't. It wasn't willful deception. I'd been treated as just another student for the last four years. Classmates and teachers alike saw through my blindness to the talents and abilities that I had to offer. They valued me as a person, plain and simple. I assumed that future employers would do the same.

I was sadly mistaken.

By the end of the day, I was frustrated and tired. Nobody was giving me a chance. I was knocked out of contention before I could even open my mouth. My very last meeting was with a local radio station. They dismissed me just as the others did, and I completely lost my cool. I raised my voice and read them the riot act for crossing me off their list just because I was blind. I think I even slammed the door behind me for maximum effect.

I was gathering my things and making my way to the bus stop

at a brisk pace to work off my anger, when a stranger stopped me midstride. "Excuse me," the man said, "is that a Seeing Eye dog?"

I was in no mood to get into yet another discussion about Kay, so I gave a quick "yes" and continued on my way.

The man blocked my path, saying, "I noticed that you were pretty upset coming out of there. Is everything okay?"

For some reason, the calm in this man's voice compelled me to tell him my whole story, unloading the day's frustrations. He listened patiently and then said, "I'm here as a recruiter for Career Day. You seem like the type of student I'd like to work for me." Now he had my attention. I asked which radio station or newspaper he was with. He replied, "None of them. My name is Freddy Kiefner, I work for the Provident Mutual Insurance Company. I think you'd make an excellent salesman." My brief bit of enthusiasm dropped away as I explained to him that I hadn't the slightest bit of interest in selling insurance. This was as far removed from my dream of a career in baseball as you could possibly get.

I shook his hand, thanked him for his interest in me, and began to make my way to the bus stop. I'd only gotten a few feet when he called out, "Have you ever heard of Morris Frank?"

He had my attention once again.

"Of course I know Mr. Frank," I said, stunned, "he founded the Seeing Eye. I wouldn't have Kay if it weren't for him. Why do you ask?" Mr. Kiefner came closer, handed me a business card, and said, "Morris works for us selling insurance. He makes millions. I've written his number down on my card. Call him, talk to him. If you like what you hear, give me a call and I'll be happy to give you a job with Provident Mutual." With that, Mr. Kiefner left.

As soon as I got home, I called Morris Frank. It was surreal, talking to the man whom I'd idolized from the book I'd read years before. He was genial, but to the point. He warned me that I might face discrimination and rejection because of my blindness, but it was my job to rise above that, whether it was while selling insurance or doing any other task. Frank assured me that with my family, my friends, other supporters, and, of course, Kay on my team, there was no way that I could fail if I kept on task.

As soon as I hung up with Morris Frank, I called Mr. Kiefner back and accepted the job.

The world was not ready for a blind broadcaster in 1962, so I followed the path that God placed in front of me. I would sell insurance for a living, until I could show enough people that I had what it took to cover the game I love, despite any limitations.

It seemed the one thing that I still couldn't ensure was my future in baseball.

6

Don't Listen to the
Naysayers, Kid!

The moment that I took my cap and gown off after my college graduation, I was hard at work studying again. This time I was learning all about the world of insurance.

True to his word, Mr. Kiefner hired me as the newest agent at Provident Mutual. He placed me with the Gillis Agency in Newark, which was run by Phil Gillis, a seasoned veteran in the insurance game. They paid me a modest base salary, but the bulk of my income would be from commissions. I couldn't actually sell a policy, though, until I was licensed by the state of New Jersey, and for that I had to pass an exam.

I spent the better part of the summer of 1962 taking the two-bus trip with Kay to Mr. Gillis's office. Once I got there, I was tutored from nine to five by Bill Lindeman, who was senior broker at the agency, and his administrative assistant, Gladys Fetch. I'd record some of the lessons, then take them home with me to study.

On September 19, I passed the state insurance exam on my first try. I was excited, because I'd already lined up my first two sales.

The mother of Eddie Reis, my old campmate, once shared with me that she had a tough time finding insurance for Eddie. Very few companies were willing to underwrite a person who was blind, deaf, and mute. When I entered the business, I reached out to her. With clearance from both Mr. Gillis and Provident Mutual, I was able to secure a policy for my friend with no hassle. The only thing required was a small addition to the monthly premium.

I also approached Mr. Rizzuto about being a client. He already had lots of policies written to cover him during his playing days and in his new career as an announcer, so Phil suggested that I insure his son. My license limited me to selling life insurance policies, so the Rizzutos bought one for Phil Jr. They actually got him the largest one available, the Rolls-Royce of policies.

I was very grateful to Scooter again, this time for giving me such an auspicious start as an insurance salesman.

Selling insurance wouldn't always be that easy. Like most sales positions, it depended largely on the use of lead cards and cold calls. Gladys would give me a list of prospective clients for the day. It was my job to phone them, convince them to meet with me, and then get them to sign on the dotted line. Gladys and Mr. Lindeman would read details of various Provident Mutual policies to me so that I could transcribe them to Braille cards. I would bring both the printed and Braille policies with me to meetings so that my potential customers could read along.

I never mentioned that I was blind when I spoke to my prospects on the phone. I didn't think I had to. Once again, I underestimated the reactions I'd get when meeting them in person.

People were polite, at first. They would open their door to me as a courtesy since I'd already called them. It was quickly evident that most had no intention of buying a policy from me. The reactions to me and to Kay ranged from mild to openly hostile. One guy even wondered aloud how New Jersey could give a blind man with a dog a license to sell insurance. It was extremely frustrating.

There were some early meetings where the prospects didn't care about my lack of sight. Those were refreshing, but I still didn't book the sales. I was too new to the insurance business.

One of the toughest sit-downs I had was with a twenty-one-year-old guy from Livingston. He spent hours debating with me about policies. I made my most persuasive case, using everything I'd learned over the past few months. He had the pen in hand and I thought that I was about to close my first cold-call sale when he abruptly changed his mind. The rejection was based on the fact that he'd been comparing my rates with those of other companies. Someone had called on him the day before to offer him a life insurance policy that would have cost him a penny less a month than ours, with payments ending at age sixty-five. After doing the math, he went with my competitor instead, thanking me for my time and sending me on my way. As I sat on the bus ride home feeling dejected, I did the same calculations. This guy wasted my entire evening and four bus fares just to save a measly $5.25 over the course of the next forty-four years!

I seemed to be getting nowhere fast. My parents, as always, were extremely supportive in my choice to sell insurance.

In addition to driving me to my appointments when he could,

Dad would give me little pep talks. He reminded me that insurance was just a necessary way station until I could make a name for myself in baseball. He wanted me to keep at it, to plow through the setbacks and excel in this new field as proof that I could successfully do anything that I set my mind to, including broadcasting. To keep me sharp, my father would quiz me on insurance policy details in between talk of box scores and batting averages.

Mom and Maureen helped out by role-playing with me. We'd sit at the kitchen table, where they would pretend to be potential clients as I pitched my assortment of policies. My sister peppered me with questions, which annoyed me at first, but actually served to make my presentation stronger. My mother bought everything I had to offer. She was my best "practice" customer.

Family members suggested leads for me to pursue and referred me to their friends and coworkers. I closed a few sales that way. To truly get ahead, I needed to broaden my portfolio. I had to take more classes to get my general license so that I could sell other types of insurance policies, such as home and automobile. The best part was that none of them required a signature. I could sell these new policies by phone and never have to have another in-person meeting. To get to the classes, I still had to take the bus.

Despite the familiarity for me and Kay, these rides were always an adventure.

I usually sat in the seat behind the bus driver when it was free. Kay would lie quietly at my feet. One afternoon, a guy got on, managing to rudely squeeze his way into the seat next to me. I could smell the potent amount of liquor on his breath as soon as he came near. He clumsily stepped all over Kay. She never flinched. As we arrived at my destination, the driver turned to let me know where we were. I began collecting my stuff, when the drunk gave me a sharp poke in the ribs. My inebriated seatmate said with a slur as I stood, "Hey, mister, I see that you're one of those blind guys. I just want to let you know to watch your step on the way out. Some big jerk left a dog under your seat!"

Navigating the streets once I got off the bus brought some crazy interactions, too.

There is a very busy intersection on Raymond Boulevard in Newark. I would wait patiently on the corner with Kay until traffic subsided a bit as the light changed, then she would walk me across. Occasionally, a Good Samaritan would see that I was blind and grab my arm to help me get to the other side of the boulevard, completely ignoring my Seeing Eye dog. I never made a fuss or protested. I simply walked along, chatting about little things like the weather, politely thanking them at the end of the short journey. One day, a guy grabbed my arm, and I began the usual routine. Something was different. Not a word was said by my mysterious companion. I figured that he was shy. When we got to the other side, I discovered the reason for the silence. "I'd like to thank you, sir," the stranger said. "It's not often that someone will allow a blind man to just grab their arm and cross." I was stunned, and replied, "Wait, did you just say that you're blind?" He quickly answered, "Yes, is there a problem?" I took his hand and had him feel Kay's harness. I explained that she was a Seeing Eye dog and offered to help him cross this busy street any time he wanted. I heard him shout "Heck no!" as he ran off in the opposite direction.

The classes paid off. I passed my test for general insurance. With the blessing of Mr. Gillis and Mr. Lindeman, I took a job at the Wolk Agency in North Bergen selling home and auto insurance. This was good for many reasons. Not only did my income rise a bit, my travel time decreased. North Bergen was less than two miles from Weehawken. Working exclusively by phone also meant no more evening meetings. I was now free to travel to the ballpark at night to renew my love affair with baseball.

Though I was busy with my studies and work in the early sixties, I'd managed to squeeze in a few visits to Yankee Stadium. Mr. Rizzuto and Jackie Farrell kept me involved in the clubhouse as guys like Mickey Mantle and Roger Maris had record-breaking seasons and the Yankees were, as usual, entrants in the World Series. The Giants were out in San Francisco, so I had to follow them from afar, except for the occasional road trip to Philadelphia to see them play the Phillies. That all changed in 1962 when the New York Mets were born.

On Friday, April 13, 1962, the Mets played their first-ever home game in New York City. It was at the Polo Grounds. John Bauman drove over with me and Kay. Sadly, since the ballpark had been vacant for five years, Barney O'Toole had taken a job in another city and wasn't there anymore. I couldn't get onto the field or into the clubhouse. The Mets were so new, their PR staff didn't know me yet. I wasn't issued a press pass, so we sat in the stands. That didn't matter much. Radios were small enough by then that I could take one to the ballpark to follow the game. I also developed the ability to tell, just from the crack of the bat, how hard the ball was hit, where it was traveling, and the distance it would go. John would quiz me with each batter, and this unique sensory experience never failed me.

I was thrilled to be back at the Polo Grounds, a place that held so many special memories for me, even if it wasn't my team playing. The Mets lost 4–3 to the Pirates. As the game ended, John and I were leaving when I heard someone shouting my name. I thought it was my imagination, but it continued, "Hey, Eddie! Hey, Eddie!" I asked John to look around to see if anyone was calling me. He then spotted my friendly greeter. It was the catcher for the Mets, Hobie Landrith.

I'd known Hobie from his days with the Giants, Reds, and Cardinals. He was always genial when I'd approach him to chat or for an interview. I hadn't seen him in a while. He was getting a lot of attention that season as the first draft pick for the Mets. Hobie called me down to the railing by the field. "I'm so glad to see you, Eddie," he said warmly as he gave me a hug, "this place wouldn't feel the same without you." I thanked him, and promised to get to as many Mets games as I could. He invited me to have dinner with him some night to catch up. Before he walked away, Hobie praised Kay for being such an excellent guide dog.

That wasn't unusual. Ballplayers seemed to gravitate toward Kay. My dog was a natural conversation starter for otherwise reluctant stars, just as she was for Ted Williams. Even managers and announcers paid special attention to her.

Casey Stengel, baseball's venerated "Old Professor," got to know me when he was in the midst of guiding the Yankees to seven World Series championships in eleven years as manager. Mr. Rizzuto was the first to introduce me to him, so Casey lovingly called me "Scooter's Boy." When I started bringing Kay around, Stengel would stop whatever he was doing to come over to greet her. This annoyed several writers, who were forced to cut their interviews short as a result. The Yankees unceremoniously let Casey go in 1960. He was hired as the first manager of the Mets two years later, at age seventy-two. The Mets started giving me passes to the Polo Grounds clubhouse in 1963. Stengel would stand in front of the clubhouse door when he saw me coming. He pretended to bar me from the room until I allowed him to pet his "girlfriend" Kay.

Russ Hodges and I kept in touch even after the Giants moved to San Francisco. He was their lead announcer now that Ernie Harwell had gone to Detroit. When the Giants were visiting Philadelphia, Russ would get me press passes, on one condition. He insisted that I bring Kay.

Hodges and Kay had a special bond, as they shared the same birthday, June 18. He was a dog lover and a passionate on-air advocate for the Seeing Eye and other services to help the blind. During commercial breaks, Russ would leave the booth to bring Kay dog biscuits and bowls of water. He even recommended a hotel for us while we stayed in Philadelphia. When I went to pay the bill, I was informed by the front desk that Hodges and Horace Stoneham, the owner of the Giants, had picked up the tab, in honor of their friend Kay.

Not every player embraced a dog in the clubhouse. Willie Mays, for instance, turned out to be a good pal to me, but he kept his distance whenever he saw Kay. Willie wasn't very comfortable around dogs, even well-behaved ones like mine.

In August 1963, as I waited outside the visiting Cardinals clubhouse to say good-bye to Stan Musial, who was retiring after that season, I heard the door open and close repeatedly without anyone exiting. This went on for half an hour. The door would open, then shut, open, then shut. It was either the wind or my imagination. I finally asked the clubhouse guard what was happening, and he filled me in. A star pitcher for the Cardinals, "Sad Sam Toothpick" Jones, was mortally afraid of dogs and would not leave the ballpark until Kay and I did so first, so he kept peeking out to see whether we'd gone, then scurrying right back inside.

Once the baseball season finished, I was able to spend more time concentrating on insurance.

Things were going great at the Wolk Agency; I was selling many policies by phone. Though the majority of calls I made were from the office during the day, I would sometimes have to make them in the evening. If it was a local call, I could easily dial from home, but if it was long distance, I'd walk to the pay phone at Charlie's Candy Store on the corner of Fiftieth to save my parents from having the extra charge appear on their phone bill.

I carried a pocket full of coins with me. I had no idea how much each call would cost. It depended on the location and duration. If the time bought with the change that I'd put in the slot ran out, then an operator would cut in on the call to let me know that I had to deposit more. It usually went without a hitch, until one day just before Christmas.

I was in the middle of a sales call when the operator's voice broke in. I was ready for this, and had started to put the change in the slot when I hesitated for a moment. Something about the female voice on the other end made me want to hear it once more. "Excuse me, sir," came the pleasant sound of the phone company employee, "if you'd like to continue the call, please deposit another ten cents." My sales call wasn't leading anywhere, and I was ready to conclude it anyway, so I bluffed a bit.

"I'm sorry, ma'am," I said, as cheerily as I could, "there seems to be a problem with the connection on this phone. Can you stay on the line after I finish my call to assist me?" She seemed puzzled, but agreed. I ended my sales call and spent the next fifteen minutes chatting with the operator.

I admitted my ruse at the outset, but she didn't hang up. Instead, this beguiling telephone operator asked me questions about my job even as I inquired about hers. The small talk blossomed from there. By the end of our chat, I'd learned that her name was Loretta, and that she was a twenty-five-year-old immigrant from Europe living in a small apartment in Jersey City with her two younger sisters.

Before we had to disconnect, Loretta mentioned that she did not own any insurance policies. I offered to help her with that. We set a time to meet at her home after the holidays. She gave me her phone number and address, then said good-bye in a singsong, whispery way that insinuated that she wanted to talk to me about more than just insurance. I had no way of writing any of her information down. I repeated it out loud over and over again on the jubilant walk back home so that I wouldn't forget.

I'd gone to the candy store to sell a policy and come away with an unofficial date. Not bad at all.

The evening of the appointment with Loretta, I made my way by bus to Jersey City, ready to dazzle her, if not with my charm, then at least with my insurance policies. I arrived at her apartment, walked up the steps, and rang the bell. I could hear her thousand-watt smile through the door as she shouted, "I'll be right there, Ed!" That happy tone disappeared as soon as Loretta opened the door and spotted Kay. She reacted to me as if I were showing up at a Yankee fan club meeting wearing a Red Sox cap.

The voice that was so warm and pleasant on the phone suddenly turned as cold as the January air outside.

I quickly realized that this would no longer be a prelude to a courtship, but a rather quick dismissal. I made a few jokes at my own expense, trying my best to recapture the magic from our call. Loretta was having none of it.

My Irish temper started to bubble to the surface, just as it had done with the recruiters at college a few months before. I chastised Loretta for being too shallow. I asked her to think of me as more than just a blind man. She said, "I'm sorry. You're a good guy, and I liked talking to you on the phone. I just can't date a blind person, so I think that you should go now."

I took my cue and had turned to leave when an unfamiliar female voice called out from the corner of the apartment, "I can!"

Loretta shouted sternly back to her, "Excuse me? What did you say?"

The new voice continued, "I can date a blind person, especially one this cute." My admirer turned out to be Loretta's younger sister Delilah. She'd been hiding in the back of the room, observing our conversation at the door, and decided to speak up before I left for good.

The fury in Loretta's voice was evident as she snapped, "I forbid you to go out with him!"

Delilah calmly replied, "I'm twenty years old now, I can date whoever I want. Mom sent me to live with you, but she didn't make you my boss!" With that, she raced over to me, grabbed my arm, and said, "Let's go, Ed!" She walked me down the steps before Loretta could object any more. Before I knew it, we were at the Loew's Theater in Journal Square, holding hands as we watched Sidney Poitier in *Lilies of the Field*. Our love grew from there.

Delilah, or "Dee" as she liked to be called, was the second youngest of ten children, nine girls and one boy. Her mother was a widow who struggled to support her family on a meager farming income. One by one, she sent her daughters over from Europe to America, with its promise of a better life and unlimited riches. Her only son stayed behind to help run the farm. Dee, as a ten-year-old, was actually sent alone to the United States on one of the last boats to come through Ellis Island before it closed for good.

The fact that Dee was an immigrant boosted her appeal with my father, who was always in touch with his immigrant roots. My mother was thrilled that I was dating. She doted on Dee, treating her like a daughter from the very beginning.

Because I obviously couldn't drive, and Dee didn't yet have a license, we double-dated a lot. Gene Mehl and his girlfriend Karen would take us to concerts in New York. Dee and I would go to dances in Jersey City with my friends Bunny Courtney, Annette Spolazino, and Maryanne Donohue and their boyfriends. George Franconero and his fiancée Arlene took us to the movies and Broadway shows. Our social calendar was pretty packed.

It was after one of those nights in New York City that George and I decided to play a joke on Arlene and Dee. As we drove back home along Boulevard East in Weehawken, with its majestic view of the famous Manhattan skyline, George asked, "Ed, what time does it say on the clock at the top of the Empire State Building?"

Stifling a laugh because I remembered that there was no such clock, I secretly checked my Braille watch and replied, "It says 10:45 up there, George."

Arlene and Dee immediately began searching for the nonexistent clock, saying, "Where is it? We can't see it!"

I continued the joke, "The one right up there, about ninety floors high, under the needle." George played along, "You're right, Ed, it is 10:45, but the hands seem to be moving slower than normal tonight."

The girls were completely baffled. "We still can't see it, George, drive around again!" they shouted. He did. Their tempers rose as we circled the block about eight or nine times, looking for the phantom timepiece. Finally, after about fifteen minutes, Arlene realized which one of us had spotted the clock in the first place and caught on to the joke. The girls weren't too happy about being pranked, but laughed about it later.

George and Arlene also brought us over to his parents' house for big Italian dinners several times. Mrs. Franconero loved having more guests to feed. George's sister joined us on occasion. Dee happened to be the same dress size as Connie Francis. After dinner, Connie would bring her in to these enormous walk-in closets and say, "Take any dress you want, Delilah. The top designers give them to me for awards shows and TV appearances. I can't wear all of them. They're yours now." My girlfriend was extremely fortunate, and I was lucky to be dating her.

I desperately wanted Dee to share my love for baseball. I couldn't wait to take her to her first game. That happened on Sunday, May 31, 1964, when the Mets played my Giants at the brand-new Shea Stadium in Flushing, Queens.

A friend in Weehawken had a job as manager of all the vendors at Shea. He agreed to give us a ride over and back, as long as we waited for him to finish his tasks at the end of the game. It was actually two games. The teams would be playing a scheduled doubleheader that day. The first game started at 1:00 p.m., and the second started at 4:00 p.m. I figured we'd be back in Weehawken in time for dinner.

Not on that day, we wouldn't.

The second game turned out to be one of the longest games in baseball history. It lasted twenty-three innings, equal to almost three separate games. I loved it, but for Dee it was overkill. She was tired, bored, asking to go home. Even if we wanted to leave, we couldn't. We had to wait for our ride. Eleven and a half hours after we arrived at the ballpark, it ended. We began watching baseball in May and didn't get home until June. That unexpected marathon soured Delilah on baseball forever.

A few weeks later, on Father's Day, Dad and I sat in the backyard listening to the radio as the Phillies' Jim Bunning pitched a perfect game against the Mets. We were excited. Dee stopped to listen for a minute and said, "I don't see what you two are so worked up about, the announcer just said that nobody has gotten on base in nine innings. Sounds like a pretty boring game to me." Clearly America's pastime still hadn't won my girlfriend's heart. We wouldn't be bonding over baseball. That's okay, we had plenty of other things to share.

In October 1964, I took Dee out for a nice dinner and proposed to her. She happily accepted. One year later we were married at Saint Ann's Church in Jersey City. We had about 150 people at the reception, mostly from my side. Five of Delilah's sisters were there. Her mother and brother declined. Getting in touch with them was tough. Their farmhouse was in an extremely rural area of Europe that wasn't connected to any phone lines. We spoke to her mother that night by placing a call to the church rectory in the closest big town, twenty miles from the farm. The pastor then sent a buggy to fetch Dee's mom. They called us back when she arrived at the church half an hour later, and we spoke to her for about ten minutes.

After a quick honeymoon in Miami, we settled into our first apartment. It was a small one, right around the corner from my parents, on Forty-Ninth Street. The proximity helped and hurt. Because Dee didn't like to cook, we spent almost every night having dinner with my folks, which put a crimp in our married life. This went on for a few months until my father took me aside quietly and told me that Dee and I needed to establish our own nightly routine as a couple, away from them, or it would be very hard to grow our marriage. He was absolutely right. After a while, we did settle in, enjoying domestic bliss.

. . . .

By 1966, MY insurance sales were steady. I kept plugging away at baseball, hoping to get my big break. It wasn't as easy as I thought. Local papers were writing articles about my ambition to cover the game, despite my limitations. Some even came to take pictures of me and my family. That was flattering, but I didn't want to be seen just as a curiosity, like one of Barnum's oddities. I wanted most of all to be viewed and accepted as a peer by the men whose columns my father had been reading to me for years. They were my idols. I aspired to be one of them.

Unfortunately, they did not welcome me into their fraternity with open arms.

These titans of sports journalism cast me aside as if I was one of the tips on the cigars they ceaselessly chomped. Despite the fact that players like DiMaggio, Rizzuto, Mays, and Williams had given me their stamp of approval, I was still made to feel invisible by the senior members of the press corps.

There were a few young guys who treated me with respect. Maury Allen of the *New York Post*, Bill Madden of the *New York Daily News*, Moss Klein of the *Newark Star-Ledger*, Bill Shannon of UPI, Arnie Leshin of the *Hudson County Dispatch*, and Harvey Zucker of the *Jersey Journal* all swapped stories with me in the clubhouse and on the field. This "freshman class" never ignored me. We looked forward to decades of working side by side covering the local teams.

None of this camaraderie mattered to the older guys. Their mistreatment of me went beyond rookie hazing; it often bordered on the cruel. I could hear them regularly mocking Kay and me.

Things were said like, "Why is this blind guy taking up seats in our press box?" and, "He's just a token handicapped reporter that Jackie Farrell brought in to make the Yankees look good." All of these comments were made in what was known as an "Irish whisper," loud enough for me to hear, but soft enough to keep from being overheard by others.

My skin was pretty thick by then. I could take any insults thrown my way by the senior press because I knew that Scooter and the players were on my side. That illusion was shattered in dramatic fashion just a few weeks into the 1965 season.

I was in the visitors' clubhouse at Yankee Stadium getting ready to interview one of the biggest stars in baseball at the time. This guy was at the top of several lists and was on his way to an MVP-worthy season. He was always known to be something of a bully, but he was such a good player that everyone ignored him or pretended not to notice. Apparently he was also the type to rip a fellow player for striking out or missing a play. But no one had warned me.

I took my spot with the other writers and broadcasters in front of his locker. I had my microphone ready and running when he arrived and everyone started firing questions at him. Five minutes in, I spoke up and asked him a question about his goals for the season. There was a moment of silence before he blurted out, "Did the blind guy just ask me that? Why the hell are you here anyway? Who let you in?"

I was stunned by the ferocity of his comments, as he continued, "You can't even see the game, yet you have the nerve to ask me about what I'm going to do this season? Here's what I'm not going to do, talk to a cripple. Is this a clubhouse or a circus?"

None of my fellow reporters said anything, but one of the other players, sensing how uncomfortable the mood was getting, tried to make a joke out of it to ease the tension. It didn't work. The guy was on a jag now and couldn't be stopped, like a loudmouth in a nightclub who just won't shut up. I was humiliated. As I walked away, he added one last parting shot by shouting, "Take your dog and get out of here, my locker room ain't no effing kennel!"

This was a complete shock. I had no idea how to respond to the ignorant tirade. What bothered me the most was that I could hear some of the senior press members laughing as all of this was happening. Not a single one of those reporters whom I'd held in such high esteem felt the need to stick up for me, or to put this Neanderthal in his place. The locker room was silent. I couldn't see the looks on anyone's faces, but I hoped that at least a few of them were quietly shaking their heads in disgust, at such naked cruelty. Jarred by all of it, I walked upstairs with my guide to the parking lot feeling lower than I had at any time since my accident.

Scooter was exiting the Stadium at the same time we were. He noticed my dejected state. Mr. Rizzuto asked me what was wrong. I brushed him off. My guide indicated silently to Phil that something had gone seriously awry. Picking up the signal, Scooter told him to go on ahead, that he would drive me and Kay home. Scooter had something important to tell me.

The ride was pretty quiet as we crossed the George Washington Bridge from New York into New Jersey. This was unusual. Mr. Rizzuto and I were normally very talkative on our drives. Somewhere around Fort Lee, Phil finally broke the silence by asking me again what was wrong. I unloaded, telling him all about the ill-fated interview. He was outraged. I confessed that I'd begun to get the feeling that perhaps a career in baseball wasn't for me. Maybe the reporters were right. I didn't belong in their league. The tongue-lashing I'd been subjected to just cemented it.

Phil was having none of it.

As he drove, Scooter reminded me that his career started out on a shaky foundation. Nobody wanted him. Casey Stengel, who was managing the Brooklyn Dodgers in 1935, told Rizzuto during a tryout for the team that he should just buy a shoeshine box and give up on baseball. Even after he was signed by the Yankees, becoming their MVP, people still doubted him. In 1956, Stengel and the Yankee brass cut him without warning. Phil just shrugged it off and moved upstairs to the broadcast booth. Though fans loved him, critics constantly hammered Rizzuto because of his homespun style and partisanship for the Yankees. He wasn't supposed to last there either, but defied expectations.

"You see, Lucas," Scooter said with fatherly concern, "I never gave up or gave in. I knew what I was capable of, even if nobody else did. You are a smart guy, you've got a college degree and know more about baseball than anybody I've ever met. This is your calling."

I interrupted him by saying, "But, Phil, none of these guys will give me an inch. They all see me as an outsider. You don't hear half of the things they have to say to me."

Rizzuto cut me off. "That doesn't matter, kid," he insisted, "I heard the same things myself. You have to turn the other cheek. Ignore them. They all have their own fears and obstacles, but they are taking it out on you because you're an easy target. These guys don't even realize what they are doing. Forgive them and move past it." His little sermon made me feel much better. "Don't listen to the naysayers, kid," stressed Scooter. "Have faith. That will get you through everything." Phil spent the rest of the drive telling me stories:

Babe Ruth was picked on because of his weight and funny-looking nose.

Joe DiMaggio was discriminated against because he was considered a greasy Italian foreigner.

Jackie Robinson, Larry Doby, and Elston Howard faced strong opposition as they broke several color barriers in baseball.

I saw his point. They were all trailblazers. Each succeeded in changing opinions through their talent, outlook, and attitude. They all had to endure rough trials. They persevered. According to Phil, if these pioneers didn't quit, I had no right to, either.

When we pulled up to the house, I opened the door to get out and thanked Scooter for the ride. He stopped me for a moment and shared one last thing. "I've been on a lot of winning teams, and some losing ones. I learned a big lesson. The way you win in life, Lucas, is by getting back up whenever you get knocked down. Don't ever stop, keep moving forward." As I headed up the stairs to my apartment, he rolled the passenger-side window down and shouted, "I promise you, Lucas, it will get better. Keep at it. Someday they will give you awards and put you in a Hall of Fame. It won't be because you are blind, it will be for the person you are, the gifts you were blessed with, and how you treat others. You've got talent, Lucas. Never stop following your dream, kid."

As he drove away, I felt like I'd just won the World Series.

. . . .

God speaks to His children in many different ways. My particular messenger just happened to be the former shortstop for the New York Yankees. That evening, after listening to Mr. Rizzuto, I discovered not only the kind of broadcaster I wanted to be, but the kind of human being. Scooter set that bar pretty high.

Buoyed by Rizzuto's pep talk, I began to work even harder to make my mark. I'd been given a small baseball trivia column in our local paper, the *Hudson Dispatch*. For a few dollars a week, I was assigned to come up with questions that would stump the most ardent baseball fans. This was a nice gig, but what I really wanted was to contribute as a staff writer, filing nightly reports from Yankee Stadium. After a year of putting in requests, in the spring of 1966 the sports editor finally gave me a few paragraphs in the weekend edition to publish my interviews.

It was a modest start, but in my mother and father's eyes, I might as well have been writing full-page columns for the *New York Times*. I was a published writer. They were just as thrilled about my breakthrough as I was.

Dee, however, wasn't as impressed. She'd grown disillusioned with married life with me, living from paycheck to paycheck. Whether or not I was finally reaching my dream mattered little to her, it was all about the bottom line. These are normal growing pains for many young working-class marriages. It seemed like Dee was magnifying them.

When she learned that we would be having our first child in

January 1967, Dee calmed down a bit. This gave her a new role to play: Mom. I was excited, but I also knew that I would have to find a bigger apartment and to add even more income.

I took a second job, selling interior decoration services by phone for a local furniture store. Combined with my insurance and baseball workloads, I was running myself ragged. It was worth it, if I could be a better provider and stand on my own two feet.

My cousin, Vince Hartnett, was the program director for a small radio station sixty miles away on the Jersey Shore called WJLK. He hired me to mail tapes of my interviews from the ballpark, which would air in snippets throughout the day. I couldn't hear the station all the way up in Hudson County, but friends visiting the shore for the summer told me that they enjoyed listening to my shows.

When my son, Edward Martin Lucas, was born on January 15, 1967, I was still looking for something more stable than the piece-meal, commission, and freelance jobs that I was doing. I really wanted to work for Hudson County in any capacity. Employment with the county automatically meant security, benefits, and pensions, which were ideal for me and my family. I hoped that all of those things would provide peace of mind for Dee, who was growing more and more anxious by the day.

I spoke to every politician I could, but was making no progress. Surprisingly, it was the intervention of Jackie Farrell that finally cleared the logjam.

Farrell, who grew up in Jersey City, asked me what I'd be doing at the end of the baseball season. I told him about my search for a county job. He reached out to his childhood friend, Mike Kusick, who ran Meadowview Hospital, the county's mental health facility.

Jackie asked Mr. Kusick if there were any openings for a guy like me, who was sharp and had many talents, but couldn't see. There was just such a position, in the public relations department. However, Kusick's hands were tied. He loved my resume. My blindness had no impact on him at all. The roadblock was that the only way to get a job with Hudson County in 1967 was with the blessing of a politician. Even that late into the twentieth century, things were still controlled by the political machines.

Another old friend was able to help me out with that.

On October 10, 1967, Connie Francis was the headliner at a big fundraising concert for the Hudson County Democratic Party. The leader of the party was a guy named J. V. Kenney, who held the reins of the county machine tightly. Nothing happened without his approval. This was my opening.

I called George and asked him to talk to Connie. I wondered if she could put in a good word with Mr. Kenney on my behalf. There was silence. I apologized for crossing a line, but George then said, "Don't worry, Ed. You're my best friend and Connie loves you. We'd be happy to help."

The next morning, I was asleep when the phone rang. Not wanting to wake the baby up, I jumped for the phone. The commanding voice on the other end said, "Hello, is this Ed Lucas?"

I cleared my throat and replied, "It is. May I ask who's calling?"

The reply was quick, "This is your boss."

I was puzzled. I managed to blurt out, "I'm sorry, you must have the wrong number."

The confusion was cleared a moment later when he said, "There's no mistake, Ed. This is Mike Kusick from Meadowview Hospital. I got a call this morning from J. V. Kenney himself. Congratulations, you now work here. Can you meet me for lunch?"

My answer was yes!

I woke Dee up to tell her the good news. She appeared to be happy, but deflated the mood by adding, "Don't do anything to blow this." Not exactly the words of encouragement I wanted to hear from my wife.

At 11:00 a.m., I kissed Eddie and Dee good-bye and took a cab over to Secaucus, where the hospital was located. I signed the papers. I was officially a Hudson County employee.

On December 6, 1968, Dee and I had our second child, Christopher Patrick. Even though I had a steady job with benefits and was making more money, she was less enthusiastic than when Eddie was born. Her biggest problem with me was that I wasn't making as much money as her sisters' husbands were. Seven of her eight sisters had married. Most were living in the suburbs. They owned houses, cars, and jewelry.

We weren't keeping pace fast enough for Dee. I pointed out many times that we weren't starving, lacked for little, and were blessed with two healthy boys. That meant nothing to my wife. My definition of the American Dream didn't seem to be the same as hers. I knew that she was depressed and I wanted to help her.

I realized that part of the problem might have come from my visits to the ballpark during baseball season. I was selling some articles and broadcasts, but not nearly enough to justify the hours and evenings away from my wife and children.

I promised Delilah that I'd cut back on my baseball schedule once the season began to spend more quality time with her. I meant it.

With the two boys, Dee would need all the help she could get. Baseball could go on the back burner. She was more important to me than anything else. By walking away from the game for a bit, I wanted to show my wife that my love for her and for my family superseded my love for baseball. I might not be able to give Delilah lots of money, but I could give her my time and full attention; surely that would help.

The culmination of Dee's depression came a few months later when—without letting me know—she left home while I was at work to fly to Texas with our children. Loretta had moved to Austin to be near her new husband's family, so Dee followed her sister for a respite from New Jersey and our marriage.

I was understandably furious, but decided to respond in a quiet, loving way. I called her and said only three words: "What's going on?" I let Dee vent for almost an hour, uninterrupted. It was productive for me to hear. When she finished, I told her how much I loved her and how much our relationship meant to me.

I asked Dee what I could do to make her feel better, to be a better husband to her. She replied that she had no idea. I suggested counseling with our pastor. I also assured her that if she came back as soon as she could, we would work together to find the solution to her woes and to strengthen our marriage. She agreed and got on the next plane.

Before she got home, I made a silent vow: My next order of business, before I did anything else, would be to do the one thing that my parents had never been able to do.

I was going to buy a house.

7

Cold Cuts and Hot Feet:
My Life in the Clubhouse

In 1965, President Lyndon B. Johnson initiated a series of social reform programs he dubbed The Great Society. One of these involved providing assistance and funds to help disabled people purchase a home. As soon as I realized that I wanted to be a homeowner, I submitted my application. As with many government programs, there are lots and lots of hoops and red tape that you have to get through before actually reaching the goal. I was very close to the end of the process in 1971 when one last roadblock appeared. This one would be almost impossible to surmount without assistance. Luckily, I'd made a few influential friends at the ballpark.

Presidents Kennedy and Johnson were in office just as my baseball career began. They very rarely got to games, so I never met them. Over the years, however, I did have the opportunity to chat with several of the men who occupied the White House.

President George H. W. Bush was the captain of the Yale

baseball team in the 1940s. He was a big baseball fan, and often went to ballgames. I was in the National League clubhouse at the All Star Game in Toronto in 1991 when the Secret Service came in, unannounced, to clear the room of everyone but the players and coaches. I was headed out the door with the crowd when National League president Bill White, Mr. Rizzuto's longtime on-air partner with the Yankees, grabbed me and said, "Not you, Ed." A moment later, President Bush walked in with former Canadian prime minister Pierre Trudeau. White introduced me to both men. Mr. Bush shook my hand and called me an inspiration to all baseball fans. One of the players stuck a ball in my other hand and urged me to get Bush to autograph it. I reluctantly asked him, and he complied. It was only later, in the press box, that my guide told me the president had signed the ball in green ink, for some odd reason.

His son, George W. Bush, was managing general partner of the Texas Rangers before he won the presidency in 2000. The younger Bush actually traveled to Yankee Stadium with the Rangers on several occasions. I was in the hallway outside Mr. Steinbrenner's office one night in the early 1990s when "W" stopped to ask me what I thought of the Rangers' roster that season. We immediately hit it off. When he returned to Yankee Stadium as president to throw out the first pitch at the 2001 World Series, shortly after the September 11 attacks, I couldn't get near him to talk, but he waved and nodded in my direction as we passed in the tunnels below the Stadium.

President Clinton moved to New York after his term of office in Washington was done. He spent a lot of time at both Yankee Stadium and Shea Stadium, so I ran into him quite often. Clinton wasn't a historian of the sport, like the Bushes, but he could hold his own. What struck me the most about him was his boisterous laugh. Also, as others have said of him, President Clinton made me feel like I was the only person in the world he wanted to talk to at that moment.

But the commander-in-chief whom I got to know best was Richard Nixon.

In between the time that he lost to John F. Kennedy in the 1960 presidential election and the time he came back to win it all in 1968, Richard Nixon moved to New York City to practice law. He was also a big baseball fan. During those years, Nixon became a fixture at Yankee Stadium. His usual spot at the games was in the owner's box, just a few feet away from where I sat. We would often talk baseball, and he knew his stuff. After his presidency ended, Mr. Nixon would travel from his home in Upper Saddle River, New Jersey, to attend Yankee games. One of the greatest moments I ever experienced was when President Nixon tapped me on the shoulder in the middle of an inning. I stood up, took my headphones off, and stopped listening to the game. "Excuse me, Ed," Nixon said, "I don't mean to interrupt the game for you, but I just finished reading your article about Yogi Berra and had to tell you at once how much I enjoyed it. You and Yogi gave me some pretty good laughs just now!"

The article the president was referring to was in that month's Yankee scorecard magazine. I'd written a column in that issue about the time that Yogi and I stood around the batting cage talking about rookie players. I happened to mention to him that one of the youngsters could hit, throw, and catch skillfully with both hands. Berra's response to me was, "Man oh man, I'd give my right arm to be ambidextrous!" That was typical Yogi.

Gene Mehl happened to be my guide the day that President Nixon approached me. In a hasty attempt to capture the moment, Gene reached into his inside jacket pocket for his camera. Before he knew it, three Secret Service agents moved him away from me and the president. They wanted to be sure that it was only a camera he was going to shoot us with.

Gene never got his picture.

When our conversation was over, I shook President Nixon's hand, and proudly said, "Thank you, sir. It's an honor to get a compliment like that from you."

He continued, "I always look forward to your articles, Ed. Keep 'em coming. If there's anything you ever need, just let me know." I appreciated the offer, intending never to have to call on him for help unless it became completely necessary.

It turned out that I did.

By the time my application for Lyndon Johnson's mortgage assistance program for the disabled had gotten to the approval stage in 1971, Richard Nixon had been president for two years. New administrations often try to put their stamp on the country by rolling back or reshaping their predecessor's programs, and this is exactly what happened under Nixon. He and Congress put a freeze on many of the Great Society funds. I wasn't too worried. My application had been submitted long before the reverses were enacted, so I was told I was grandfathered in. The funds were supposed to be guaranteed for me. Knowing that, I'd already made a bid on a house on the west side of Jersey City.

The clerk in charge of approving my loan, however, wasn't so certain.

I was at work on the afternoon of Monday, May 3, when I received a call from a man at the Federal Office Building in Newark, New Jersey. He was phoning to let me know that I couldn't have the loan from the government due to the Nixon rollbacks. I calmly explained my grandfather clause to him. Still, he wouldn't budge. We went back and forth for over an hour discussing the fine points of government programs. Both of us felt strongly that we were right. My frustration was leading to anger when I decided to put a succinct end to the debate. "What's the bottom line here?" I said. "I only have a few days to complete my bid on this house, and I don't want to lose it. What would it take to get this loan approved?"

I could hear the sarcasm and self-satisfied snark dripping from the other end of the line as the clerk smugly replied, "The only way you are getting this money from us, Mr. Lucas, is if the president of the United States himself calls me and tells me that it's okay."

I broke into a huge grin that he couldn't see from his side of the call. "Thank you very much." I hung up the receiver to disconnect. A second later, I picked it up and dialed the White House.

The next morning, as I was getting ready for work, our doorbell rang repeatedly. I asked who it was at such an early hour. I recognized the nervous voice on the other side of the door right away. It was my telephone debate partner from the day before. A phone call wouldn't do. This clerk drove all the way from Newark to personally hand me papers with presidential approval for a loan in whatever amount I needed. He said very little to me, with the exception of humble apologies that continued from the time he walked up the front steps to our apartment until he got back to his car.

Dee and I were now the proud owners of our very own home.

We closed the deal on Friday, May 14, and moved in on the following Monday. It wasn't a mansion, but was just enough for us. The house was on Nunda Avenue, which is a dead-end street that borders a large county park. It was perfect for the boys to explore and play. There were three bedrooms, two bathrooms, and two levels. The bus stopped just up the street, so my commute was made a lot easier.

One of the other things I wanted to do for Dee now that she was back home was to get her a car. With a little help from Mr. Kusick, double shifts at work, and other small sacrifices, we were able to buy a family-sized station wagon. I also paid for Dee to take driving lessons.

One night, shortly after we moved in, Eddie called me into his room. It was long past his bedtime, but he was full of energy. He wanted me to read a few pages from his favorite Disney storybook. This is a rite of passage that almost all parents share as their children grow up. I desperately wanted to experience it, too, but I was prevented by my limitations. I offered to recite a fairy tale for Eddie from memory, but he was insistent. He wanted to read the book along with his father. I was trying to come up with another way to satisfy him when Dee burst into the room to find out why there was such commotion. Eddie said, "I want Daddy to read me a story and he doesn't want to!" Dee said, "He's blind, he can't read it. Your father will never be able to read books to you!"

I was sure that she didn't mean any harm with her remark, but I was crushed.

Around the same time, I began to notice that Kay was slowing down. Dogs usually have a ten- to twelve-year life span, which is great for the families that love them. Even when they naturally start to age and lose vision or mobility, pets are usually allowed to live out their days curling up quietly at their master's feet. For Seeing Eye dogs, it's quite different. As working dogs, they are subjected to the same chronological limitations as athletes. Thirty-five or forty is considered young in human years, but baseball players see their skills deteriorate so fast at that age that even the best choose to gracefully retire. Seeing Eye dogs at a comparable age in dog years can't climb steps or move at the same pace as their master, making them no longer fit to work. This heartbreaking realization came to me when Kay couldn't repeat even simple tasks that she'd done thousands of times. I had to make the tough decision to retire her and to take on a new partner.

I called the Seeing Eye. Our house was too small to be able to keep Kay and a new dog, even if I wanted to. They suggested that I bring her back to happily live out her retirement years on their farm with another owner. I went back to the Seeing Eye for my second dog. Eddie and Chris were still too young to feel the loss like most kids would, but Kay was more than my pet, she was an extension of me. I wondered if I'd be able to welcome and adapt to a new partner. Would the heartache end?

Three weeks later, I left the Seeing Eye with my new dog, Flo. She was a black Labrador. Flo moved at a different pace. Kay would stop on a dime at street corners. Flo would reduce speed as she approached the same corners. Flo was noticeably slower. Their training was exactly the same, but all dogs—like humans—have different personalities and styles. I had no choice but to adjust to her. Months after Flo came to live with us, I was still slipping up and calling her Kay. I loved my new dog, but felt the loss of my partner of over a decade, and it made me sad.

To cheer me up, several friends and family members came over to meet Flo and to bring housewarming gifts for her, Dee, and the boys.

I'd already been blessed in my life with a great gift, a sense of humor. I used it as a way to get through dark moments. My visitors knew this, so we spent hours trading punch lines, laughing long into the evening. It was just the tonic I needed.

ONE OF THE people who was the most supportive during that time was also, without a doubt, the funniest man I've ever met.

Jerry Molloy was the living definition of the cheery Irishman, always ready with a joke. He was a Hudson County legend, not only for his encyclopedic memory of great comic lines, but also for his role as a baseball and basketball coach for three different local teams. Jerry held the New Jersey record for wins with over one thousand at each school. The guy was tireless.

He had such a great sense of humor that Jerry was an extremely popular after-dinner speaker. Eventually, New Jersey named him toastmaster general, an honorary post that took him all over the state entertaining crowds. Jerry definitely knew how to make me, and everyone else who crossed his path, laugh. He also encouraged me to develop my own banquet speech, one that would highlight my life in baseball and all that I'd accomplished since my accident.

My baby picture, 1940.

A studio portrait for Easter, at age 4, with my sister, Maureen, age 2, 1943.

Standing outside our home at the Lafayette Gardens Housing Project in Jersey City, 1947.

A school picture from P.S. #22, age 9, just a few years before the accident that would take my sight away forever.

A photo article about me and my broadcasting goals that appeared in The Jersey Journal *in 1956.*

LISTENING .N—Eddie Lucas (standing) entertains his sister Maureen and his parents Mr. and Mrs. Edward Lucas (seated left to right) with tape recordings of some of the interviews he has had with major league ballplayers. Eddie, who lost his sight five years ago hopes to make a career of interviewing sports celebrities.

In the dugout at New York's Polo Grounds in 1957, with Giants manager Bill Rigney and friends.

My graduation from the New York Institute for the Blind, 1958.

Celebrating my graduation with Maureen, my Dad and Mom in our Weehawken apartment, 1958.

The Seeing Eye class of summer 1958. I'm second from the right with Kay, my first Seeing Eye Dog.

My first big interview—with superstar Willie Mays—at the Polo Grounds. It was his last day as a New York Giant—September 29, 1957.

With Mickey Mantle on Old Timer's Day in 1977. Though he was an American icon, Mick was still among the the most humble and generous people I was ever blessed to know.

Sharing a laugh with Mr. DiMaggio at his locker on Old Timer's Day in 1978.

Sitting in the Yankee dugout in 1980 with Scooter and Yogi. I'm proudly wearing my gold blazer and purple tie, the symbols of my long association with the Lions Club.

On the field in 1979 with my second Seeing Eye dog, Flo, and the late Yankee captain Thurman Munson, a gentleman in every sense of the word.

With my personal home run hitting tutor, Reggie Jackson, in 1980.

After Dee walked out on our family, I had to raise the boys all by myself. I'd often take them to work with me at the ballpark. Here we are in the stands at Shea Stadium in 1974.

My sister and my parents were, as always, there for me when I needed them the most. They watched the boys when I couldn't. This is Mom and Dad at Eddie's First Holy Communion, in 1975, at Saint Aloysius Church, Jersey City, with Chris and Maureen's son, Jeffrey.

Bob Diehl, Yankee relief
pitcher Goose Gossage,
and me in 1981.

Bob Hope giving me a few
golf pointers in 1981 as my
guide, Angelo, looks on.

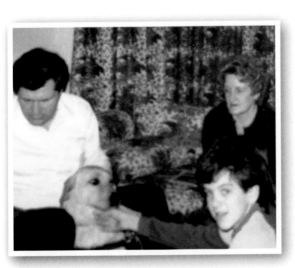

At the Seeing Eye with my third
dog, Bessie, my son Chris, and a
family friend, 1982.

Yankee pitcher Dave Righetti, with me and my fourth (and last) Seeing Eye Dog, Tommy, in 1984. Dave was trying to "see" the locker room just by hearing, like I do, so he closed his eyes for a few minutes while we chatted.

Posing with "The Donald" and Chris in 1990. One of the rare times you will ever see Mr. Trump out of his customary business attire.

Allison and me on our first date at Yankee Stadium, with our matchmaker, Phil Rizzuto, 1991.

The story of my long battle to win back custody of my boys made headlines all over the world in 1980. This is just one of the hundreds of articles that appeared. I'm still touched and humbled by the outpouring of support and love that came our way.

Doing the job that I love the most, broadcasting, with my mentor, Phil Rizzuto, on WPIX in 1990.

Scooter and me at our annual charity golf outing in New Jersey, 1998.

In October 1998, this was one of the last photos taken of me, the boys and my mom together.

At a party in 1999 with Sister Anthony Marie, the teacher who changed my life.

With Cal Ripken, Jr., and my lifelong best friend, Gene Mehl, in 1996.

I've known Yogi Berra for more than fifty years. He looks the same to me today as he did when I first saw him in 1947. What an amazing guy.

With slugger Barry Bonds in 2000. His late father, Bobby, was a dear friend.

Me, Johnny Damon, and Chris in the Yankee dugout, 2007.

With Chris and the King of Queens himself, actor Kevin James, outside the Mets locker room at Citi Field, 2013.

Turning the tables on one of my broadcast interview idols, Larry King, in 2008.

At the 2008 Hall of Fame reunion in Cooperstown with Willie Mays, almost 51 years to the date of our first interview.

I've been blessed to know several U.S. presidents. Here I am with Bill Clinton at Shea Stadium in 2007. I was quite impressed with his extensive baseball knowledge. (Photo courtesy of Bill Menzel Photography)

In the dugout at the new Yankee Stadium with The Captain, Derek Jeter, in 2009.

Outfielder Nick Swisher in the clubhouse pouring champagne all over me after a Yankee playoff division series win in 2010.

At a dinner in 2013 honoring Academy Award winner Robert DeNiro, who was Mr. Rizzuto's favorite actor.

I bonded with Robin Williams over our love for the San Francisco Giants.
(Photo courtesy of Bill Menzel Photography)

At Citi Field in 2013 with Chris, Eddie, my daughter-in-law, Sharon, and my grandson, E.J.

With my lovely bride, Allison, at our historic home plate wedding at Yankee Stadium, March 10, 2006.

Just moments after the wedding, we posed outside the Yankee clubhouse with actor/director Penny Marshall, who flew out just to share in our special day.

At my 75th birthday party, January 2014, with the whole Lucas family—Eddie; his wife, Sharon; E.J.; Allison; Chris and his two boys, Adam and Sean. I thank God every day for the joy they've all brought to my life.

To give me firsthand experience, Jerry would take me along with him to speaking engagements. We traveled to breakfasts, luncheons, and dinners from Cape May to Mahwah. I was learning from the master, filling my repertoire with jokes for all occasions to help round out my presentation. We usually wound up back in Jerry's hometown of Hoboken after we were done. He would bring me to a social club to hang out with his best friends Dolly and Marty, who just also happened to be the parents of my favorite singer, Frank Sinatra.

One night, we came home extremely late from a dinner in central Jersey. Jerry was the emcee. He spent hours after the affair ended chatting with admirers and giving advice about speaking. By the time we got back to Jersey City, it was pitch dark. Jerry drove down my block, pulled up to the house, and began walking me to the front steps. I knew right away that something was amiss. My house had steps leading down, this staircase was going up. I stopped Jerry and said, "This is wrong."

He asked me how I could possibly know that if I couldn't see where we were. He insisted that I was mistaken. When I explained, Jerry took out a match and read aloud the number on the mailbox. I started laughing. "Jerry, that's three numbers away from my house; I'm telling you this isn't the right place." He sheepishly agreed.

When he finally brought me to my steps, I turned around and asked, "Would you like me to drive you home, too, Jerry?"

A few months after that, Jerry was booked to speak at a Knights of Columbus pancake breakfast in Camden. It was about one hundred miles south of Jersey City. There was no such thing as satellite GPS back then. Jerry was hopelessly lost. After driving around in circles, we finally pulled up to a banquet hall, but Jerry still wasn't sure if it was the correct location. He left the car running, got out, and said, "Stay here, Ed, I'm going to head inside and see if it's the K of C breakfast. If it is, I'll come right back for you."

Forty-five minutes later, I heard him shouting, "I'm so sorry, Eddie!" as he dashed in a panic toward the car.

When Jerry had entered the hall to see if he was in the right place, they immediately escorted him to the dais because it was his turn to speak. Jerry was so flustered that he completely forgot about me. Three-quarters of the way into his talk, he stopped midjoke and screamed, "Holy smokes! I've got to get back to the parking lot!"

We both used that story in our speeches for years.

I wasn't going to the ballpark much, because I'd made my promise to Dee. I missed baseball, but the respite came at the right time. The Yankees were in an uncharacteristically horrible slump. After decades of being the gold standard in sports, the team had fallen hard. The farm system was decimated, legends like Mickey Mantle had retired without suitable replacements, and the league had expanded. From 1965 to 1972, the Bronx Bombers wound up at or close to the bottom of the standings. This was bad for fans, but even worse for freelance writers and broadcasters like me who covered the team. The formerly hapless Mets were now the toast of the town. I still hadn't made many connections with the Mets, so I didn't enjoy as much access with them as I did with the Yankees. Nobody was buying stories about the Yankees unless they involved scandals or slinging mud, and that just wasn't my style.

Nevertheless, I nurtured my love for the game in other ways.

My son Eddie was now old enough to be able to play baseball in the backyard with me. My father bought Eddie a kid-sized Wiffle ball and bat for his fifth birthday. As soon as the first nice weekend day came along, Eddie begged me to go outside and play with Grandpa's gift. I couldn't wait.

Dee had gone out shopping with Chris to get him new shoes that day, so it was just me and Eddie alone in the backyard. We used the house as a backstop. I set Eddie up at a makeshift home plate. I walked a few feet away and told him to say something so I'd know in which general direction to throw the soft plastic Wiffle ball. After more than a few tries, Eddie connected.

My son got his first hit!

Other than the cries of Eddie and Chris when they were born, this was the sweetest sound I'd heard in years.

We spent the next thirty minutes or so repeating the routine. I would pitch the ball, Eddie would swing. If he hit it, the trajectory was so slow that it would only take me a minute to find the ball. If he missed, the ball would bounce off the house and roll back to me. Either way, we were able to play this father-son game without interruption.

Then Eddie suggested that we switch sides.

I agreed, but told him that he would have to let me know when he was throwing the ball so that I could take a guess and swing at it. He lovingly replied, with that endearing logic that little children often possess, "No, Daddy, you don't understand. We're switching places. Now I'll be the blind one, and you can see!"

I hugged him and continued our game, filled with mixed emotions over his innocent request.

A few days before that, I'd had a conversation with a fellow graduate of the New York Institute for the Blind named Barbara. As we caught up on old times, Barbara told me that her son, like Eddie, had asked her to read stories to him at bedtime. She shared the same frustration that I did. Barbara was thrilled that she'd found a company called Twin Vision for the Blind in Tarzana, California, that provided books for blind parents to read along with their children.

Twin Vision was founded by a sighted woman, Jean Norris, in 1959. She'd heard a blind parent at a meeting express the same concern that Barbara and I had. Norris, who was adept at Braille, took action. She transcribed several books into Braille, with the printed version and illustrations on one side of the page and the raised dots on the other. They were an immediate hit. Within a few years, she was shipping thousands of these Braille children's books for free to blind parents and youngsters all over the United States.

Barbara had been using the Twin Vision service for a while. She was very happy with them. I signed up for it. The night the first book, *Pinocchio*, arrived, I sat down on the edge of Eddie's bed and read it side by side with him. As happened with the little puppet in the story, a transformation occurred. A whole new world had opened up for both of us. To Eddie, I wasn't his "blind" father, I was just "Dad." There were no more strings on me.

Eddie's little brother, Chris, was being teased by the other kids in first grade a few years later. They were telling him that their fathers could do things that I couldn't do. Chris shut them all up at once by saying, "Oh, yeah? Well, I bet that your dad doesn't have special powers like my dad does. He can read to us in the dark!" Twin Vision had turned me into a superhero.

My wife didn't share that view.

. . . .

Delilah got a phone call in May 1972 that brought her to tears. I could hear her crying from the other room, so I rushed over to console her. My first thought was that something terrible had happened to her mother back in Europe. Dee's explanation stunned me. She said, "It's not my mother, it's my little sister, Eva!" This was shocking. Eva was four years younger than Delilah, and had just moved out to California to look for work.

I asked, "Is your sister okay? Did she get hurt?"

"No," Dee sobbed, "she's getting married!" Now I was really confused. I thought wedding announcements were supposed to be happy news. When it came to my wife and her sisters, they weren't.

Dee's siblings always had a competitive streak. Each one had to outdo the other. Only one of them still lived in Jersey City like we did. Her sister Stella married a county employee, had several children, and was very happy staying put. She was often treated like the black sheep in the family. For the other sisters, life in America had to be onward and upward.

I asked Dee why she wasn't happy for her sister. "Happy?" she screamed. "Do you know what her fiancé did to celebrate? He took her to Chez Madeline, the most expensive restaurant in Fresno. It's one hundred dollars a plate! Then they got on a plane to Hawaii for a two-week vacation."

I still didn't understand why this wasn't cause for joy. I reminded Dee that we'd been pretty blessed ourselves lately, with the new job, the house, the car, the boys . . .

"You call all of this a blessing?" she said, getting more agitated than I'd seen her in a while. "I'm cooking hot dogs and taking my sons to the swings on the playground, while my baby sister is eating at five-star restaurants and flying to Maui. Where's the blessing in that?"

Delilah stormed off into our room and slammed the door. I wanted to give her some space, so I slept on a cot in the room with our sons. The next day, when I arrived home from work, Dee was waiting outside. It was a Friday afternoon, so I thought that she might want to go out to dinner.

She had other plans.

Dee put the handle of a heavy suitcase in my hand and said, "Feel this." I knew what it was, but not why it was there. Her next words hit with a thud. "I'm leaving." I was thrown off balance as I replied, "Leaving what?" She shot back with, "You, I'm leaving you. I can't do this anymore." I stood there silently for about ten minutes, too stunned to respond.

Finally, I broke the silence by asking Dee why she was leaving, and how long she'd be gone this time. "This isn't like Texas," she said. "I'm leaving forever. I'm not coming back. This marriage is in no way what I pictured it would be. I need to go somewhere to find myself."

In a combination of confusion and defensiveness, I fired back, "Find yourself? What is that supposed to mean? Whatever is wrong, we can work together to make things right."

Delilah sighed and said, "That's just it, Ed. I don't want it to be work anymore. Marriage should be easy. Everything should be simple. My sisters don't have to do much and everything is taken care of for them. I want that, too, and it's clear I'm never going to get it with you."

At that moment, one thing became shockingly clear to me: No matter how much talking or reasoning I did, there would be no convincing Dee to change her mind. My marriage, like my heart, was shattered irreparably.

Once I let that reality sink in, I turned to the most important matter of all, my boys.

Luckily, Eddie and Chris were with my parents at a zoo in New York City for the day and didn't witness any of this.

"What about our sons?" I asked.

The sound of her voice was as cold and emotionless as I'd ever heard, "You can keep them."

I wanted to be sure that I was hearing her right, so I asked again. "You're leaving me and them? You'll come to see them on weekends or something, right?"

The silence that followed from her told me all that I needed to know.

"I can't take them with me," said Dee. "I want to travel and to discover the kind of person that I should be. I have to explore that alone. The boys would just get in the way." The last remark really upset me.

"Get in the way?" I was shouting now. "These are your children! You're just going to leave them without saying good-bye? What should I tell them?"

"You're a writer," Dee said. "Make up something creative."

Suddenly, incredible sympathy for what my wife must have been going through welled up inside me. I couldn't imagine anything that might haunt her so much that it would push her to just give up and leave everything she loved behind—especially her children. She must have been in deep torment.

Before I had a chance to ask her to stay long enough to see her sons, a cab pulled up. Dee rushed into it with her bags, telling the driver to take off as fast as he could.

That was the last we saw or heard from her for almost a year.

In April 1973, Dee got in touch with George Franconero, who was then acting as my lawyer, to let him know that she was officially filing for divorce with the state of New Jersey and annulment with the Church. She would give up her rights to the house and grant me full custody of the boys.

She never even bothered to show up for the hearings in court.

Four weeks later, Dee married a guy named Burt, whom she'd met the previous November. He was a Yugoslavian immigrant who owned a chain of successful butcher shops in New York and New Jersey. They bought a big house in the suburbs and had eight children together over the next decade.

I was sad to see my marriage end, but I wasn't bitter. I wished Delilah, who was now going by her middle name—Beverly—well in her new life. Occasionally, she would call to ask for Eddie and Chris to come and visit her. I never said no to her requests.

My sister Maureen and her husband Jimmy moved into the house on Nunda Avenue with us to help out. Their son Jeffrey was born just a few months after Chris, so he and the boys became like brothers. We converted one of the rooms on the lower level into a bedroom for me, and Maureen took the master room. It was a perfect living arrangement.

For the first time in a long time, we had peace and calm.

MORE THAN A few friends made the joke that I was now free to go on "blind" dates. I laughed heartily along with them. Once again, God's gift of humor was my lifeboat in rough waters.

Still, something important was missing. I kept hearing the siren call of baseball. Perhaps it was just the voice of Scooter, who let few broadcasts go by without asking, "Where's that huckleberry Lucas tonight?" The time was right to head back to Yankee Stadium.

Jackie Farrell reached out to me after the divorce to see if I needed anything. He also invited me to come over to the Bronx to meet one of the new owners of the Yankees, a shipping magnate from Cleveland named George M. Steinbrenner III.

Mr. Steinbrenner put together a group that bought the team on what happened to be my thirty-fourth birthday, January 3, 1973. He promised to be a "silent owner," but that didn't last long. After seeing how badly neglected the Yankees, and their ballpark, had been by their previous owners, CBS, he took action.

The old guard of reporters mocked George for his plans to re-habilitate Yankee Stadium and the team. These were the same guys who had ostracized me a few years earlier. For many of them, this was their parting shot. They were close to retirement age. A new wave of broadcasters was taking their place, and I felt more at home with this crowd. Many of them, like Warner Wolf, Sal Marchiano, Chris Berman, Jon Miller, Bob Uecker, and Al Michaels, welcomed me warmly when I came back to the press box.

George Steinbrenner joined the group that greeted me. In our very first meeting, I was surprised that he asked me how I was doing and even how my boys were. Jackie Farrell and Mr. Rizzuto had told him my story a few weeks earlier, and the new boss showed genuine concern for me. I was astounded.

Before he left, George said, "Eddie, you're part of the Yankee family now. I expect to see you in that seat almost every game."

Who was I to disagree with him?

My seat actually moved a few New York interborough bridges over in 1974. George decided to give Yankee Stadium a facelift after fifty years, so the team had to move to Shea Stadium in Queens for two seasons. They shared it with the Mets. Luckily, I'd already had a guided tour of the new ballpark, provided by one of its biggest heroes.

Outfielder Ron Swoboda saved the World Series for the Mets in 1969 with a miraculous catch in Game 4. That made him an instant Mets legend. I had gotten to know him a few years earlier, when he was a rookie. I once interviewed him for my radio show about his feelings on breaking into the majors. He stopped midchat to turn the tables and to ask me a question.

Swoboda wanted to know how I lost my sight. When I told him about my boyhood accident, he followed by asking me if anyone had ever taken me around a major league park to describe it up close. I said no. I spent the next forty-five minutes walking with Ron as he helped me better visualize Shea Stadium by running my hand along the outfield wall, touching the bases, and traveling the length of the warning track.

This would come in very handy now that the Yankees were playing there.

A renewed winning mentality was instilled in the Yankees under George Steinbrenner. Shortstop Gene Michael, catcher Thurman Munson, and outfielder Bobby Murcer were three of the Yankees who really embraced it, helping to build the team back up. I was lucky enough to develop close relationships with all of them. They made it much easier for me to do my job, paving the way for me to be accepted as just one of the guys in the clubhouse.

Gene Michael was known as "Stick," not for his prowess with a wooden bat, but for his tall and lanky frame. Though he wasn't the biggest star on the team, Michael was definitely the shrewdest. Gene was a master at the "hidden ball" trick, which he demonstrated for me several times during interviews. He was usually the first player to greet me when I came into the clubhouse. When his playing career ended, Stick became a Yankee for life, holding every job imaginable with the team—coach, manager, GM, scout, executive—everything except for peanut vendor.

Thurman was a bit more complicated. He was Rookie of the Year when he came up with the Yankees and was the leader of the team, on his way to becoming captain. Thurm could be mercurial, and wasn't a fan of the media. He rarely granted interviews. For some reason, he and I had a pretty easygoing relationship right from the start. Munson knew that I was a reporter, but didn't mind talking to me. I was able to tell what mood he was in as soon as I walked in the door. I gave him room on days that he wasn't up for conversation. Thurman liked that. He told other players on the Yankees, and around the league, that I was a guy they could trust. I appreciated that. Thurman and I developed a mutual respect.

Bobby Murcer was, like Mickey Mantle, a kindhearted and talented Oklahoma boy. He took over Mantle's position as the Yankees' primary slugger. He also treated me just as well as his predecessor had. Murcer's sense of humor was amazing. I can't recall a day that went by without the two of us joking with each other before and after games.

Bobby had something unusual at his locker stall. He placed an old-fashioned rocking chair in front of it. He would sit there conducting interviews as he rocked back and forth. Murcer claimed that the soothing motion helped him to recover from the various aches and pains that came from playing baseball. It definitely set him apart.

One evening, I was talking to Bobby about the two outstanding defensive plays he'd made in that night's game. He spent ten minutes giving me some great quotes. Five minutes in, I noticed that something was different. Murcer was standing up. I commented on it. Bobby said that the rocking chair had developed a small crack, which he repaired. He wasn't sitting on it, allowing the glue to dry properly. As I was putting my tape recorder away, I said, "Thanks for the interview, Bobby. I have to say, though, this is the first time I've ever spoken to a player who actually admitted to being off his rocker!"

Unfortunately for Murcer, the move to cavernous Shea Stadium in 1974 hurt his home run swing. He hit only two dingers that year, way down from his average of over twenty-five a season. The Yankees traded him to San Francisco in 1975 for another hard-hitting Bobby. His replacement became one of my closest friends in baseball.

BOBBY BONDS ONLY played for one season with the Yankees. It was a memorable one. He hit thirty-two home runs in 1975, stole thirty bases, and scored almost one hundred runs. He was one of the first of George Steinbrenner's big player acquisitions. He came up in 1968 with the Giants and was a protégé of Willie Mays, so I got to know him even before he arrived in New York. Like Thurman, Bobby didn't really trust the media. Nevertheless, he always took the time to talk to me. I wanted to know his feelings about the game. Bobby was fascinated with the details of my life as a blind reporter. It was a two-way street.

The thing that really caught Bobby's attention was my ability to tell where the ball was going just by the sound of the crack of the bat. Every day at batting practice, Bobby would call out, "Eddie, do your thing!" I'd then predict, with about 99 percent accuracy, where the ball was going to land. Players and fellow broadcasters would gather around to watch.

Over the years, people have asked me to describe what it sounds like to hear a ball hit and to know instantly where it's going. It's an innate sense that just comes naturally to me, so it's hard to put into words, just like it would be hard for you to describe what "salty" tastes like, without using that exact term. The closest analogy to my unique method of following a game would be the echolocation that bats use in caves. They hear sounds bounce back to them, enabling them to tell where they are and where they are headed. The volume and pitch of a baseball bat making contact tells me all I need to know as it rings through the ballpark. To my sensitive ears, a long home run sounds almost like a cannon being fired. A weak fly ball reminds me of a champagne cork popping, and an infield hit is reminiscent of twigs snapping underfoot. The direction is just a matter of listening for the echo. I've always been able to tell the difference, without fail.

At the end of the 1975 season, Bobby finally found a way to stump me. I stood by the batting cage feeling as confident as ever with my sonic feat. Bonds grabbed me in a bear hug and said, "You're never wrong about what goes on at the plate, are you, Eddie?" I agreed with him. "Okay, smart guy," he said, as he chuckled, "let's try this. The next player who gets up, tell me whether he's black, white, or Hispanic."

That was one trick I couldn't pull off.

During the summer, Bobby would occasionally bring his ten-year-old son, Barry, to the ballpark. Like other players' kids, Barry would sit in the clubhouse while his dad was on the field. He would also play pickup ball games with other children in the hallway outside the locker room as Bobby did interviews. Barry was a great kid, very respectful and courteous. Bobby raised him well. Like his dad, Barry was curious to know more about my blindness. Bobby would sometimes ask me to look after his son when he had to go upstairs to talk to the boss, or to do a national TV interview in the studio. To pass the time, I'd hand Barry my Braille watch. He loved it. Barry and I started a great relationship that lasted throughout his own stellar twenty-one-year career in the 1990s and 2000s with the Pirates and Giants.

And, of course, my two boys traveled with me to the ballpark whenever they weren't in school.

CHRIS LOVED TELEVISION, radio, and movies, so he'd sit with the camera operators, engineers, and producers, learning how a broadcast is put together. Eddie was more into sports. He would be downstairs, joining in those pickup hallway games with the players' sons, some of whom went on to great heights. How many kids can say that they got to toss a ball around with future superstars like Barry Bonds, Cal Ripken, Jr., Roberto Alomar, and Ken Griffey, Jr., when they were very young? My Eddie can. The boys were enjoying some unique experiences.

I never wanted my sons to feel like they were missing out on anything because of my disability. Perhaps I even overcompensated for it. I tried to take the boys everywhere. I felt the need to do things that any other father would, even to go some places that others wouldn't or couldn't.

The Loew's Journal Square Theater in Jersey City, the same place where Dee and I had our very first date, showed special Disney double features on Saturdays in the 1970s. The boys really enjoyed Disney films. When we weren't at the ballpark, I'd take them by bus to the movies. We had a little ritual. We'd stop at Boulevard Drinks, next door to the theater, for a hot dog and Lime Rickey lunch, then to the movies. When the films were done, we'd walk to the Canton Tea Garden, where my parents used to treat my sister and me in the 1940s, for a big Chinese meal.

The double feature usually started with a classic Disney animated film, finishing with a modern live action one, like *Herbie the Love Bug* or *The Apple Dumpling Gang*. Unlike today, they didn't have thirty minutes of commercials and previews before the movie. The theater used piped-in classical music as a preshow. The music would end abruptly, the curtain would open, and the film would begin. I'd generally seat the boys, then head to the lobby for popcorn and candy, getting back just in time for the start of the film.

One week, the bill was *Fantasia* and *The Boatniks*. We ran late that day, so we took our seats with a few minutes to spare. I went to get the popcorn and rushed back into the theater just after the appointed starting time. I still heard the classical music playing, so I figured I was okay. Ten minutes later, still no movie. I checked my watch. Twenty minutes had gone by and all I heard was classical music. Finally, I leaned over to Chris and said, "When is the movie going to start?" He whispered back, "It already started, Daddy. It's been going on for a while!"

Nobody told me that *Fantasia* had been rereleased in the 1970s with certain cuts to shorten the running time. This newly edited version actually removed the little bits of dialogue that existed between the classical music segments. I had no idea what was happening.

I'd taken my sons to see a cartoon that essentially amounted to a silent movie for me.

Chris was fascinated by magic when he was young. He wanted me to hire a magician at every birthday party, communion breakfast, and lemonade stand opening that he had. I kept a guy named Prince Jasper pretty much on retainer.

Jasper was a classic showman, with the requisite tuxedo, doves, linking rings, and fire-eating. Chris idolized him and imitated his every move. I took Chris and Eddie to magic shows all over New York and New Jersey. As a special treat, I even got private backstage lessons from both Harry Blackstone and Doug Henning when they were appearing on Broadway.

Eddie was more of an athlete. I decided to take my boys to a dude ranch in upstate New York so that we could spend a week enjoying the genuine cowboy experience. Horseback riding was a big selling point for the resort, so we signed up for lessons.

This would be the first time on a horse for each of us. There were about fifteen other people in the group. Our instructor helped us get comfortable in the saddle on our individual horses. Mine was named Tachyon. The instructor explained that we would all follow him in line slowly down a dirt road, which would eventually branch off into three different trails. They were marked EASY, HARD, and EVEN THE CRAZIEST HOLLYWOOD STUNTMAN WOULDN'T ATTEMPT THIS ROUTE. When we arrived at the fork, my horse decided to break from the pack and go his own way.

Guess which trail he picked?

The instructor screamed in horror as soon as he saw Tachyon bolt down the dangerous path. I hung on for dear life. Before I knew it, the horse was jumping and ducking, with me trying to follow its body movements. At one point, Tachyon was racing down a trail that had low-hanging limbs. Sighted riders might see them and know enough to duck, but I couldn't. I was being repeatedly smacked in the head with tree branches.

It was like something out of a Three Stooges movie.

Finally, I was able to pull the reins tight enough to get the horse to stop. The others caught up to me, and the owners apologized profusely. Other than a few scratches, I was fine. Eddie and Chris, who had watched my adventure helplessly from atop their horses, came over and said, with shrieks of laughter, "That was awesome, Daddy. Do it again!" I declined.

My time as a cowboy ended that day. I'd stick to talking about sports instead.

IN APRIL 1976, Yankee Stadium reopened. The team was home again. Mr. Steinbrenner and the city did an amazing job. I was excited to be attending my nineteenth straight Opening Day. The team itself had also gotten a facelift. Former second baseman Billy Martin was now the manager, bringing not just his fiery temperament but also a link to the great 1950s teams that had been missing. Thurman had developed into a true leader and had the team primed for another dynastic run. Superstar pitcher Catfish Hunter was a big free agent acquisition for George. Sparky Lyle was now the game's dominant closer.

Things were looking up in the Bronx.

The Stadium was jam-packed. American flag bunting ringed the stands and old-timers from every Yankee championship team were introduced.

Mr. Steinbrenner had given me something I never had before, a permanent assigned seat in the press box with my name engraved on it. The chorus of voices ridiculing my inclusion in the New York media's inner circle was growing smaller, but they were still there. George was determined to silence them completely.

Just before game time, a familiar voice said, "Hey, Eddie, glad to see you. Do you mind if I take that empty seat next to you?"

I'd know that voice anywhere—it was the Yankee Clipper himself, Joe DiMaggio!

"Not at all, Mr. DiMaggio," I said, as I started to take my radio out of the bag and set up my headsets.

Joe inquired, "What are you doing?" I told him that I needed to listen to the game on the radio to be able to follow what was happening.

DiMaggio's next remark took me by surprise. "Put those away, kid. I'll do the play by play for you."

And so he did. For the next nine innings, I listened with rapt attention as one of the greatest baseball players ever sat next to me calling his team's 11–4 win over the Twins in their newly remodeled home.

I've had many surreal moments in my life, but the day that Joltin' Joe became my own private announcer definitely ranks close to the top.

Scooter had his own table in the new press dining room. By then, he was an iconic part of Yankee broadcasts. He was also one of the best-known voices in the country. The rock singer Meat Loaf featured Phil on his hit single "Paradise by the Dashboard Light," and Scooter was doing commercials for a place called the Money Store that ran on local TV incessantly. Phil was famous beyond the world of baseball. Celebrities from all areas began to flock to Yankee Stadium in the late 1970s. It was, once again, the "it" place to be. Most of them made a stop to see Mr. Rizzuto as he held court at his little spot in the dining room.

Bob Sheppard, the Yankees' longtime public address announcer, usually sat with Phil. If Robert Merrill, the legendary Metropolitan Opera singer, happened to be at the Stadium, he would be there, too. Scooter always reserved a seat for me. This gave me the opportunity to break bread with many people whom I admired.

Mr. Rizzuto's table was like the couch on *The Tonight Show*.

Former U.S. secretary of state Dr. Henry Kissinger and I once spent a half hour in the dining room having a heated debate over the merits of the designated hitter rule. In the middle of our discussion, Dr. Kissinger stopped to ask me if I could speak a little slower because my Jersey City accent was confusing him. I didn't have the heart to tell the Nobel Peace Prize winner that I actually only understood every other word he was saying in his trademark thick Teutonic tone.

Michael Douglas liked a conversation I was having with him so much that we continued it on the dugout bench after dinner. I sat with the Oscar winner for over an hour talking about his favorite baseball teams and players. He knew what he was talking about. Douglas would have made a great sportscaster.

When Billy Joel mentioned to me in between bites that he was a big fan of Johnnie Ray's music, we started quoting lyrics from the former teen idol's greatest hits to each other. I told the Piano Man about the Victrola I got for my birthday in 1952, and the speech about Johnnie Ray that my dad made to me as he presented me with the records. Joel loved hearing that. A few years later, Billy included Johnnie in his rapid-fire list of icons on his hit single "We Didn't Start the Fire." I've always wondered if our dinner conversation had any influence on that.

In the 1970s some of my wardrobe selections were—to say the least—a bit colorful and garish. I wasn't alone. Many players and reporters were clad in the same kooky outfits. (As a blind man, I can say that I had a built-in excuse. I'm not sure what the other guys are using for their defense.) One night, the Court Jester himself, Danny Kaye, stopped by to nosh with Mr. Rizzuto and me. Once he got a good look at the multicolored checkered suit I was wearing, Kaye shouted—to nobody in particular—"Does anyone have a good set of earplugs? This boy's jacket is so loud, they can hear it all the way over in Brooklyn!"

Mr. Rizzuto's best friend, Yogi Berra, was a coach on Billy Martin's '76 ball club. He was the same old Yogi, a baseball lifer. I couldn't imagine him out of a uniform. He and his wife, Carmen, were also devoted supporters of local charities. Yogi invited me to a benefit golf tournament and dinner at the Montclair Country Club in New Jersey. I accepted, even though I had no idea how to play golf.

That was solved by their special guest for the day.

Bob Hope was the featured speaker and honoree at Yogi's affair. He was treated like a visiting dignitary. People lined up in the morning to meet the legendary comedian. They all wanted to shake his hand and say hello. Yogi brought me to the front of the line to introduce us. When Hope saw me, he asked if I'd be golfing that day. I said no, explaining that I'd never been on the links.

Hope was astounded. "Nobody ever taught you how to golf? I want to tell ya, you're missing out on a great game!" He then made an interesting suggestion. "Let me teach you, Ed."

This was another moment that I would add to the surreal category.

Before I knew it, Mr. Hope had fetched a set of left-handed golf clubs for me. He stood behind me and taught me how to swing. It was a bit different from a baseball bat. I followed him to the golf course and put my newly learned lessons to use. After a few tries, I connected. I couldn't see where it landed, of course, but Hope let out a cheer that let me know I'd made it to the green.

We spent the rest of the afternoon on the links chatting about life, baseball (he was part owner of the Cleveland Indians), and golf. Mr. Hope shared with me how nervous he was the first time that he learned how to play golf, while he was still on New York's vaudeville and burlesque circuit in the 1930s. "I didn't want to embarrass myself on the course," he mused. "I used to spend all of my free time underneath the Fifty-Ninth Street Bridge shooting balls into the East River for practice." Bob also told me not to worry about the final tally. "Years ago, Bing Crosby told me that my score should equal my height," Hope said with a chuckle as he lined me up for a putt. "I usually wind up shooting my weight!" He assured me that I'd get better at golf over time, with practice. "I've been playing this game so long now, Ed, that they write my handicap in Roman numerals!"

When the day, and our lesson, was done, Mr. Hope suggested that we take a photo. We were already inside, so someone set up a makeshift tee on a platform and snapped the shot. My guide, Angelo, crouched behind me. It's one of my favorite pictures.

I saw my Hollywood golf teacher a few times after that at the Stadium. He never failed to ask, "How's your swing, Ed?"

A few days after the event, I ran into Yogi in the Yankee locker room. He asked how I enjoyed the day at his outing. I told him all about my golf lessons. Yogi said, "No kidding? You can golf now? Maybe you and me should get out there and play each other."

I answered, "Great, Yogi. I'd love to. When and where do you suggest?"

Yogi thought about it for a minute and proposed the Montclair Country Club on the following Monday, which was an off day for the team.

"What time do you want me to meet you, Yogi?" I asked, innocently.

"I dunno," he said, "any time you want to play, I'm ready."

I smiled and answered, "Okay, let's play at midnight."

Yogi was indignant. He shouted, "Midnight? There's no light on the course at midnight. I won't be able to see a thing!"

"Well," I said drily, "that will make us even, won't it?"

The ballpark was a fun place to hang out and work, but I still wasn't selling many stories. The Yankees were getting better, and I'd earned the respect of players, but I needed that one big interview to get the attention of station managers and editors. That breakthrough came on a cold Sunday afternoon at the end of the season.

The Yankees were on the path to their first postseason appearance in over a decade when the hapless Tigers came into town on September 12, 1976. The biggest story for them that year was their rookie sensation, pitcher Mark Fidrych.

Because of his height, long, curly blond hair, and quirky habits on the mound, Fidrych had been dubbed "The Bird," after Big Bird of *Sesame Street* fame. Earlier in the year, he beat the Yankees in Detroit on a *Monday Night Baseball* game that set ratings records. The whole country was in love with him and his story.

By September, Mark was completely burned out and overwhelmed by the media attention. A gentle soul, he preferred anonymity instead of the microscope that he was under. Since New York was, and is, the media center, everyone wanted a piece of him. Reporters followed him everywhere. Fidrych decided that he didn't want to answer the same questions over and over again. He wanted to find one reporter whom he could trust to come up with a fair line of inquiry, one who wouldn't try to dig up dirt or push him to talk trash.

I asked Mark for a little bit of his time, and he granted it. I was the one he chose.

Perhaps it was because Fidrych saw that I had the respect of his manager, Ralph Houk, who'd been the skipper of the Yankees in the early 1960s. Maybe "The Bird" watched me joking around on the field before the game with Thurman Munson, who was similarly press shy. Whatever the reason, the wunderkind pitcher spoke to me for over fifteen minutes while he dismissed almost everyone else.

I didn't realize that Mark was giving me a somewhat exclusive interview until I got up to my seat in the press box. Several of my peers began asking me to play the interview for them. I suddenly understood the value of what was on my tape.

I could have sold the contents to any number of radio stations for quite a price. That went against my ethics. In the interest of professional courtesy and fairness, I allowed anyone who wished to freely take quotes and snippets from the interview to do so. I imposed one condition. They were not allowed to twist the words in any way that would smear Fidrych. They all agreed.

Mr. Rizzuto noticed, and praised me for my teamwork. That was all the compensation I needed.

This free distribution of something in limited supply might seem like stupidity, or acting against my own financial interests. The opposite actually happened.

Within days of the interview, my phone began ringing with offers to submit stories and interviews about and with the Yankees to radio stations, newspapers, and magazines all over the United States. I was suddenly in demand.

I'd been praying for years for this moment to arrive, waiting on God's timing. It was finally here. I thanked Him for the opportunities and lessons He'd given me, the people He allowed me to meet along the way, and the ability to laugh through any adversity.

All of these gifts had prepared me for the next moves, onward and upward.

8

Not Above You, Not Beneath You, but with You

Things got much busier for me after that night in September 1976. The Fidrych interview boosted my profile and prospects.

Thanks to a dramatic last-inning playoff home run from Chris Chambliss, the Yankees advanced to the 1976 World Series. They were swept by the Reds. George added one more crucial piece to the team in 1977 by signing slugger Reggie Jackson, Catfish's former teammate on the A's and the biggest free agent on the market. Billy Martin led them right back to the playoffs and a World Series victory. In 1978, the clubhouse exploded with infighting and Martin was fired midseason as the team fell far behind the Red Sox. Despite all the turmoil, they came back to win it all that year, too. The clubhouse had become, as Sparky Lyle so memorably dubbed it, "The Bronx Zoo." Suddenly, everybody wanted to know about the

Yankees. It was like following a real-life soap opera. My workload increased exponentially as a result.

Flo was an excellent guide dog, but there's one thing she couldn't do: drive a car. To get to Yankee Stadium, I needed a guide who was willing to pick me up after work at Meadowview and drive me to the Bronx. The evenings usually ended late, but there were perks. My guides sat with me at Mr. Rizzuto's table, escorted me around the clubhouse and field, and watched the game from reserved seats in the press box.

I had no shortage of volunteers.

Many of my guides were friends I'd known for years. Some of them were people I'd met along the way as a proud member of a club that helped me to repay all of the kindness I'd been shown and the assistance I'd been given.

I knew of the Lions Club from their fund-raising drives in support of Holy Family and Camp Marcella before, during, and after my time there. I discovered that they weren't just from New Jersey, but an international organization, founded in Chicago in 1917 by Melvin Jones. Their motto was "We Serve." The idea caught on right away. Clubs popped up all over. Even Babe Ruth was a Lion. Helen Keller made a speech at their convention in 1925 urging Jones and his Lions to become "knights of the blind." They've been involved in that cause ever since, growing to millions of worldwide members, all dedicated to assisting blind people.

It was at one of Jerry Molloy's speaking engagements in February 1970 that I first met Bernie and Dottie Pryor. We were seated at the same table. Bernie was a lively guy. Dottie was even more fun. In between jokes, they asked me if I was a member of any service organizations. I'd always wanted to join one. These types of clubs were a great way to build relationships, while at the same time doing good for the community. I was looking for exactly that kind of situation. There were many worthy ones in Hudson County that I could choose from, including the Elks, Kiwanis, Rotary, and Moose Clubs. Bernie Pryor just happened to belong to the Lions.

Over the course of the evening, Bernie convinced me to come to a Lions meeting, to discover what they were all about. I liked what I heard. His club, called the North Hudson Lions, met once a month in Union City and had more than forty active members. Many of these guys hadn't missed a meeting in years. They raised tons of money for blind people all over New Jersey.

I wanted in, but had to attend three more times before I could be officially proposed for membership. In June, Joe Liccardo, the club's president, called me to let me know that I was officially a member. Five other guys would be joining the club with me.

The North Hudson Lions didn't have their own building. We usually met at a local restaurant. As president, Joe was allowed to pick which restaurant, club, or catering hall the induction ceremony would be held in. Since it was a very special occasion and a large incoming class, Joe decided to have a little fun. He booked the Playboy Club on Fifth Avenue in New York.

The place wasn't as risqué as it sounded. It was Playboy in name only. The owners tried to convey sophistication and refined elegance instead of sordid lowbrow tackiness. They did, however, have a staff full of women wearing Playboy bunny costumes. I was told that all of the servers walked around in black satin bunny outfits, replete with ears and a tail.

I couldn't see them, but I was blushing anyway.

Joe, who spotted my bright red cheeks, brought me up to one of the bunnies and said, "My friend here is blind; do you mind if he feels your tail?"

A second later I heard a weird snapping noise. The next thing I knew, the bunny placed her cotton tail, which she'd already unbuttoned from the back of her costume, in my hand. She laughed and said, "Go ahead, feel away."

A few years after that, someone sent me a copy of *Playboy* in Braille. It contained only the text, no pictures. I could legitimately say that I was one of the few guys in America who read *Playboy* "just for the articles."

There were some great guys in the North Hudson Lions Club. In addition to being my guides at ballgames, they would pick me up just to socialize with them on evenings and weekends. The Lions had become my second family. I was proud to wear their bright yellow jacket with the Lions logo and the accompanying purple tie. In 1975, I was elected club president. I chose a more modest banquet hall for the induction. Joe Liccardo and his wife, Helga, were extremely helpful. They would assist me with whatever I needed to make the club run more efficiently. One of our members, Don MacAteer, became governor of our Lions District, 16A, a year later. He honored me by naming me his deputy. My blindness wasn't a factor at all to him, or to the others.

It was at those District 16A meetings that I came to know Bob Diehl of North Bergen, a man cut from the same cloth as Mr. Rizzuto. Bob, and his wife Marge, owned a construction materials plant that supplied many of northern New Jersey's contractors. He did very well for himself and his family, but never showed off. Bob was extremely humble and generous, quietly giving vast sums to charity each year. He also gave generously of his time. Like Jerry Molloy, he seemed to have an unlimited fountain of energy. Bob was willing to go anywhere at any moment, especially if it meant helping others.

Bob was a huge sports fan. He loved the Yankees and had season tickets to the New York Giants football team, which played right up the road from us in the Meadowlands. My son Eddie was just as passionate about the football Giants. Bob would often give his tickets to Eddie, who would sit and enjoy the game with Bob's son, Robert, who was around the same age. The boys were also big hockey fans. They bonded over their love for the New York Rangers. Marge and Bob would often have me and my sons over for dinner, and would also bring us along as volunteers for the various charity clothing drives and food banks they organized through their church. I was happy that the Diehls could expand my boys' appreciation for what it meant to be a family that has fun together while giving back to their community.

AFTER ONE OF these dinners with the Diehls, in March 1977, Bob dropped the boys off with Maureen at the house and then gave me a ride back to Weehawken, to my parents' apartment. My father wasn't doing so well physically, and I needed to be with him.

My mother had first noticed the symptoms a few months before. Dad was losing a lot of weight. His skin was turning yellow. He went to a bunch of doctors before finally being diagnosed with cancer. He was tough, and he fought it with all of the energy and prayers he could muster. The battle took a lot out of him. On this night, he was a shell of himself.

I walked into the living room to talk to him. I could tell right away that it was pretty bad. His voice was raspy and weak. In an effort to cheer him, I brought up our favorite subject, baseball.

"Hey, Dad," I said, trying not to betray the worry in my voice, "in a few days, spring training games will be shown on TV. I think our Giants are playing the Mets on Saint Patrick's Day. That should be a fun one to watch. The Yankees face the Red Sox two days later, on Saint Joseph's Day."

There was silence for a moment. Dad then turned to me and whispered, "I won't be here, Ed."

I didn't understand. "Where are you going, Dad?" I thought that he might have a doctor's appointment or something.

He made a sound like someone who wanted to cry, but couldn't. He reached over, squeezed my hand, as he'd done thousands of times before when I was young, and said, "I just won't be here."

I understood his message. Nothing more needed to be said. The two of us sat there quietly, hand in hand, until he fell asleep. I helped my mother get him to bed. He'd dropped so many pounds by then that I was almost able to pick him up with one hand.

My mother asked me to stay. I took a few vacation days from work, then called my sister to let her and the boys know where I would be. I slept in my old bedroom. In the middle of the night, I heard a crash coming from my parents' room. I made my way there as fast as I could. My father had fallen from the bed and was lying on the floor. After determining that he was all right and hadn't broken anything, I helped him back up and went back to sleep.

A few hours later, I awoke to heartbreaking screams from my mother that will haunt me forever. "He's gone! He's gone! Oh, God, he's gone!"

My father had passed away, peacefully and quietly, in his bed.

The next few days were a blur.

I somberly made the necessary arrangements. Relatives and friends came from all over the country for my father's wake and funeral. Guys from his union broke down in tears and had to leave the room. Bob Diehl and my other fellow Lions formed an honor guard for Dad, though he wasn't actually a member.

Those tributes were incredibly touching and meant a lot to me and to my family. They were a fitting way to say good-bye to the man who was, and always will be in my eyes, the biggest Giant of them all.

I was numb for several weeks. Even after the baseball season started, I couldn't really enjoy it. My heart just wasn't in it. Then I remembered how much my father loved the game, how he'd taught me to be just as passionate about it.

Dad would want me to embrace baseball as much as I had during any other tough time in my life, especially now that I'd proven myself. I couldn't give up. I would honor his memory with my work. When I got to the Stadium, Mr. Steinbrenner was one of the first to express his condolences to me. Billy Martin was also extremely sympathetic.

Jackie Farrell had retired by then, but the Boss, along with the many PR guys who served under him during his tenure, made sure that I had complete access to the whole ballpark. George and Billy set the tone. Everyone else followed.

Billy Martin was a close friend of Mr. Rizzuto. The whippet-thin manager fancied himself a cowboy, but he was, in reality, an Italian-American kid from the urban streets of Berkeley, California. Even though I was Irish, he called me "paisan," which is Italian for "friend." He'd kiss me squarely on the cheek every time that I saw him. We got along great. Martin could be tightly wound, prone to temper tantrums, but he knew how to win. The public rarely saw his lighter side. He was a decent man and quite the practical joker.

More than once, as I waited in the clubhouse for an interview, Billy would silently grab my arm and walk me around. Thinking it was my guide, or a security guard, I'd follow along. Before I knew what was happening, he would lead me right into the showers, turning them on at full blast. As I stood there drying off, I could hear his distinctive high-pitched laugh, which gave him away as the culprit every time.

Martin never actually admitted that he did it.

That might sound like a cruel trick to play on a blind man, but I loved it. Baseball players have a long history of playing practical jokes on each other, and on those whom they consider one of the "boys." By subjecting me to his shower prank, Martin was sending a clear signal that I was now a member of this exclusive fraternity. I was free to be hazed.

The master of practical jokes was Sparky Lyle. He was having a Cy Young–caliber season in 1977, but still found the time to tease me and others. Every time I'd walk into the locker room, Sparky would toss towels in my general direction. Most would whiz harmlessly by. I would actually catch some, just by reflex alone. When that happened, Lyle would shout loudly to the clubhouse guard, Charlie Zabransky, "Arrest him, Charlie, he's trying to steal our towels!"

Sparky also loved giving hotfoots. I was not immune to them.

A "hotfoot" is a time-honored baseball trick in which a player will sneak up on another player or reporter while he is giving an interview in the dugout. The unsuspecting victim then has a match or two placed gently in the back or side of his shoe, with the head facing out. When the moment is right, the prankster will light the match head and slink away to watch from a distance. As soon as the flame from the slowly burning head reaches the victim's shoe, it's hot enough to be felt. The general result is a startled yelp. I had more than one interview interrupted by Lyle's antics.

So one day, I had my guide distract Sparky as I snuck a match into his shoe. I'd pranked the prankster. Turnabout is fair play.

Sparky was later joined in the bullpen by another intimidating closer, Rich "Goose" Gossage. He was a country boy from Colorado and, like Lyle, had an excellent sense of humor. Goose used to kid me incessantly.

I often rushed to get to the ballpark, sometimes making mistakes with my wardrobe. Most players were discreet enough not to mention it. My pal Goose spoke his mind. After spotting an error in my footwear one afternoon, he called me out on it. "Hey, Eddie, do you know that you are wearing one black shoe and one brown shoe?"

I gave him the first explanation that popped into my head. "Of course I know that, Goose. I have a pair just like them at home."

My guides were also in Goose's line of fire.

I brought my son's pediatrician, Dr. Frank Cardiello, with me to a game. Goose spotted him and said, "Geez, Eddie, you have a different person with you each day. Who is this clown?"

I wanted to pull a fast one on Goose so I said, "This is Dr. Frank Cardiello. He's my eye doctor."

Goose came right back with, "So you're Eddie's eye doctor? Let me tell you, that's one heck of a job you did there, Doc. You evened his eyes out!"

Reggie Jackson, who happened to be walking by, was horrified. He chastised Goose. "You can't say that to Eddie! He's a good guy!"

I eased Reggie's concerns. "It's okay, Reggie. I'm pretty fortunate to be blind. That means I don't have to stare at Goose's ugly mug every night."

Without missing a beat, Goose topped me. "You're even luckier than you think, Eddie. Yogi's coming out of the shower right now without a towel. You don't have to see what we're seeing."

Even my sons weren't above the genial banter.

Chris was waiting for me in the clubhouse after a game. He told me that he was hungry. I promised to get him something to eat once we left the Stadium. He wasn't happy. Despite having eaten his fill of hot dogs and Cracker Jack, Chris kept loudly moaning that he wanted something to eat. He was putting on a world-class show. The whole locker room could hear him, including Goose.

Gossage called out, to nobody in particular, "If someone doesn't shut this kid up, I'm gonna give him a knuckle sandwich!" He was just kidding, of course, but Chris misunderstood the warning. He rushed over to Goose's locker and said, "You have a sandwich for me, Mr. Gossage? Can I have some mustard on it?" Goose, and everyone around him, burst into laughter. To this day, whenever Goose sees Chris, he asks him if he wants a knuckle sandwich.

I took Chris to his first Old-Timers Day game in 1978. He was nine years old. I was thrilled to be able to introduce him to the men who shaped my life and childhood. Eddie had already been to one, but this was all new for Chris. He loved it. As the ceremony was about to start, I sat in the dugout with Chris. I heard a familiar clacking of spikes on the runway. It was Mickey Mantle's trademark gait. I told Chris to run over and say hello to him before he had to take his place on the diamond with the other Yankee veterans.

Chris approached the legendary center fielder. He was too young to have seen the Mick play, but he'd heard all of my stories. Mantle was his hero. Chris shared that with Mickey as soon as he got close enough. Mantle, who was quickly surrounded by throngs asking for autographs and handshakes, had a habit of sometimes brushing off admirers, depending on his mood.

He asked Chris how a kid his age could say that he idolized him if he wasn't even alive in the 1950s and 1960s. "It's because my daddy told me all about you." As he started to walk away, Mickey asked, "Oh, yeah, who's your dad?"

When Chris identified me, Mickey froze in his tracks.

Mantle came back over to Chris, leaned down to his level, put his arms on his shoulders, and said, "Kid, I hear people telling me that I'm their hero every single day. I want to tell you something. Your dad is *my* hero. You are very, very lucky."

With that, Mantle resumed his trot out to the first-base line for introductions, leaving my son standing there, in awe of him for reasons that were deeper than anything that had to do with baseball.

On the ride home later that night, Chris casually mentioned what Mickey had said. I was glad that my son couldn't see me in the front seat as I tried my best to hide the tears that were streaming down my cheeks. Now I knew how Mickey felt that day back in 1954 when he had his emotional encounter with my friend Eddie.

WHEN I WASN'T at work, baseball games, or Lions meetings, I spent most of my time with Eddie and Chris. We loved being with each other. They were getting to know what life was like for me, helping me to adapt to any situations that came our way. They also began to develop an innate empathy for anyone who was facing challenges. What my boys didn't appreciate was the reaction that my blindness would sometimes bring out in people, especially when we'd go out to eat.

Waiters and waitresses were the ones who seemed to slip up the most. I lost count of the number of times that a server would walk over to our table, look directly at Eddie while pointing at me, and say, "What does he want to eat?" Eddie, who got more and more annoyed each time it happened, would snap back, "He's not deaf, he's only blind, ask him yourself!" I'd gently chastise Eddie, as I felt bad for the waiter, who'd made an innocent mistake. Invariably, the server would compound the error by screaming loudly at me when asking for my order, as if an increase in volume would suddenly restore my eyesight.

A woman once stopped by our table to say to Chris, "I want to tell you that your father is amazing. I was sitting over there eating, and I watched him the whole time. Not once did your dad miss his mouth. Good for him."

Chris, who had even less tolerance for silly remarks than Eddie, answered her quickly. "I was watching you, too, ma'am, and I want to congratulate you."

This confused her. "Congratulate me? What for, my dear?"

He looked at her innocently and said, "You were eating the whole time without a mirror in front of you to look at yourself, and you didn't miss your mouth once. Good for you!"

I had raised my sons to be respectful to their elders, but I let Chris's answer slide, just this once.

I also got Eddie and Chris involved in Lions activities. We marched in many parades together. They stood with me as I sold small white canes, which was a Lions signature fund-raiser. The Lions were the first organization to require canes to be made of white reflective material rather than dark wood. They helped reduce the number of traffic accidents involving blind pedestrians.

It was important for me to demonstrate to my sons that service to others was the best ideal that they could strive for. They learned this golden rule in church on Sunday, and when they read the Bible at home, but the Lions were helping me to show it to them up close.

Lions founder Melvin Jones once observed that you can't get very far in life until you start doing something for other people. I believe that with every ounce of my soul. One of the reasons that I joined the Lions Club was that I loved the toast that they make at the beginning of every meeting. This toast actually sums up my personal feeling that no matter what circumstances come my way, good or bad, I'm no better or worse than any of my brothers and sisters on this planet. We are all in this together, so we should try to make life better for each other.

The nine powerful words that Lions recite when we gather and raise our glasses are: "Not above you, not beneath you, but with you."

In the summer of 1979, the New Jersey Lions decided to try something new. We put together a twenty-four-hour telethon that would air on what was then the new medium of cable television. I was part of the planning committee. Seton Hall University generously donated their broadcast facilities for our use. New York radio legend "Cousin Brucie" Morrow agreed to emcee for the entire event.

I was asked to secure talent to fill in the airtime. There were plenty of local bands, magicians, and performers that were ready to volunteer, but the Lions wanted to get a bigger viewing audience by having big-name guests. They asked me to call on some of my friends from the ballpark.

The Yankees were away that weekend, so when I asked Thurman, Goose, and the others, they had to decline. At least I could say I spoke to them about it. They each offered their support. Some, like Bobby Murcer, made generous donations. Mr. Rizzuto agreed to miss work to join us for the telethon.

At the All-Star Game a few years before, I'd met a hot young comedian and actor named Robert Klein. He was writing an article for a sports magazine and wanted to get to know some of the players. I kept crossing paths with him, and we became fast friends. Any time Robert was at the stadium, I'd get him access to the inner circle of players. He was a great guy, always appreciative of my efforts on his behalf.

Robert was starring with Lucie Arnaz in the Broadway show *They're Playing Our Song* when I was looking for telethon guests. He had just been nominated for a Tony Award for his role. He'd also completed his second comedy special for a seven-year-old cable channel called Home Box Office. I asked him if he would come on to do his act for us. He said yes without hesitation.

Fellow Lion Tom Gartley drove me over to New York on the day of the telethon to pick up Robert. It was Saturday, so he had some time between the matinee and evening shows. We met him at the stage door and then raced over to South Orange. Knowing that he had to get back, I'd asked Robert to stay for only twenty minutes or so. He gave us two hours and then raced back to Broadway just in time for his evening show. He was a huge hit on our telethon. The phones rang more during his time onscreen than for anyone else, including President Jimmy Carter.

President Carter, another fellow Lion, had taped a special message from the White House, to be shown during the prime spot on our show. He still couldn't top Klein's jokes.

The telethon raised more for blind charities in New Jersey than any event had up until that time.

A few days later, I was on the field at Yankee Stadium. It was a warm, late July Wednesday night. Thurman came over to me. He asked me how our telethon did. I was touched that he remembered. Sensing that he was in a happier than normal mood, I took a bold step.

Munson had just published his autobiography, with the help of Jackie Farrell's successor, Marty Appel. Someone bought me a copy, so I asked Thurman if he would sign it for me. Reporters usually never ask players for autographs, but Thurman was an old friend and I wanted a keepsake for Eddie and Chris.

He feigned indignation and said, "Everyone knows that you're a Red Sox fan, Eddie, why would I sign for you?" I laughed as he followed with the obvious question, "If you're blind, why did someone buy you my book? You can't read it! It's just a paperweight!"

I told him that my son Eddie was reading it to me.

"Okay, buddy, I'll tell you what," Thurman said with a rare grin, "you bring the book tomorrow night. I'll quiz you on some of the chapters. Get the answers right, and I'll sign it for you."

Thurman did indeed ask me a bunch of questions as we stood on the field the following day. He was turning the tables and interviewing me. I passed his test.

This was a more laid-back version of Munson than I'd ever witnessed, despite the fact that the team was way behind the Baltimore Orioles in the standings at that point. Perhaps winning the World Series the previous two seasons and being the captain of the Yankees had taken some of the pressure off him. Whatever it was, he signed the book, and even posed for a picture with me and Flo.

During the game, my guide noticed that Thurman hadn't added Chris's name to the inscription. I caught up to him after the game. Ron Guidry had given up only three hits for a 2–0 win over the Angels, so everyone was in a good mood. I asked Munson if he would write something for Chris on the note he put to Eddie. He said, "I'd love to, but we're going on the road tonight and I've gotta run. See me when I get back next Friday and I'll do it for you. Be ready to answer more questions!"

He slapped me on the back, leaned down to pet Flo, and headed out the clubhouse door.

That was the last time I ever saw him.

One week later, on August 2, 1979, Thurman Munson, a licensed pilot, was killed in a tragic crash as he was practicing landing procedures in his new Cessna plane.

His locker remained untouched in the clubhouse until they built the new Yankee Stadium, where it was moved intact to the Yankee Museum.

I miss him every time that I'm at the ballpark.

In 1979, Hall of Fame pitcher Catfish Hunter announced his retirement from baseball at age thirty-three. He had been diagnosed with diabetes, which can often cause loss of vision and clarity. I had a pretty good relationship with him, but Hunter was a lot less outspoken than Goose or Sparky. Catfish called me over one day to ask me about blindness and how I coped with it. I referred him to some organizations in his home state of North Carolina, including the Lions Club. He became a member of the Lions, like Babe Ruth before him.

Bob Diehl was with me when All Star second baseman Willie Randolph took me aside to talk about the diagnosis of juvenile diabetes that he'd just received for his daughter. Since Willie lived in New Jersey, Bob and I were able to help him even more with referrals. Willie was grateful. I'd already known Randolph for years, but he and Bob developed a friendship that day.

Reggie Jackson was another guy whom Bob got to know well. Jackson was the brightest star of the Yankees by that point. His three home runs in one World Series game in 1977 assured that his number 44 would be retired by the Yankees, and that he'd have a spot on the wall in Monument Park. They even named a candy bar for him.

The biggest knock on Reggie that people made was that his ego was enormous and he was full of himself. It was completely untrue. I never experienced any of that. Jackson was one of the most gracious ballplayers I ever met. He loved giving interviews, which were always fun because he often referred to himself in the third person. He once told me, "Always remember, Ed, Reggie Jackson is here for you."

He wasn't kidding.

After a game in which he smashed two big home runs, including a game winner, the crowd around Reggie's locker was three deep. Bob and I made our way to the back of the crowd, and I lifted my microphone in the air to try to catch some of what he was saying. It didn't work, so I asked Bob to take me over to Guidry's locker.

I'd get Reggie some other time.

While I was busy talking to Guidry, Reggie crossed the room and startled Bob with a tap on the shoulder. "Hey, Bob," he said, "is Eddie mad at me?" Bob assured him that I wasn't. Jackson continued, "I noticed that Eddie was at my locker but didn't ask me a single question. You guys just walked away. I hope I didn't do anything to get him mad. Tell him I'm sorry that I didn't get to talk to him today."

When Bob shared what Reggie said, I realized just how far I'd come. This was almost the exact same situation I'd encountered in 1965, except that this time the superstar with the crowded locker wasn't humiliating me, he was offering an apology for not being available. I said a silent prayer of thanks for the journey.

I was hired by a national sports magazine to do a feature story on Reggie. They wanted to know what it was like for him to calmly stand at the plate and produce the amazing results that he did. Reggie agreed to the interview, with one condition. He was going to share the experience by actually showing me what it was like to bat at home plate in Yankee Stadium.

Bob Hope had been my golf tutor, Joe DiMaggio had been my announcer, and now Reggie Jackson was going to teach me to hit home runs. My list of surreal moments just kept getting longer and more surreal.

We set aside a few hours before a game. Reggie went through every single step of his process, with a photographer from the magazine snapping away. It was, by far, one of the greatest interviews I've ever been given.

When our lesson was done, Reggie was heading to the locker room to prepare for the game. I called out, "Wait a minute, Reggie, you forgot to teach me the most important part."

He turned back around. "What did I miss, Eddie? I had a checklist, I'm pretty sure I covered it all. Whatever it is, I'll work on it for you."

My answer set him off in fits of laughter. "You forgot to show me how to keep my eye on the ball!"

Bob Diehl once told me that taking me to games was an experience that money couldn't buy. Others seemed to share the same opinion, even members of the clergy.

Our local church parish, Saint Aloysius, was filled with baseball fans. The Reverend Charlie Christell was especially excited the day that

I asked him to escort me to a game. He soaked up every minute of it. When I made the introductions in the locker room, some of the players were surprised that I had a priest with me. They tried, and failed, to curb their language. Others treated him like just another guide.

At one point, I couldn't locate Father Christell. It turned out that a player who was in a bit of a slump had asked him to bless one of his bats. Several players followed, and a line quickly formed. It took us another fifteen minutes to get out of there. The Yankees wound up having one of their best nights ever at the plate.

Our archbishop, who was visiting the parish a few weeks later, heard about Reverend Christell's night at the ballpark. He asked if he could take me over sometime. Of course I agreed. Neither man wore his clerical garb. Until I identified them by their title, nobody had a clue that they were men of the cloth.

This almost got the archbishop in big trouble.

I didn't realize it, but he'd brought little plastic baggies with him to the game. While we were standing on the field behind home plate watching batting practice, the archbishop bent down to fill them up with the same dirt that DiMaggio, Mantle, and Berra had walked on. This was a big no-no, expressly forbidden by Yankee Stadium security.

Within seconds, several burly security guards surrounded the archbishop. They were intent on escorting him down to the holding cell underneath the stands behind first base. Once they spotted the special ring that he wore to signify his role in the Church, they all blessed themselves, apologized, and backed off as swiftly as they had descended. We were escorted up to the press box instead.

Mr. Steinbrenner always got a kick out of that story.

The Boss was one of my biggest supporters. It was a courtesy that he extended to my family, too.

My mother was sitting in the stands with Eddie and Chris during the 1977 World Series. It was a freezing cold night in October. They were bundled up, but still shivering in the face of the fierce fall winds. George happened to look down and recognize my boys. A few minutes later, one of his staff members arrived at their seats to take the three of them into a heated room to watch the rest of the game in comfort.

Mr. Steinbrenner never mentioned it to me or made a big fuss.

George was caricatured by the media and fans as a blustering tyrant, but he was always secretly dedicated to helping others in need without seeking any praise. His favorite saying was, "If you do something good for someone and more than two people know about it—you and the other person—then you didn't do it for the right reason." Mr. Steinbrenner, like Bob Diehl and the rest of my fellow Lions around the world, is an excellent model for service and philanthropy.

I was happy that my mom got to see how the owner of the Yankees treated me, and my family, like his own. I hoped that she realized, as I did, that none of this would have happened were it not for the results of her letters to ballplayers on my behalf twenty-five years earlier.

She helped to put God's plan for me into action. I know that my dad felt that way, too.

My mother was all by herself in the Weehawken apartment, so in 1979, I began looking for a bigger place to live. Maureen's second son, Brian, was three years old. Eddie, Chris, and Jeffrey were on the verge of their teens. The house on Nunda was now too small for us to be comfortable. Mom agreed to join us in purchasing a new home. Ideally, we would find a multifamily house so that my sister could have her own floor, and the boys and I could live on the lower level with their grandmother. We would be together as a family. It was very exciting.

I'd worked hard to create a normal life for me and my sons, one full of love, faith, peace, and happiness.

Things looked very bright, with my family and with my career.

I had no idea that my dreams for future bliss were about to be dissolved by a piece of my past.

9

I Refuse to Believe That
Justice Is Blind

I spent the early part of 1979 looking for a new home. Nothing panned out. The original loan for Nunda Avenue was paid off, so I had a little more flexibility with price than I did the first time. My mother and Maureen were helping, too. Still, we didn't find anything suitable until Eddie happened to look in the real estate section of the paper one summer day.

"This is perfect, Dad!" Eddie said when he spotted the picture of the two-family home. I took his word for it and contacted the Realtor listed. Eddie was right: it was an amazing house, and in just the right location. Union Street was only about ten blocks away from Nunda Avenue. The grammar school that Eddie, Chris, and Jeff attended was three doors up from the house. Their middle school and high school would be within walking distance.

We took a tour of our prospective new home. The owners were the parents of one of Chris's classmates. They built the house from scratch in the 1950s and kept it in excellent condition. Eddie loved the big finished basement and rec room, which would be perfect for having his friends over for air hockey, electric football, and Strat-O-Matic Baseball tournaments. Chris was thrilled that there was a pool in the backyard and a shed large enough to put on shows. The second floor was almost as large as our whole house on Nunda. Maureen, Jimmy, and their kids would have lots of room up there. I made a bid, which was accepted. The closing came on the Feast of the Assumption, August 15. We all moved in a week later.

On September 18, I was having lunch at work when I got a call from Maureen. I thought perhaps one of the boys might have been sent home sick, or that there was an issue with the new house. The news was more shocking than I'd imagined.

Our postman asked my sister to sign for a certified letter to me from a law office in Bergen County. It looked very serious and official, so Maureen wanted me to know about it right away. I asked her to read it to me. I'm glad that I was sitting down when she did.

Dee was suing me for custody of the boys.

For reasons I still can't understand or explain, my ex-wife had decided—after eight years of separation and divorce—to seek full and complete custody of Eddie and Chris. Her lawyer wasn't just asking for shared parenting, Dee wanted them to live with her permanently, granting me occasional visitation.

The boys had seen their mother whenever she, or they, wanted to. They had been spending vacations with her, some holidays, summers, and some weekends at her new house. Dee's husband, Burt, was a decent guy. I admired him for his work ethic and dedication to his faith. Eddie and Chris got along well with him. They also loved seeing their younger half-brothers and half-sisters, who ranged in age from six to one. I thought that Dee and I had a good parenting arrangement worked out.

I was mistaken.

Mr. Kusick let me go home early. My mind was racing. What would I tell my boys? How could I explain that they faced the possibility of living apart from me for the first time in their lives? I certainly couldn't handle that outcome, and I didn't want them to worry about it. As soon as they walked in the door, I sat them down at the kitchen table to talk. Both of them were in as much shock as I was.

Divorce was still somewhat uncommon back then, heated custody trials even rarer. There were television shows about single dads, like *Andy Griffith*, *My Three Sons*, and *Diff'rent Strokes*, but none of them dealt with custody issues. The Academy Award–winning film *Kramer vs. Kramer* did cover the subject, but was months away from being released. This would be an uncharted experience that my boys and I would have to get through together.

The summons said that I had thirty days to file my response, or Dee would win by default. My first order of business was finding a lawyer. George Franconero had gone into private practice in Essex County as a business attorney by then. He offered to help, but suggested that I find a lawyer from Hudson County who specialized in family law and knew the court system there.

My finances were stretched pretty thin, so I had to settle for an attorney on the lower end of the scale. The division of family services came by our house to check on our living conditions. We passed that inspection handily. I believed that any judge would be able to see that I'd been raising my boys for eight years, and that things should stay the same. Whether my lawyer was high-priced or not shouldn't make a difference. That was another miscalculation on my part.

We were assigned a court date in November. My lawyer did minimal preparation. When the day arrived, I brought my mother, my sister, Father John Bauman, my father's sister Josephine, and her son Dennis with me to testify. Shortly after the judge entered the courtroom, he called my lawyer and Dee's lawyer into his chambers to confer in private. When they came back, my lawyer put his hand on my shoulder and whispered, "I think this ruling is going to be the best thing for you." Not a word of testimony was given in open court.

The judge asked us all to stand as he delivered his decision. The words still burn a hole in my heart. "It is the opinion of the court," he stated in a monotone, "that Mr. Lucas, as a blind man, is unfit to be a single parent. His children are approaching the teen years, and I have no confidence that he will be able to handle them properly. I therefore find it in the best interests of those boys to avoid a trial and to place them permanently in their mother's custody, no later than five weeks from today. Mr. Lucas will be granted one weekend visit per month."

Outrage consumed me as I shouted, "How is that fair, your honor? I've been raising these boys all by myself. You didn't even hear from anyone that I brought with me. I'd like a trial. That can't be too much to ask, can it?"

Unmoved by my plea, the judge gave me an ultimatum. "Mr. Lucas, you have two choices. You can either agree with my ruling, giving your boys to their mother, or you can resist it and request a trial. If you choose the second option, I will immediately have your sons named wards of the court. The boys will be split up and placed in separate foster homes until a decision is reached, and that could take months. Which road would you like to go down, Mr. Lucas?"

I was anguished. Then I remembered the biblical tale of King Solomon, from the first book of Kings, chapter three. The king, in that passage, showed his wisdom by offering to mediate a dispute between two women who claimed to be the mother of a particular baby. Both wanted the infant for their own. When King Solomon ruled that the child should be cut in two so that each could have their own half, one of the women said, "No, just give the baby to the other so that it won't be harmed." King Solomon immediately knew that she was the true parent. She was willing to make a tough sacrifice for the sake of her child. I had to do the same for the boys.

With a heavy heart, I swallowed hard and agreed to the judge's ruling. He asked if anyone in the courtroom wanted to voice their objection. My relatives and friends desperately wanted to, but stayed silent out of respect for me. With that, the judge said, "Thank you, Mr. Lucas. This court rules in favor of the plaintiff. Case dismissed."

Two months after Dee had filed, it was over. The boys would be moving in with her just after the holidays. I was disconsolate. Eddie and Chris were just as upset. They put up a brave front, but I could hear the sorrow in their voices as they prepared to leave home.

A few weeks later, I was at a Lions meeting. By then word had spread among my fellow Lions about what had happened in the trial. After the meeting was over, a few of us stayed in the restaurant to chat. Don MacAteer said emphatically, "Ed, what happened to you isn't right. The judge railroaded you, and that lawyer you had was useless. You need to appeal the decision."

I appreciated his sentiments. "I'd love to appeal, Don, but I don't even know how to go about it."

He was quick with his reply. "You need to get a good custody lawyer. In fact, you need the best!"

I asked, "And who is that?"

Don answered, "I have no idea. Starting tomorrow, you and I are going to search." Within a week, we found him.

Howard Danzig had a thriving family law practice in Morristown. A few years earlier, he had lost custody of his own child and was determined to help other fathers who might be facing the same fate. The courts in New Jersey overwhelmingly favored mothers in custody disputes. The same was true throughout the United States. Cases like mine, which involved an appeal, were mostly uphill battles. The chances of winning were minuscule. If he agreed to work with me, Howard was going to be the guy coming up in the bottom of the ninth with the bases loaded, down three runs, with two outs, hoping for a miraculous game-winning grand slam.

He was just the man for the job.

DON DROVE ME out to meet with Danzig on January 8, 1980. His first words to me were, "Tell me your story, Ed." I went through the whole day in court for him.

When I mentioned that Father John was in the row behind me, Howard stopped me and said, "Wait—a priest was there?" I told him that I'd known John since our days in college together. "Father John heard everything the judge said to you, even the part about you being unfit because you are disabled?"

I said yes. For the next two hours, we went over my relationship with Dee from the first meeting at her sister's apartment until our last in court. Howard took pages of notes.

When he was done, he stood up and said, "I'll take the case!"

I paid his retainer so that we could get started, but secretly worried that I might not have enough to cover his one-hundred-dollar-per-hour fees over the long haul. Howard didn't seem concerned about that; he wanted to get started right away on the appeals process.

Howard went to Hudson County to meet with the judge in person to ask for a change in the ruling. As expected, he was summarily dismissed. The judge insisted that we had no reasonable grounds for appeal. Howard disagreed. He claimed that I had been unfairly discriminated against, because my blindness was cited as the sole factor in the verdict, without a word of testimony from either side being heard. He then said that he'd be taking my appeal to the superior court.

The judge laughed at him.

This appeal was quite a gamble. The superior court was not in the habit of tossing out rulings in family law cases unless they involved abuse or harm to the children. Dee would certainly never harm the boys. Her request was the same as mine. We both felt that the children belonged with us. All my lawyer was asking for was a fair hearing, with testimony and expert witnesses.

In early February, Howard told my story in front of three New Jersey superior court judges. He was persuasive enough to get their attention. They removed the original judge from the case and asked Hudson County to assign another judge, with instructions to have a bench trial that included testimony. They also ordered psychiatric evaluations for me, Dee, and the boys.

Howard had done it! And this was only the first step. At least now I'd be able to make my case in open court. Howard wasted no time in getting to work. He asked me for a list of everyone that I'd known since Dee and I met. He wanted to interview and take depositions from as many friends, coworkers, and relatives as he could. If I was going to testify that the boys belonged with me, Howard wanted to present as strong an argument as possible.

Eddie and Chris were now living with their mother in Bergen County. My house, and my life, felt empty. The only solace came from where it always had, my faith. Prayer strengthened me, giving me a peace and hope that would otherwise be lacking. There was no guarantee that my prayers would bring the outcome I wanted, but they did promise that I would not be abandoned during my ordeal. That was a great comfort.

I continued to ask the saints in heaven to pray for me. I also turned to a living saint.

In 1917, three shepherd children in Fatima, Portugal, saw the apparition of the Virgin Mary on a hillside. The visitation became world famous, the subject of several inspirational books and movies. My mother and father were particularly attracted to the story of Our Lady of Fatima. One of the children on that hillside, Lucia, became a Carmelite nun and was living in a convent in 1980. I wrote a letter to her, which explained my story. I asked Sister Lucia to pray for me.

To my amazement, she wrote back. It was a nice note, encouraging me to honor God and to wait patiently on His timing. She assured me that all things would work together for good. Sister Lucia also enclosed a special set of rosary beads to assist me in my prayers.

This was a very touching gesture on her part. I continued to write to her over the years, and she would write back.

It was a special correspondence that lasted until her death in 2005.

The appellate trial was scheduled to begin on September 15. The new judge had a reputation of being fair, but this was still Hudson County. The likelihood of his changing a verdict already rendered by one of his colleagues was slim. But at least we were being given a fighting chance.

Rather than travel all over New Jersey and New York trying to get depositions, Howard decided to set up one day in which potential witnesses could come to him. We held the meetings at my house. My mother had it catered. From 9:00 a.m. until 9:00 p.m., more than fifty people came by to talk to my attorney. Between that marathon session and his many phone calls to my friends in the Lions and in baseball, Danzig had gathered enough testimony to more than vouch for my abilities as a single father, disabled or not.

I was thrilled with the amount of work he was putting in, but still worried about the looming bill. Every time he told me that he'd spent another hour or two on my case, I heard a silent meter running in my head. Howard had been focusing almost exclusively on this trial, so his income was largely dependent on me and the timely payment of his fees.

The pressure was getting to me. I called Howard in the hopes of working out a payment plan. Even if it took me decades, I would find a way to pay him all that I owed him and more. He'd certainly earned it, win, lose, or draw.

The moment he answered the phone, I said to Howard, "I need to talk to you about my bill." I didn't want to waste any time with small talk, I wanted to address the big issue. I had anticipated every answer that he could give, except for the one that actually came out of his mouth. "Don't worry about it, Ed. Your bill has been paid in full."

I dropped the receiver. Surely I had heard him wrong.

He repeated, "Your bill has been paid in full." I said, in disbelief, "Paid by whom?" Howard said, "The easier question to answer is, who didn't pay? My mailbox has been flooded for weeks with checks. Once I began making calls asking for testimony on your behalf, people started sending me money for your legal fees. Most of them asked me not to tell you that they did it."

I wanted to cry. I still want to, recalling all their kindness.

"I can't name names," Howard said, "but almost everyone that you've met in your life has pitched in to help you out. The Lions, alumni and teachers from Seton Hall, Holy Family, PS 22, and the New York Institute, county workers, your dad's union—even Mr. Steinbrenner and the Yankees!—players, writers, and broadcasters from all over baseball, all of them and more have contributed. You've touched and inspired a lot of people, Ed. These are your true friends, and they are showing you just how much they love you."

Just like George Bailey in Frank Capra's *It's a Wonderful Life*, I guess I had an angel watching over me—in fact, a whole team of them. My life was indeed wonderful, no matter how the trial turned out.

. . . .

BY THE TIME we arrived in court, Howard had devised an excellent strategy. Rather than calling witness after witness, he selected five representatives from five areas of my life, each of whom would testify to a different aspect of my parenting.

Bernie Pryor spoke for my fellow Lions, explaining that I often involved my boys in our service activities, giving them firsthand experience in contributing to the community and being productive members of society.

Dr. Cardiello testified about the physical health of my sons. He proved that they were not neglected and had a well-rounded life. My mother took the stand to bear witness to our close-knit family life.

Phil Rizzuto represented the Yankees, speaking to the judge about my ability to balance my job in baseball with fatherhood, a lifestyle that he and other players and broadcasters knew all too well. "I've spent the better part of my life away from my family," Scooter said on the stand as his voice broke with emotion. "It was hard missing all of those special moments because I had to be at the ballpark. For six months a year, my kids followed me through the TV." He stopped for a moment to compose himself, then continued. "What Eddie has done—and I think he's been incredibly successful at this—is to make his boys part of his team. He spends as much time as he can with them, not because he's required to, but because he wants to. Eddie really enjoys being with his children, and everyone can see that, including them. In my scorecard, I'd definitely mark that as a home run. I hope that you do, too, your honor."

The most effective witness was Norma Kreitzer, the wife of my first trainer at the Seeing Eye. She was the director of the New Jersey Commission for the Blind. Norma was also totally blind herself. Norma had children of her own, so Howard asked her many questions about the capability of a blind person to be a parent. Even under cross-examination Norma never wavered, offering strong and compelling arguments for our side.

Howard wanted me to take the stand on my own behalf. This presented him with a unique problem. One of the many effective tactics in a lawyer's arsenal is to set up visual cues with clients before they give testimony. A stroke of the chin, for example, or the crossing of arms, might indicate that the lawyer wants his client to stay silent on one point, or elaborate on another.

It was just like the signs that coaches give to players in baseball. But visual cues would be lost on me. We did consider verbal ones, but a cough or a loud tap isn't as subtle or as easy to cover as something that can be seen with a sideways glance.

We decided to prepare as much as we could by going over the probable lines of inquiry from the other side, relying on that role-playing exercise to put me at ease on the stand.

Dee's lawyer, surprisingly, didn't ask that many questions in cross. He also called very few witnesses for her. She testified. So did Burt, and some of her sisters, but that was it.

Essentially, both of us were making the same case. We wanted to have our children live with us. Neither of us could prove that the other was unfit, or that the children would suffer in the other's home. It was a toss-up.

The puzzling question was still why Dee chose to seek custody now, after all the time that had passed. Eddie was thirteen and Chris was eleven. If she'd just waited another few years, they would both be old enough to make up their own minds about who they wanted to live with, and the courts wouldn't have to be involved at all.

Howard seemed worried. When we broke for lunch, he took me aside and confided that he couldn't tell which way the judge was leaning. We'd done our best, but that might not be good enough. He said, with great worry in his voice, "To my knowledge, a father has *never* won custody of his children from the mother in New Jersey. No judge wants to break precedent." That was gloomy enough. He then added, "From what I understand, a disabled person has *never* won custody from a nondisabled spouse in the United States. I just want you to be prepared for the worst, Ed."

I felt bad for a second, then I reflected on that word: *never*. It was a word that I'd heard many times. "A blind person will *never* amount to anything besides begging on the streets." "A student has *never* graduated Seton Hall with a guide dog." "There's *never* been a successful disabled sportscaster." "Someone that lost their sight will *never* hit a baseball, ride a horse, or play golf."

So many times, with God's help, I'd blown right past all of the *never*s. I had completely erased the word from my vocabulary.

I was fully confident that through His strength I was about to do it once again.

The final pieces of testimony that the judge needed to hear did not come in open court. He wanted to talk to Eddie and Chris before making his decision. The psychiatrist had evaluated us a few weeks before. He gave us a passing grade, but the judge wanted to get to know my boys beyond what was on paper or said on the stand.

Nobody was allowed to be in there when the conversations occurred. They would be off the record. Each boy would go in by himself. Eddie was first. To put him at ease and to break the ice, the judge spoke about baseball and football before getting down to the question of where Eddie preferred to live. Even that wasn't asked directly. The conversation revolved around daily life after school and the differences between Jersey City and the suburbs. Eddie was in there for over an hour and a half.

When it was Chris's turn to go in, the judge used the fact that he had a grandson born the same week as Chris to set the tone. They chatted about TV shows popular with Chris's age group at the time. The conversation gradually drifted from *Batman*, *The Dukes of Hazzard*, and *H.R. Pufnstuf* back to where Chris wanted to live. Like Eddie, he spent more than ninety minutes inside but also came out smiling.

If either one of them realized what they just said would have a direct impact on the judge's decision, they didn't let on.

The trial concluded just a little over a week after it started, on September 23. By then, it had made news in several national and international papers. I was getting calls and cards of support from all over the globe.

Two days later, on Thursday, September 25, which just happened to be Scooter's birthday, we were notified by the court that the judge had reached his decision. We were asked to reconvene in his courtroom at 1:00 p.m. Eddie and Chris were in school, so they wouldn't be in court when the verdict was read.

A big crowd gathered inside. The tension was thick. The judge's words seemed to come out in slow motion as he spoke. "Having found no legitimate reason to deny Mr. Lucas the right to bring up his children, and having found no evidence that his disability would render him in any way incapable of carrying out his responsibilities as a parent, I hereby overturn the prior ruling and order that his children be immediately returned to his custody, which I am awarding to him on a permanent basis."

All I can remember from the moment after that was the deafening roar that went up from the assembled crowd and the bear hug that Howard gave me as he shouted, "You did it, Ed, you did it! You made history! You beat the odds!"

As I was saying a quiet prayer of thanks, I heard, through the chaos, a familiar noise. It was my mother, sitting behind me crying tears of joy, just as she had every other time I'd gotten past an impossible barrier. We embraced, and I joined her in the flow of happy tears.

Everyone came back to the house on Union Street to celebrate. The flow of well-wishers continued long into the night. I finally got to bed around three, exhausted and relieved that it was all over.

MANY PEOPLE ASKED me, and continue to ask, which piece of testimony do I think swayed the judge to make such a historic decision? I honestly don't think that it was anything that anyone said or didn't say, either in court or in the judge's chambers. My feeling is that he based his verdict on one thing only: love.

I'm not trying to claim that Dee doesn't love the boys. I know that she does, probably just as much as I do.

What I mean is that all things being equal, the only factor the judge had left to go on was which home radiated the most warmth and love for Eddie and Chris. Fair or unfair, I had an eight-year head start on my former wife. The majority of my boys' lives were spent mostly with me, my sister, their cousins, and my parents. The Lucas family didn't have a lot of money, a mansion, or all of the latest gadgets. We did, however, always have an overabundance of love and deep faith. It was something that I remembered fondly from my childhood days. We could always call on and rely upon our loving family members, who were there for us and never abandoned us, no matter the situation. I tried to create the same atmosphere for my sons. I took the verdict as a sign that I'd succeeded.

Eddie and Chris returned to Jersey City a few days later. The three of us, naturally, went out to celebrate in the one place that had become a second home for us: Yankee Stadium.

The Yankees were on their way to the playoffs once again in 1980. I took the boys to one of the last games of the season, versus the Tigers, on Thursday, October 2. It was a great evening. The team got its 101st win of the season, Reggie hit his fortieth home run, and Goose closed things by striking out three and allowing just one hit over two innings for his thirty-second save. The players were all in an excellent mood when the game was over.

The Yanks were on the road when the trial ended, so this was the first time I'd be seeing them since. Scooter had already told everyone the decision, something I discovered when I walked into the clubhouse and heard cheers from the team. Bobby Murcer, who had rejoined the club, gave me a big hug and told me how happy he was for me. The other players invited Eddie and Chris to eat from the postgame buffet of cold cuts. Some of them even brought bottles of Coke over to my sons, just as the Giants had done to me almost thirty years before.

Chris, still confused about the term, kept asking Goose why there were no knuckle sandwiches included with the cold cut spread. Everyone was having a great time. It was just the party my boys deserved.

I stood to the side of the clubhouse, smiling as I listened to Eddie and Chris joke around with the Yankees. I realized at that moment just how many times I'd been blessed in my life. I was humbled by the thought. I wanted to pay those blessings forward.

We are called, as good stewards, to give at least 10 percent of our time, talents, and treasure back. I was determined to give even more. My goal was to bring as much hope and opportunity to others as I had been given.

With the help of Scooter, Bob Diehl, the Lions, Mr. Steinbrenner, and many more special people who would come into my life, I was ready to do just that.

10

Does Home Plate Look
Like a Dinner Plate?

Chris wrote a letter to Mr. Steinbrenner in October 1980. He expressed his thanks to the Boss for all of the support that he, and the Yankees, had given to our family over the years, especially during the trial. I knew that my son was writing to George; what I didn't know was that he'd included a special request in the letter.

The boys had heard the story of my accident thousands of times. They had also heard how their grandmother, along with the Giants, Dodgers, and Yankees, helped to pull me out of my deep depression. Chris remembered me saying that my dream as a boy was to throw out the first pitch in an important game. He wanted that dream to come true.

In his letter, Chris asked Mr. Steinbrenner to think of me when he was making selections for ceremonial first pitch honors at Yankee Stadium. George sent a very nice reply, promising to put me on the list when the Yankees reached the World Series. They missed out in 1980, but did return to the Fall Classic the following season.

The Yankees would be playing their old rival, the Dodgers, in the 1981 World Series. It would be their third championship match with Los Angeles in five years. A few days before the series began, George's PR director called me.

I had made the list!

The plan that Mr. Steinbrenner laid out was for Hollywood legend Jimmy Cagney to throw out the pitch before the first game. Cagney's most famous role was as George M. Cohan in the classic 1941 film *Yankee Doodle Dandy*. He won an Academy Award for the part. The guy was a living legend, a New Yorker through and through, and a true Yankee.

The second game was to feature Mr. Rizzuto, who had been the 1951 World Series MVP versus the Dodgers. I would be throwing out the pitch alongside him, to honor the thirty-year anniversary of his MVP award, and the unique friendship we developed starting that year. The Yankees would then go on the road to Dodger Stadium for Games 3, 4, and 5. Game 6 honors would go to Joe DiMaggio, who was celebrating the fortieth anniversary of his fifty-six-game hitting streak. Game 7's ceremonial first pitch would be handled by Don Larsen. Twenty-five years earlier, Larsen pitched the only perfect game in World Series history. That also happened against the Dodgers.

I was excited; Chris was even more thrilled. One of my childhood dreams was about to come true in front of millions, thanks to my son. Then the commissioner stepped in to alter the plans.

Bowie Kuhn, baseball's head honcho, gave an order that no

celebrities or politicians were allowed to throw out World Series first pitches. It had to be someone connected to baseball. I made the cut—but Jimmy Cagney did not! George was forced to rescind the invitation to the silver screen icon. After a mad scramble, Joe DiMaggio agreed to move up his appearance to Game 1.

There was immediate outrage from Jimmy Cagney fans throughout the world. How could he be humiliated like that? To prevent an international black eye for baseball, Commissioner Kuhn reversed the order.

Good news for Cagney, bad news for me.

Rizzuto and I were bumped from Game 2, so that the Oscar-winning actor could throw out the pitch without having to wait another week. Don Larsen moved his game up from 7 to 6. Scooter and I were then rescheduled to throw out the first pitch at Game 7.

Sadly, that game never happened.

The Yankees lost to the Dodgers in six, giving L.A. the championship. I saw Mr. Steinbrenner after the game. His team had just been defeated, but all he was worried about was that my feelings would be hurt. George apologized profusely and asked me to say sorry to Chris for him. I appreciated that. He told me that I'd be at the top of the list the next time the Yankees got to the World Series.

They didn't return for another fifteen years.

George also asked me what charities I supported. I named a few, like the Seeing Eye and Holy Family. Over the years, he quietly sent large checks to all of them. That was the type of man George Steinbrenner was. He was a kind soul. He never hesitated to help those in need, or to donate to good causes. I deeply admired him for that, and I tried to emulate his philanthropic spirit.

. . . .

Shortly after that, Holy Family hired a new administrator. I'd kept in touch with Sister Anthony Marie and the nuns who shaped my life, but times were changing by the early 1980s. Most school districts were assimilating blind students, which was amazing progress. It spelled doom for schools like Holy Family, which were dedicated solely to helping the blind. In an effort to keep afloat, the nuns welcomed students with other major disabilities. The increased workload was proving too much for the sisters to handle, so they turned to lay teachers and administrators.

Herb Miller was a born leader. As soon as he took the job as administrator at Holy Family, he put into motion a plan for the school that went beyond the walls of the building. He became a passionate advocate for the blind. Herb and his wife, Zinnia, loved the students as if they were their own children. Herb wasn't shy about mingling with politicians and businesspeople to gain needed support for the school and to help create new laws making life easier for the disabled. He was already doing that on a local level, but wanted to broaden his horizons.

He reached out to me for help.

Other than the occasional fund-raising drive and speeches to Lions Clubs around New Jersey, I hadn't done much directly for my alma mater. Herb asked if I would give him a hand in promoting the school and his mission. I leaped at the chance. I wasn't officially an employee of Holy Family, but I became Herb's teammate. It was the start of a productive partnership.

My list of guides was pretty long. I had no shortage of volunteers to take me to games. Even so, Herb became my most frequent companion, followed closely by Gene Mehl and Bob Diehl.

The Yankees of the 1980s were a fun group, though a little tamer than the Bronx Zoo 1970s crew. Sparky, Reggie, and Goose were gone by then. There were a few holdovers. Willie Randolph, Ron Guidry, and Graig Nettles were among the last links to the championship teams. All three would be named Yankee captains. Two young guys, first baseman Don Mattingly and pitcher Dave Righetti, made an immediate impact and became close friends.

Mattingly started joking with me almost from the first day he arrived. He would tease me about everything from my escorts and wardrobe, to the size of the microphones and recorders I used. I played right along with him, and even pulled some pranks of my own.

I was standing with Herb Miller at Yankee outfielder Dave Winfield's locker, interviewing the future Hall of Famer about an upcoming series with the Detroit Tigers, when Charlie, the clubhouse guard, came over to say, "You have about ten minutes left before I have to close the locker room, Eddie."

I checked my watch and said, "Got it, Charlie, I'll leave in ten."

Mattingly happened to see me check the watch, missing the part where I flipped up the glass to feel the Braille. He was astonished. Racing over from his locker, Don said, "Eddie, how the heck can you tell time with a wristwatch? You can't see that thing. It probably doesn't even work. C'mon, you probably just wear it for show!" I took the watch off and handed it to him, so that he could see that it was functioning like any other timepiece.

This frustrated Mattingly no end. He could see the Braille on the inside of the glass, but didn't realize there was a secret button to push to flip the glass up. He spent the next three minutes feeling the face on the watch again and again, as several players looked on with curiosity.

Finally, he gave up. Mattingly handed the watch back to me and said, "Eddie, I don't know how you do it, pal. You can feel those bumps through the glass and I can't. That's amazing!"

"Well, Don," I replied with a grin, "some guys can hit curveballs, some can't. Some guys can feel Braille through glass, some can't. We've both got our talents."

As Herb walked me toward the door and away from Mattingly, I turned to him and called out, "Hey, Don!" As soon as I had his attention, I held my wrist up, pushed the button, and revealed the secret of the watch. Other players roared with laughter. I had to run out the door to avoid the barrage of towels the freshly pranked Mattingly good-naturedly tossed in my direction.

DAVE RIGHETTI, LIKE Ted Williams and several other players, loved seeing my dog. I would bring Flo with me whenever I could. Dave always took time to pet her. Flo was very well-behaved in the clubhouse. One afternoon, she started jumping around and barking. This was totally uncharacteristic. It went completely against her training. I couldn't figure out what was spooking her until a few days later when Graig Nettles shared with me that he'd brought a sonic dog whistle into the locker room and was blowing it to see what Flo would do. Only she could hear it.

Players were actually pranking my dog! I don't think any other media members could say that.

By the end of 1981, Flo began slowing down to the point where she had to retire. Once again, I was heartbroken, but knew that she would be happier on the farm. Another three-week trip to the Seeing Eye brought me together with my third dog, Bessie.

She was a yellow Lab, and was definitely more active and alert than Kay or Flo had ever been.

A few weeks after Bessie came home, she showed us just how remarkable she was.

In December 1981, my sister, Maureen, gave birth to her third child, a daughter whom she named Erin Rose. Bessie loved the baby. Whenever Maureen came downstairs with Erin and my dog was off duty, Bessie would stay close to my infant niece.

One Sunday evening in April 1982, we were all seated at the table for our weekly family dinner. Bessie was lying at my feet. Erin was in a bouncy seat that had rollers, so that she could move around the room. Without warning, Bessie bolted from my side, raced over to Erin, and knocked her little bouncy seat a few feet backward.

The baby started crying.

As they ran to comfort Erin, my mother and sister yelled at me to scold Bessie for scaring the baby. Then they realized what actually happened. Someone had left the door to the basement slightly ajar. It was an opening small enough that nobody noticed it. Nobody except Bessie, that is. When my dog saw how close the baby was getting to the door, Bessie realized that one push by Erin's bouncer would open it, sending her forward into a dangerous tumble down the stairs.

Bessie used her Seeing Eye training to take action and to save a child's life.

My dog was a hero.

Almost exactly a year later, Bessie would prove her heroism once again, with an act of canine bravery and sacrifice that still brings me to tears.

I was in the middle of my nightly 11:00 p.m. routine of walking Bessie when I heard an odd sound coming from down the street. I quickly identified it as that of a car scraping and smashing into other cars. Union Street had a tavern at the end of our block. Occasionally, patrons would drink too much and get behind the wheel. The Jersey City Police Department usually did a great job at stopping them. Tonight, one of the drunks got through their net.

My brain processed the fact that a car was speeding out of control, on a direct course toward me. I froze. I wanted to react, but my body was gripped by fear. Not Bessie. She recognized the danger as soon as I did. Before I knew what was happening, my dog ran in front of me and knocked me backward, just as she had done for my niece.

I was safe.

Bessie suffered for her heroism. Her leash was violently ripped from my hands as the car struck her head-on. She was dragged one hundred yards up the block. I sat on the ground in shock, screaming for help. My neighbors ran out of their homes to come to my aid.

Unfortunately, the driver had escaped the scene and was never caught, leaving Bessie's crumpled and bloody body in the middle of Union Street. She was rushed to the emergency animal hospital, but it was too late.

I held my brave and lovely partner in my arms as she breathed for the very last time.

It took me a few months to return to the Seeing Eye for another dog. Several players expressed their condolences. Dave Righetti was especially kind. His career was in full bloom by then, as the heir to great Yankee pitching legends. I told him that I thought he was next in line to throw a no-hitter, something no Yankee had done for a quarter-century. He laughed at the notion.

On July 4, 1983, I was at the Seeing Eye, listening on the radio as Righetti struck out Wade Boggs of the Red Sox to complete a no-hitter. I was thrilled for him, but felt bad that I couldn't be there to congratulate him in person. When I saw him at the Stadium a few weeks later, accompanied by my new dog, a male black Lab named Tommy, Dave gave me a ball inscribed: "To Eddie, You predicted it! Dave Righetti 7/4/83." Then he whispered, "That's for Bessie."

Holy Family had an annual fund-raising variety show that was languishing by the time Herb Miller came along. He was always looking for new ideas to help the school, or trying to revitalize old ones. This show would be a perfect project for us. The benefit gala had actually been started by my mentor Jerry Molloy in the 1950s. Jerry passed away in 1977, so it was an honor to follow in his giant footsteps. Just as I had done for the telethon a few years earlier, I reached out to celebrity friends to participate in the gala show to raise the profile. Ted Brown, a local radio legend from WNEW, presided over the show and would often arrange for singers and comedians to appear on the bill. Established names like singer Jerry Vale and up-and-coming talents like comedian Joy Behar all pitched in.

Dolly and Marty Sinatra were big supporters of the school throughout their lives. They were both gone by then, but Herb thought it might be a good idea to honor them posthumously. We reached out to Frank Sinatra's representatives in California to let them know about our show and the tribute to his parents. To our amazement, we got word that Old Blue Eyes himself was so touched by Holy Family's salute to his mother and father that he was going to drop by the benefit show to represent them and accept on their behalf.

There were some conditions. Mr. Sinatra would not be performing, just making a short acceptance speech. He would only stay for about thirty minutes. We were not allowed to publicize his appearance at all. They were all fair requests. Herb and I were just excited that one of the biggest stars in the world would be on hand to speak to supporters of the school.

I was as excited as I've been at almost any other time in my life. I'd be meeting my musical idol. I couldn't wait to share stories with him about how kind his parents were to me.

We kept the secret pretty tight. Nobody knew about our special guest.

The night before the show, I got an urgent phone call from California. Sammy Davis, Jr., had died. Given that he was one of Mr. Sinatra's best friends, naturally, plans had changed. Funeral arrangements were being made in Los Angeles, and there was no way Sinatra could come to New Jersey for the show. Of course, we understood.

Nevertheless, our benefit show was still a big hit. We made more money for Holy Family that year than any other. Herb and I wondered if we could schedule other events, perhaps even with Scooter's help.

Mr. Rizzuto was one of the greatest advocates of charities for the blind, including Holy Family. Like Russ Hodges in San Francisco, Scooter would use much of his air time to mention them, in between giving play by play and the score. He also donated 100 percent of his fees from speaking engagements and royalties from his books to the school and other worthy causes. Coupled with his long career as a broadcaster and player, this made Scooter one of the most beloved Yankees ever.

The team knew what a treasure they had in Rizzuto. In 1985 they announced that Phil would receive their ultimate honor. His uniform number 10 would be retired, and a plaque featuring his likeness would be added on the wall in Monument Park, Yankee Stadium's fabled miniversion of the Hall of Fame. The ceremony was set for Sunday, August 4, before a game against the Chicago White Sox.

John Fugazy, the director of special events and promotions for the Yankees, made a very special request of me. He wanted me to be the keynote speaker for Phil Rizzuto Day at the Stadium. The speech would be made during the ceremony, in front of fifty-seven thousand fans and live on TV. I accepted without hesitation. This would be a chance for me to publicly thank Scooter for helping to change my life. I wanted the world to know what a terrific guy Mr. Rizzuto was. Fugazy was giving me the perfect opportunity to do so.

I was asked to put together a two-and-a-half-minute speech describing the unique friendship Mr. Rizzuto and I had developed over thirty-four years. The words came easy to me. I spent months paring them down to a streamlined talk that would fit into the time limit. When I finally had it at the 150-second mark, Fugazy called me again. He realized that WPIX, which would be televising the event to an audience of millions, wanted to add commercial breaks. To accommodate them, I needed to cut thirty seconds from my keynote address.

The solution was simple. I'd originally planned to mention each of Phil's children by name. If I just omitted that part, since they would probably be mentioned by others anyway, I could shave off the extra time. It worked. I now had a neat and concise two-minute talk.

Bob Diehl was my guide that afternoon. The Stadium was completely sold out. Even the press box was jam-packed. I stood on the field before the game as several Yankee sponsors and teammates presented gifts to Phil, Cora, and their kids. The *New York Daily News* even gave him a live cow, named Huckleberry. As Phil went to greet his new "pet," the cow nudged him, promptly knocking him to the ground. Phil, showing the trademark humor that endeared him to his admirers, popped right back up with a huge grin on his face.

Twenty minutes into the ceremony, my name was called by emcee Frank Messer, Phil's broadcast partner. Bob walked me up to the microphone at home plate. I took a deep breath.

Home plate at Yankee Stadium is hallowed ground. This was the same spot on which Lou Gehrig made his famous "luckiest man on the face of the Earth" speech in 1939. I was following in some huge footsteps. For a moment, I was overwhelmed by the task.

After my initial nervousness disappeared, I began my two-minute speech. I had the cadence and timing practiced to the second. I also made one big error. I hadn't factored in the feedback that comes from the public address system at cavernous Yankee Stadium. There is a natural delay of a second or two from the time you talk into the microphone until it comes out of the speakers. This causes a weird and jarring echo. Even experienced singers get thrown when they try to perform the National Anthem from that spot. My timing was way off. I abandoned any hope of keeping to the allotted two minutes. Winging it was the best option.

I had a feeling that I might be going over my time limit. Nobody was saying anything to me, so I figured it was okay. What I didn't know was that the WPIX camera crew was frantically waving at me to finish up. Unlike Howard Danzig, who realized that hand gestures wouldn't work for me on the stand, these guys had no clue as to how to signal me. I was unwittingly causing agita for the director of the broadcast. Bob Diehl finally put an end to it by walking over, tapping me, and quietly saying, "They want you to finish, Ed."

The added minutes didn't ruin things after all. The pregame ceremony finished on time and without a hitch. Phil was delighted and humbled by the day's tributes. He and Cora took me aside to thank me for being a big part of it. I told them that there was no way I'd ever be able to repay all of the kindness and friendship they'd shown to me. A public speech in his honor was the least I could do.

I owed my career and so much more to the Rizzutos.

I now had a regular baseball column in the *Jersey Journal* called "As I See It" and a monthly column in the official scorecard magazine of the Yankees, sold at the ballpark and on newsstands. Twenty-four-hour sports programming on cable TV and talk radio was in its infancy. They would call me on as a guest for local and national TV and radio shows. I enjoyed talking baseball with hosts like Art Rust, Jr., Barry Farber, Ed Randall, Bill Daughtry, Spencer Ross, Richard Neer, and Ann Liguori on stations like Sports Channel, ESPN, WOR, WABC, and WFAN.

WMCA radio, AM 570, gave me a Saturday-afternoon show of my own. I cohosted it with Howie Karpin. Howie was a local guy who knew the rules of baseball inside and out. He now serves as official scorer for both the Yankees and Mets. During our show, Howie and I would take calls from fans, have guests like Mr. Rizzuto, Hall of Famers Richie Ashburn and Ralph Kiner, and play prerecorded interviews. It was some of the most fun I've ever had covering the game.

John Sterling also hosted a show on WMCA and would have me in to chat. He had an amazing voice and an almost encyclopedic knowledge of sports. In WMCA's overnight spot, they had an energetic kid, Chris Russo, fresh out of college. He was dubbed "Mad Dog." Chris was a fellow Giants fan. He and I bonded right away. He was funny, a breath of fresh air in the sometimes stuffy sports world. I enjoyed his work, and figured he'd get pretty far. "Mad Dog" now has his own channel on Sirius/XM Radio and is one of the most famous broadcasters in the United States. John Sterling went on to become the esteemed voice of the Yankees for a whole new generation of fans. It couldn't have happened to two nicer guys.

My friend Eddie Dunphy introduced me to Kevin Williams early in the 1980s. Kevin was the station manager at WOBM radio in Toms River, New Jersey. He'd heard my interviews and hired me to cover baseball for the station, which had a large audience in the South Jersey area. I did that for almost twenty years. All-Star pitcher Al Leiter, a Toms River native who came up with the Yankees and was a three-time World Series champion with the Toronto Blue Jays and Florida Marlins, once told me that he loved listening to me on WOBM when he was younger.

In addition to the sports shows on traditional radio, I did work for two stations dedicated to blind listeners. One was called EIES of New Jersey, the other was In Touch Network. I would do interviews with the players like I did for WOBM and WMCA, but these had a different angle. The questions I asked dealt with things that sighted people take for granted.

I would encourage the players to describe what it looked like to enter Yankee Stadium for the first time, or to see a play develop. Some even described their uniforms. It sounds simplistic, but many radio hosts and broadcasters overlook things like that. Michael Kay, who is the face and voice of the Yankees YES Network, is a notable exception. He takes special care to always describe home and visiting uniforms for blind listeners. One of Kay's most famous on-air phrases is his description of the Yankees' classic home uniform: "They are wearing their crisp white jerseys, with an interlocking NY and pinstripes and no name on the back . . . of course."

I'd sometimes take questions from blind listeners on In Touch. They were very incisive. I didn't lose my sight until I was twelve, so I had an image in my head of what a ballpark looked like. Anyone who was born blind had no sense of this. As a result, I was asked things like, "Is the foul pole thin like a fishing pole or thick like a flagpole?" "Is a dugout actually dug out of the dirt or like a little room on the field?" "Does home plate look like a dinner plate?" I tried my best to answer them all, giving thanks to God that He was allowing me to share what I knew with other fans who couldn't actually see the game they loved.

When I give banquet, corporate, and after-dinner speeches, the organizers sometimes want me to leave time for questions and answers. It's at these events that I've gotten some interesting inquiries from sighted people, who are curious about what life is like for a blind person and broadcaster.

Here are some of the most frequently asked:

"Are your other senses even stronger? Are you able to feel, taste, and hear things better than us?"

This is the biggest misconception about blind people. The comic-book hero Daredevil has these powers, not me. The only thing that I can honestly say increased a bit after my accident was my sense of audio perception. It's what helps me to identify which direction baseballs are headed just by the crack of the bat. It also comes in handy when trying to differentiate voices. Some people say, "I'm better with faces than names." I don't have that option. I can remember others only by their voice.

Bob Sheppard was sitting in the Yankee dining room when he called me over to his table to solve a dilemma for him. NBC had hired two sportscasters who were identical twins, Doug and Don Gould. Try as he might, Sheppard just couldn't tell them apart. He asked me over to decipher which brother was which. It wasn't that hard for me, but others were relying on their visual cues. Their voices were as different to me as a redhead would be from a brunette for sighted people.

Speaking of colors, knowing the difference between them comes naturally to most sighted people. It's one of the hardest concepts to get across to the blind. There is just no way to describe colors. Think about it. If I asked you to tell me what "yellow" looks like using only words, it would be impossible.

I can conceive of colors because I saw what they looked like, but my palette is limited to the primary ones. When a player tells me his uniform includes teal, burnt orange, or metallic purple, I'm clueless. The only baseball "colors" I'm familiar with are Red Schoendienst, Vida Blue, and Dallas Green.

Another question I get often: "Do you have to feel someone's face to know what they look like?"

This is a popular myth about blind people, perpetuated by Hollywood. You know the scene I'm referring to. Someone without sight reaches out, puts his hands all over another person's face, and then miraculously knows exactly what he looks like. Not only is that unsanitary, it's just not true. I rely on something I call "mental mapping" to see people. It's their voices that give me an image of their faces. My idea probably doesn't match reality, but it doesn't have to. It's unique to me.

Reggie Jackson once asked me what I thought he looked like. My description made him seem larger than life, like a mythical hero, à la Paul Bunyan. He liked that better than the reality.

On Old-Timers Day one year, I asked Mickey Mantle to take a picture with me. Like Thurman, he joked about a blind person wanting a photograph. "You can't even see the photo, Eddie," Mickey said with a chuckle, "how do you know I won't be making faces at you the whole time?"

I told Mantle that he looked the same to me as he did on his rookie baseball card in 1951, before I lost my sight. I still pictured him with a full head of shining blond hair, a chiseled body, and a thousand-watt grin.

Mickey grabbed me and shouted, "I like the way you think, kid! Let's do it!"

I use the mental mapping to build actual maps in my head, too. Long before everyone's car was giving them directions via GPS, I was able to get around with my own internal system. I think that my aptitude for math and simple geometry helped.

I'd committed so many streets, highways, and shortcuts to memory that I could usually help my escorts get around detours or traffic.

One of my guides knew that I'd memorized several shortcuts to the Stadium, so he had a friend of his call me for directions. I walked him through it step by step over the phone. Later that year, I was at a Lions event when I was introduced to a member of a club from South Jersey. He said, "Your name is Ed Lucas? That's so funny. I took directions to Yankee Stadium from a guy with that name who drives his car over there all the time. Do you know him?" I laughed. "Know him? He's standing right in front of you!" The guy was left speechless.

It works indoors, too.

There was a blackout at Yankee Stadium during a game. It only lasted for about fifteen minutes. While we were waiting for the lights to come back on, one of the reporters said aloud, "This is terrible. I have to use the bathroom really bad, but it's too dark for me to see anything. I have no idea how to get from here all the way over there."

Blind guy to the rescue!

I didn't need lights, of course, so I spent the next few minutes helping my fellow broadcasters make their way back and forth from the press box restroom until the power returned. There's no line in the box score for "bladders saved" but if there were, my name would be listed with a few of them that night.

The strangest question I ever got was, "Do you hang out with guys like Ray Charles, Stevie Wonder, and Ronnie Milsap?" It's like they think we have a little club of blind people that has secret meetings. I respect these guys for their tremendous talent and use of their gifts, but I've never actually met them. We have our blindness in common, but I'm no more connected to them than I am to people like Bruce Springsteen, Queen Latifah, and Bon Jovi because we all happen to be from New Jersey.

José Feliciano, the Grammy-winning blind singer of "Feliz Navidad" fame, was introduced to me when he sang the National Anthem at Yankee Stadium. He told me that he admired my work, and I repaid the compliment. One of his escorts wondered why I didn't wear dark sunglasses as Feliciano, Charles, Wonder, and other blind people did.

Unless it's a sunny day that calls for it, I've never worn sunglasses. This is something that I feel strongly about. It stems from seeing the beggar on the streets when I was young. He was wearing dark glasses. As with the cup and cane he had, I always associated those glasses with helplessness. I realize that's not the case with most blind people. They wear their glasses to cover their eyes or to protect them. But I don't need them, and try hard not to get pigeonholed into other people's image of what a blind person should look and act like.

Sometimes stereotypes about the blind can be used for humorous purposes.

I was at a party with Bowie Kuhn when I decided to have a little fun with him. I walked over and said, with as straight a face as I could manage, "Mr. Commissioner, I believe there's a job in baseball that I'm extremely qualified for. I'd like to apply right now." Kuhn, who was with a large crowd of reporters, was puzzled. He politely replied, "What job is that, Ed?" My answer, "Umpire," brought the house down.

The umpiring job wasn't offered, but lots of other opportunities were pouring in. A Japanese company had developed a new kind of baseball that was dimpled. They claimed it would help avoid injuries to young players. I was hired by them to do endorsements in the United States and Japan.

Speaking engagements were also becoming more frequent. After much inner debate, I decided to leave Meadowview County Hospital to pursue these other interests, and broadcasting, full-time.

I established a company called No Cup or Cane to handle all of the requests for my time. Exiting Meadowview also gave me the opportunity to devote more energy to fund-raising for charities dear to my heart.

Herb had some excellent high-profile ideas to support the children at Holy Family. One of them was to have an auction featuring items from the Yankees and Mets.

I'd been visiting Shea Stadium and the Mets more often since they hired Jay Horwitz, one of the best PR men in the business. Jay treated me very well, and helped me get access to some of the star players on the Mets as they began their incredible rise to championship status in the mid-1980s. I became close friends with catcher Gary Carter, pitcher Dwight Gooden, and outfielder Darryl Strawberry.

When Darryl heard I was having an auction, he personally went around the clubhouse collecting autographed items from his fellow Mets superstars for me.

The Sisters of Saint Joseph offered their beautiful residential facility on the cliffs overlooking the Hudson River for the auction. We set a date for late August, on a Saturday evening following a Yankee day game. Scooter came to help auction some items from the Yankee old-timers. Jay Johnstone, the eccentric former player who was then a Yankee broadcaster, acted as master of ceremonies. Yankee catcher Bob Geren showed up to represent the team and to mingle with fans at the auction.

It was a smash hit.

Thousands were raised for Holy Family that night. Herb was ecstatic. Even so, Mr. Rizzuto proposed a bigger, bolder, idea. He wanted to have a celebrity golf tournament.

This would be a massive undertaking. Celebrity tournaments were a lot of work. I told Scooter that I had no idea where to start. He assured me and Herb that we could do it.

He was right.

After a few bumps and a steep learning curve, we were able to build the Phil Rizzuto Celebrity Golf Classic into an annual highlight of the New Jersey fund-raising calendar. Not only did we get golfers and companies from all over the state and beyond on board as supporters, celebrities flocked to be involved with Mr. Rizzuto and to spend the day hanging out with him. We had his buddies, like Yogi, Mickey, and Whitey, of course, but stars from every arena also joined the fun. Meat Loaf, Jerry Orbach, Dick Vitale, Mick Foley, Rod Gilbert, Phil Simms, Pat Cooper, Gary Carter, and Tony Lo Bianco were just a few of the luminaries who pitched in to help.

Over the course of twenty years, we raised millions for Holy Family. Herb was astute enough to use the prominence of Scooter's tournament to bring even more awareness in Trenton and in Washington, D.C., to the needs of blind people in New Jersey and around the country. He did more than almost anyone else for the cause.

My contribution was to talk about the tournament with the celebrities gathered at Scooter's table, gently nudging them to get involved. Phil's deep humility prevented him from actually talking about the golf classic himself. He would always call it "The Eddie Lucas Tournament" even when doing on-air commercials and promotions for his own event.

Chris was with me after a game one day when we ran into Donald Trump, who was uncharacteristically dressed in a Yankee jersey. I spoke to Mr. Trump for a few minutes about the golf tournament. He asked me a few questions about my career. As we were walking away, Trump grabbed Chris and said, "Are you twenty-one yet?" When he replied no, the Donald followed with, "When you are, take your dad to my new casino in Atlantic City. We have Braille slot machines now. He'll love them!" I thanked Donald for his invitation. He ended by saying, "The only thing we don't have yet, Ed, is Braille playing cards."

Little did he know, I carried just such a deck around in my bag.

Don Mattingly actually challenged me to a hand of poker one night. I pulled out my trusty Braille deck. He dealt himself a royal flush and then said, "You know, Eddie, I've never played with anyone who admitted to having a marked deck like yours!"

Dan Schlossberg, the author of *The Baseball Catalog* and thirty-two other books about the sport, is one of my closest friends. He decided, in 1989, to help fulfill the promise that George Steinbrenner had made to me almost a decade before. The Yankees came close to pennants during the 1980s, winning more games than any other team, but kept missing out on the postseason. It was clear that I wouldn't be able to throw out a first pitch during a World Series at Yankee Stadium. The Giants were another matter.

My father's favorite team was doing pretty well for themselves in San Francisco. Led by slugger Will Clark, they were cruising to a playoff berth in 1989. Inspired by Chris, Dan wrote to Bob Lurie, then owner of the Giants, making the same request my son did. Mr. Lurie knew of me, and of my history with the Giants. Not wanting to risk a situation like 1981 when there was no seventh game, or—heaven forbid—that the Giants would somehow miss the postseason, the owner declared September 12, 1989, Ed Lucas Day at Candlestick Park.

Like Mr. Rizzuto, I was going to have my own day at the ballpark!

Gene Mehl had lots of frequent flier miles built up, so he offered them to me for the trip out to the West Coast. He would be my escort, since he had business meetings scheduled in California around that time. Herb Miller also made the trip, to be with me when Gene wasn't available. Dan had an assignment in Milwaukee, so he couldn't go. He'd be with us in spirit.

It was a wonderful autumn night in northern California for a ballgame. It was also my first time in San Francisco. The Giants featured my story on the scoreboard, then introduced me to the sixty thousand fans. I was escorted to the mound. Pitcher Rick Reuschel stood next to me, encouraging me all the way. This was the moment I'd dreamed of since I was ten years old.

I could imagine and feel my dad looking down and smiling at me with pride.

As I raised my arms for the windup, catcher Terry Kennedy took a few steps back. He was prepared for a soft ceremonial toss, but I'd asked some guys like Dave Righetti, Al Leiter, Goose Gossage, and Dwight Gooden to give me pointers before I left New York. My pitch moved right down the center, hitting his glove smack in the middle.

Nobody clocked it, but I'm sure my pitch would have won a carnival prize or two that night.

When the ceremony was over, I had to leave the field by way of the stands, since the game was about to start. As I walked up the steps to our box seats, a fan grabbed me and hugged me. I was startled. Then I listened to the person's voice. It was familiar, though I hadn't heard it in over twenty-five years.

Barry Baum had been a classmate at Seton Hall. After graduation, he moved to San Francisco to practice dentistry. He was also a Giants season ticket holder. As he gripped me tight, Barry said, "I'm so happy that I was here to see this, Eddie! Congratulations, pal, you've led such an amazing life!"

I thought about Barry's comment on the three-thousand-mile plane trip back home.

God had indeed blessed me with an amazing life, and I continued to be grateful to Him for that.

There was still one thing missing from that life, a special someone to share it with.

Scooter, ever the resourceful shortstop, was about to provide an assist for me there, too.

11

Bride of the Yankees

Hillside, New Jersey, is a small town of twenty thousand people, not far from Newark Airport. It was here that Phil and Cora Rizzuto settled in the 1940s to live and raise their family.

The Rizzutos loved their town and were fiercely loyal to the businesses in the area. Everything they needed, they tried to do close to home. When they wanted to get flowers for someone, they would stop by a shop less than a mile away. There were two workers at the florist in particular whom they were fond of, an aunt and her niece.

One day, Phil was talking to the aunt, Marlene Greene, when he noticed that she seemed a bit down. He asked her what was wrong, and she told him that her niece, Allison, was having difficulty with her vision. This was frustrating to them both, and they didn't know what to do.

Scooter knew.

He said, "I have a friend, Eddie Lucas, who is blind. Maybe he can help lift her spirits. Is it okay if he calls Allison?" She agreed, and I made the call that would start me on a road to lasting joy.

ALLISON PFEIFLE WAS born prematurely, along with her twin sister, Lorrie. For three months they were kept in an incubator. The increased oxygen caused damage to her developing retina cells. Her sister had no ill effects. Allison struggled with her vision throughout childhood and had problems in school. Unlike Jersey City, with its PS 22, her town didn't offer programs for children with limited sight, so she slipped through the cracks.

Despite the setbacks, Allison was a devoted sports fan and even played catcher on her high school softball team. After graduation, she went on to earn a degree in biology and education at Kean University, then followed that by finishing in the top percentile of her class in nursing school at Seton Hall. It was during a routine eye checkup while working as a nurse that Allison was diagnosed with retinal detachment. Several unsuccessful operations were performed. She was then sent to Dr. Freeman in Boston, one of the best eye doctors in the world. He repaired her torn retinas by attaching buckles, but the vision loss was irreversible and permanent. She could not work as a nurse again.

Allison's aunt Marlene, whom she lived with, urged her to take the job at the florist. She could use her skills in a productive way without having to worry about a long commute to work, or traveling at night.

When I called, I spoke to Allison about the challenges we both faced. We knew from the first few moments that there was a strong connection between us. As soon as we hung up, we couldn't wait to speak to each other again.

For three years, from 1988 to 1991, we continued our frequent phone calls, never once meeting in person.

That might seem odd, but we were at a bit of a disadvantage. I lived in Jersey City and she lived thirty miles south. Not much of a distance, but she might as well have lived in Saint Louis, San Francisco, or São Paolo for what it was worth.

I couldn't just hop in my car to visit Allison, and she couldn't, either. We made the mutual decision to keep our relationship confined to phone calls, because it would be too heartbreaking to meet each other, then have to endure long stretches of separation.

On June 21, 1991, I decided to bend our little agreement and surprise Allison with a visit to her shop. My friend Carl Holtzberg was taking me to the Yankee game that night. I asked him to make a detour. Allison was cleaning the front of the store when I walked in. She recognized me right away. I didn't have to say a word. We hugged for what seemed like thirty minutes. I stayed until she closed the shop.

Carl and I got to Yankee Stadium late that night. I didn't mind at all.

Our phone calls increased in regularity and intimacy.

And then: We were officially a couple.

The very first date that we went on was to the ballpark. Allison was a big Mets fan, so I arranged for us to have four tickets to a game at Shea Stadium versus the Dodgers. Another couple drove us to the game, and we all sat together. Around the sixth inning, one of Allison's friends leaned over and whispered, "I think Ed really likes you." She was right. Allison was the perfect woman for me, one who cared more about Shea Stadium than Chez Madeline.

I chose Los Angeles as the opponent for a reason. Allison's favorite player was my pal Darryl Strawberry, who had collected the signatures for my auction. Darryl was now playing for the Dodgers, and I brought her to meet him after the game. He was very gracious to her, taking a photo with us and signing one of his bats to mark the occasion.

A few weeks later I took Allison to Yankee Stadium. Scooter was thrilled to see us together. Our diminutive matchmaker invited Allison to sit at his table and helped me to show her around the House that Ruth Built.

In 1994, Mr. Rizzuto got an interesting phone call of his own. After years of being passed over, he was told that the National Baseball Hall of Fame would be including him in its class of inductees that year. Fans all over the country cheered the news of this long overdue honor. Allison and I booked a trip to Cooperstown for the July ceremony as soon as we heard.

The amazing coincidence of that summer was that Leo Durocher was posthumously chosen to go into the Hall of Fame alongside Scooter. I would be there with my girlfriend to watch the two men who gave me a huge lift when I needed it receive their well-deserved rewards.

Phil retired from the Yankees two years after that, ending a seven-decade run that he was told would be impossible for a little guy like him.

My dog Tommy passed away around that time, the longest-serving Seeing Eye dog I ever had.

I did not return to Morristown for another Seeing Eye dog. Chris and Eddie were old enough to help me get around. I wasn't commuting to Meadowview anymore, so Tommy was basically a stay-at-home dog by the end.

Baseball also changed a bit in the 1990s. Clubhouses were no longer the raucous, freewheeling places that I was accustomed to. Things were more businesslike. Players still joked around, but there wasn't as much horseplay with the media. Nobody would be throwing towels or giving hotfoots anymore.

A new crop of Yankees came up in the 1990s: Bernie Williams, Mariano Rivera, Andy Pettitte, and Jorge Posada were four of the players who helped Gene Michael and Buck Showalter build the core of a dynasty. They were all very open to the media, and behaved in a classy manner that fit the hallowed uniforms they were wearing.

In 1995, an overseas magazine was doing a story about my life and wanted pictures of me and Allison on the field at Yankee Stadium. They couldn't send a photographer, so we had to bring our own camera. The problem was that we had nobody to take the pictures. Allison happened to be talking about our dilemma when the Yankees rookie shortstop, Derek Jeter, heard her.

Derek came over and said, "Would you like me to take some pictures of you, Mr. Lucas?" He then took the camera from Allison and proceeded to spend the next few minutes snapping shots.

This was no ordinary Yankee rookie.

The poise, grace, decency, and composure that I sensed in Derek

Jeter early on was reminiscent of guys like Joe DiMaggio, Willie Mays, Stan Musial, and Thurman Munson. Like them, he had the qualities of a leader and classic exemplary role model, both on and off the field. It was quite clear that his future would be a bright one with the Yankees.

In the twenty years that followed, I got to know Derek better. I discovered that we had many things in common. Though he was raised in Michigan, Derek's mother's side of his family was also made up of Irish Catholics from Jersey City. Derek's maternal grandfather, Sonny Connors, is actually a Hudson County legend. One of the biggest high school gyms in the county is named for Sonny. Derek used to come back to visit New Jersey during the summer in the 1980s, when he was a boy. His grandmother loved the Yankees, and he would watch the games on TV with her. Derek grew up listening to Phil Rizzuto and told everyone that he was going to be the Yankees' shortstop one day, just like Scooter had been.

The part of Derek's story I identified with the most, though, was the love and dedication shown by his parents, Dorothy and Charles. Early on, they taught Derek and his younger sister, Sharlee, that goals in life could be achieved, but there was a price. Nothing would happen without hard work, dedication, and respect for themselves and others. Dorothy and Charles, who has a Ph.D. in psychology, drew up contracts for their children to sign, which set in writing what was expected of them. Derek once told me that his parents always saw great potential in him, thanks to the gifts that God had blessed him with, even during the rare times when he lost sight of that himself.

That sounds a lot like my own parents.

Like Munson before him, Derek led his team to a two-decade, almost uninterrupted string of postseason appearances and championships. Jeter was named Yankee captain in 2003. Thanks to Derek and to the other young players who came up with him, the Yankees were once again the biggest team in sports. Their success even allowed the Yankees to replace the eighty-five-year-old Yankee Stadium with a twenty-first-century streamlined version in 2009.

I'm still getting used to it.

The Yankees also started their own television network, called YES. I participated in many programs on Yankee history and was hired to report on the last few seasons of old Yankee Stadium. I even won an Emmy Award for my work. Ernie Harwell, who, like Scooter, was nearing his own retirement after sixty years, saw me on one of his last trips into New York with the Tigers. He embraced me and said, "I knew you could do it, Ed. I'm glad you stuck with it."

I flashed back to the day in 1952 when he had me as his guest in the broadcast booth and gave me advice that I carried with me throughout my career. I was happy to share this moment with him.

That same year, I was inducted into the Irish-American Baseball Hall of Fame. This officially recognized branch of Cooperstown is located in Manhattan, at Foley's on Thirty-Third Street. My fellow honorees were Vin Scully and Walter O'Malley, two Dodger legends.

It meant a lot, because they were not only honoring me, but my dad, my mom, and all of the Irish men and women in the Lucas and Furey families who preceded me.

At that induction, a reporter said to me, "Ed, you've been pretty lucky in life, how do you feel about that?" The answer that came to mind was a quote that Father Kerry had shared with our class at Seton Hall years before.

It was from Seneca the Younger, a Roman theologian and friend of Saint Paul. He said, way back in the first century, that "luck is just hard work meeting opportunity." I've lived by that ever since.

God placed people and events in my life that helped me to succeed, but if I hadn't been totally prepared, mentally, emotionally, physically, and spiritually, those opportunities would have passed me right by. You have to keep yourself ready and in position to receive the blessings. As Dr. Charles Jeter always pointed out to his son, nothing comes easy; hard work is always the biggest key to the equation. The only place success comes before work is in the dictionary.

It took some hard work for Allison and me to keep our relationship going. We hit some rough patches, but we hung in there.

In the early 2000s I had a skin cancer scare. Allison was right there with me as I recovered from my operation. By this time, I was living alone in the house on Union Street. My mother had passed away in 1999, Maureen five years later, and Eddie and Chris left to start their own families. Allison's Aunt Marlene died the same year as my mother, so she was alone in her house, too.

The time was right for us to get together permanently.

On Thanksgiving morning 2005, I asked Allison to marry me. She said yes.

My next question was, "Would you like to get married at home plate at Yankee Stadium?" She said yes to that, too.

Neither of us had any idea whether such a thing was even

possible. Turns out it wasn't. Nobody had ever been married at home plate.

We began looking into other options when Rick Cerrone, the Yankees media relations director, called us. I'd known Rick for years, from the days when he ran his own national baseball magazine. He asked if we were the ones who put in the wedding request. When I said yes, he said, "I want you to call Gina Chindemi, who organizes our Stadium events."

I phoned her the next day. She said, "I have to meet you." I was curious why. "Mr. Steinbrenner gave me strict orders never to allow anyone to get married at home plate. I was going to say no to you, too, but the Boss told me to say yes. I asked him why, and he said, 'It's because Ed Lucas is part of our family.'"

We decided to have a small service in a chapel on the campus at Seton Hall, where we would be married by a priest, but the main event would be in front of a large crowd in the Bronx at the Stadium known worldwide as the Cathedral of Baseball.

Allison and I spent the next few months planning our wedding, which was scheduled for Friday, March 10, 2006. We invited more than 150 guests. Phil and Cora weren't feeling well enough to make it, but Mrs. Rizzuto gave Allison her fur coat to wear, just in case the March winds made the Stadium too chilly.

Chris wrote a letter to Steve Rushin at *Sports Illustrated* telling him about my life and upcoming wedding. Rushin wrote a full-page article that appeared in the February 27 issue of the magazine.

That story opened the media floodgates. Suddenly, my phone started ringing with calls from reporters asking to cover our wedding. Rick was getting the calls, too, at the Yankee spring training camp in Tampa. Once word got out that this would be the first-ever wedding at home plate in Yankee Stadium, it became a news-worthy event.

Rick took the pressure off Allison and me by running all requests through the Yankee PR office. There would now be more reporters at the wedding than guests. Cerrone set up a post-wedding press conference in the Yankee media room with the Yankee banner behind us, just like the players and managers have after their games are over. All three network morning shows wanted an exclusive interview and coverage of the wedding itself. Bob Dotson of NBC's *Today Show* had always been one of our favorites, so we went with him.

A few days before the wedding, Dotson and his crew set up an interview in Mr. Steinbrenner's private box. It was freezing. There was snow all over the Yankee Stadium field.

This was shaping up to be a very chilly wedding indeed.

On the morning of the wedding, we woke up to an unexpected weather forecast of sunny and seventy-five degrees. It was an amazing day, unseasonably warm for early March.

But an even bigger surprise occurred when we arrived at the Stadium. What had been snow-covered and dormant a few days before was now vibrant and fresh. Mr. Steinbrenner asked his grounds crew to make the Stadium look just like it would for Opening Day, even though that was almost a month away.

The wedding itself was like a fairy tale. A judge from the Bronx presided. Eddie read the familiar passage about the virtues of love from Corinthians, chapter thirteen. Chris read a poem about life and baseball written by former pitcher Jim "Mudcat" Grant. Irish tenor Ciaran Sheehan, who starred in *The Phantom of the Opera* on Broadway, sang "Always," Irving Berlin's famous love song in 1942's *Pride of the Yankees*.

Finally, Allison and I got to say "I do" on the very same spot where so many of our heroes had their own memorable days in the sun.

As soon as the wedding was over, we were rushed to the press room for interviews. There was standing room only. It felt weird to be on this side of the interview table.

Someone asked Allison why I picked Yankee Stadium for a wedding venue and she said, "Because he wanted to give me the biggest diamond possible."

Eddie thought ahead and brought two bats, a ball, and a glove as props for wedding photos. They brought us back out to the pristine field, with the red, white, and blue bunting and the scoreboard that said CONGRATULATIONS ED AND ALLISON ON YOUR SPECIAL DAY! We posed with the bats over our shoulders. I held a light-colored stick, and Allison had a dark one, which contrasted nicely with my black tuxedo and her white wedding dress. The next day, several newspapers ran that photo with the headline BRIDE OF THE YANKEES.

The reception was held upstairs in the private Yankee club. Allison and I sat in a booth shaped like a gigantic catcher's mitt as well-wishers came over to talk to us. The room was adorned with pictures of the Yankee players and their greatest moments. It felt like just the right place to celebrate. Actress and film director Penny Marshall was there, along with producer Elliot Abbott. They had made *A League of Their Own* and were interested in learning more about my story. We were happy to have them among our guests.

Toward the end of the evening, one last surprise from Mr. Steinbrenner was announced. He couldn't be there himself, so the Boss sent a congratulatory note, which was read aloud by Chris. George was returning the check that Allison and I had written to cover the cost of the wedding. He was taking care of the whole tab himself. It wasn't a small amount. He insisted that family members should not pay for the use of their own house.

As he had so many times before, Mr. Steinbrenner left me in awe of his generosity.

I hope George doesn't mind that I just told more than two people about it.

I saw Mr. Steinbrenner for the final time at the All Star Game in Yankee Stadium in 2008. It was the last year at the old Stadium and they were using the pregame ceremonies to honor all of the legends who played there. I happened to be in the Monument Park area out by the bullpen in left center. Chris was my guide that night.

Toward the end of the introductions, George was brought to the bullpen gate in a golf cart. They were going to ride him around the perimeter of the Stadium to hear cheers from the fans in honor of the six championships he'd helped to deliver them. He was right next to us. When Chris told me he was there, I leaned over and said, "Thanks for everything, Boss. I love you." George looked over at me. Unable to speak, he gave a thumbs-up and nodded. I couldn't see this gesture, but I could feel the warmth that came my way from him.

Two years later, I was at the All Star Game in Anaheim, California, with Chris when we got an early morning phone call that

Mr. Steinbrenner had passed away. It was a sad day, but it also made me happy that people were finally lifting his self-imposed moratorium on stories about his generosity. The Boss didn't want to ruin the public image of himself as a stern taskmaster prone to firing and rehiring managers, players, and employees. He asked everyone to keep quiet about his charitable works until he was gone.

The world would now know the George Steinbrenner I had known for years.

GOING TO ALL Star Games and Hall of Fame inductions gives me a chance to catch up with players I might not ordinarily get to see on a regular basis. When Goose Gossage was put in the Hall in 2008, I was in Cooperstown to cheer him on. The president of the Hall, Jeff Idelson, invited me and Chris to be his guests at the gala party the night before. Most of the living Hall of Famers were there.

Chris was in the corner chatting with Reggie Jackson when both of them noticed Willie Mays enter the room. Chris came to get me. We approached the "Say Hey Kid." Willie was losing his sight and was moving a bit slower, but he was still as sharp as ever. He greeted me with a cheery, "Hey, Eddie, how you doin', man?"

We talked about old times at the Polo Grounds and my very first interview, in 1957. I told him that I still had the photo of it that Uncle Eugene snapped. There were others waiting to talk to Mays, so I said good-bye. Before I had a chance to walk away, Willie grabbed my arm and said, "How 'bout another picture?" With that, he and I did our best to try to re-create the pose from fifty-one years earlier.

Herb Miller was with me at the All Star Game in Boston in 1999. They introduced a special "Team of the Century" before the game. Fenway Park erupted in cheers for ten minutes when Ted Williams was brought out. He was the greatest Red Sox player of them all and was taking a long-overdue bow. Herb made sure that I got to see Ted before he left the park. Williams rarely appeared away from his Florida home, and I wanted to thank him for all he'd done for me.

As soon as we got close, Ted snapped to attention. "There you are, Eddie! I see you over there. Where's Kay? How come you didn't bring her?"

I didn't have the heart to tell Mr. Williams that Kay would have been almost thirty years old in human years at that point. He shook my hand, said hello to Herb, and left with a big grin.

It was a magical night.

The Celebrity Golf Classic had been running smoothly for two decades. Herb and Scooter made sure that the students at Holy Family, and blind children all across New Jersey and throughout the United States, got as much funding as they possibly could, thanks to our tournament.

Unfortunately, we suffered two major losses in rapid succession.

Herb Miller died suddenly in October 2005. It was a shock. He was relatively young and in good health. Other than the stress of running the school and constantly seeking new methods of fund-raising, he was a carefree guy. My heart broke for Zinnia and their children.

Holy Family was never the same after Herb's death. The nuns shut the doors to the building completely a few years later, and it was eventually demolished. The school that I lived in and loved was gone forever.

And then Phil Rizzuto passed away in 2007. He had been in ill health for years, but it was still a crushing blow. Allison and I got to see him a few times toward the end at his assisted-living facility. He was still the same old Phil. Though his voice was weaker and he was confined to his room, the spirit of the little man whose heart was as big as all of Yankee Stadium shone through.

I AM CONSTANTLY inspired by such things as Derek Jeter's Turn 2 Foundation, Don Imus's Ranch for Children with Cancer, Curtis Granderson's Grand Kids, the Michael J. Fox Foundation, the David Ortiz Fund for Children, Oprah Winfrey's Leadership Foundation, Danny and Marlo Thomas's Saint Jude's Children's Hospital, and other examples of celebrities leveraging their fame to give back to their communities, helping thousands of worthy causes in the process. The Yankees have also continued George's philanthropic endeavors. Thanks to Media Relations Director Jason Zillo and George's children, Jennifer, Hank, Jessica, and Hal, the team instituted an annual event called HOPE Week. Not only do the Yankees donate to these charities, they highlight them for an entire week at the ballpark and on television, encouraging fans to be supporters.

It's an organization using the power of its brand for good.

To emulate all of these inspiring examples, Allison and I began the Ed Lucas Foundation in 2012. It's meant to provide support and guidance to blind and disabled people and the organizations that assist and serve them throughout the United States and the world. Bob Diehl passed away in 2010, but his fellow Lion, Herb Bodensiek, was a man cut from the same cloth. He had lots of experience setting up foundations, and gave me excellent guidance. Several other people, like Tim Courtney, Rich Cutter, and Joe DiDio, and old friends like Gene and Karen Mehl, and the five Dunphy siblings (Eileen, Ann, Eddie, Mary, and Regina), were instrumental, along with Mr. Bodensiek, in helping me and Allison get the foundation up and running.

One of the events that directly led to the Ed Lucas Foundation was Strikeouts for Scholarships, a partnership created by David Nussbaum between WCBS Radio, Seton Hall, and the New York Yankees. For three seasons, beginning in 2008, ten dollars was donated for each strikeout thrown by a Yankee to a special fund set up to help disabled students at Seton Hall. The public was encouraged to match donations. It was very successful, but limited to one school. Allison and I wanted to expand it to benefit students from any college, as well as any disabled children, adults, or senior citizens facing their own uphill battles.

Many people wondered what would happen to the golf tournament after Phil's death and the closing of the school. Gene Michael, who was largely responsible for putting together the Yankee team that won all those World Series championships in the late 1990s, stepped in to fill the large void left by Scooter. He wasn't replacing Mr. Rizzuto, just carrying on his legacy. Thanks to Gene, the Golf Classic, renamed in his honor, is still going strong.

In the years to come, I hope to expand the reach and scope of the Ed Lucas Foundation, following the pattern set by Derek and the others. More and more people each day are left facing a life of blindness and disability due to injury, disease, or aging. We would like to be a beacon for them.

If you'd like to learn more about what we do at the Ed Lucas Foundation, I invite you to visit us at www.EdLucasBook.com. There's even a link there where I will send you a bunch of gifts to help you get started on making a difference in your own community.

I have been blessed many times over, and it has humbled me. Whenever there were moments that I could have thrown in the towel and completely given up, God placed people in my life to lift me up and to keep me moving forward. You can be that person for someone, too.

Several of the people I encountered in my journey just happened to be Hall of Famers. It's a special title, given to those who excel in a certain area. That seems like an unreachable goal for many, one reserved for icons and immortals. Nothing could be further from the truth. Each and every one of you has the opportunity to be a Hall of Famer in the eyes of someone in your life, in a quiet and meaningful way. It's easy to do.

My obstacle just happens to be blindness, but everyone has his or her own mountain to climb. Whether it's physical, psychological, financial, emotional, or otherwise, we all face battles at several points in our lives. If you just take the time to recognize and empathize with those who are going through rough waters, reach out to them and lend them support in your own way, you will be a Hall of Famer to them.

My passion just happens to be baseball, but if you follow your own passion and live it to the fullest, you will quickly discover the rewards that come from it. Doing that helped me to carve out a successful career in sports despite my limitations, but it just as easily could have been law, education, science, entertainment, or dozens of other vocations if that's where my heart took me. It was more about the drive than the journey. By following your own passion and working hard at it, you are enriching not only your own life, but those of others who are watching, especially your children and family members. Once they see you proving that anything is possible if you set your mind to it, no matter what the naysayers claim, you will be a Hall of Famer to them.

My faith just happens to be Roman Catholic Christianity, but if you look to a higher power, no matter what your denomination or creed, it can help bring you comfort in times of crisis. This has always worked for me and my family, putting into action the lessons from the Good Book we heard from the pulpit. When you shift your focus from yourself onto others, treating them as you'd like to be treated—the central tenet of almost every religion—your life will improve in the process. It seems like a contradiction, but I've discovered that the more I do for others, the happier my own life becomes. If you take some time out of your busy day to perform an act of kindness for a friend, or even a complete stranger, you will be a Hall of Famer to them.

My service organization just happens to be the Lions International, but I encourage you to join a club in your local area. It doesn't matter whether it's the Lions, Kiwanis, Rotary, B'nai B'rith, the Knights of Columbus, the Elks, or other similar clubs, they are all outstanding organizations that gather like-minded people to give back to their communities while offering opportunities for personal growth and networking. By joining a local service club and becoming an active volunteer in helping those in your community who need it the most, you will be a Hall of Famer to them.

So many wonderful things have happened to me in my life that I feel it's my duty to give back, to comfort others and to help them realize their dreams. I encourage you to do the same. We are all on a journey home; it's how you treat others along the path that makes the difference.

Always be there for other people. Be the shoulder to cry on, the ears to listen sympathetically, the eyes to recognize suffering, and the arms to hold someone tight when that person is hurting. Do all of these things, and I promise you that when you round the bases for the final time, you will be welcomed home at the end of the game with love by God, who will surely include your name on the list of life's Hall of Famers.

Acknowledgments

My humble thanks to Almighty God, who blessed me with an amazing dad, and also gave me the gifts to be able to help co-write and share my father's inspirational story with the world. I'm also grateful to God for all the family, friends, acquaintances, role models, and teachers that He has placed in my life along the way. The moments and lessons in my journey with them—the highs and the lows combined—led to the creation of this book. I couldn't have properly told my dad's tale without those experiences. Thank you, Lord, for providing them.

—CHRISTOPHER LUCAS (ISAIAH 64:8)

My deepest appreciation goes to our literary agent, Jennifer De-Chiara, who believed in this project from the beginning and was passionate enough to see it to fruition, and to Marie Lamba, who first brought it to Jennifer's attention. To Mitchell Ivers, Natasha

Simons, Jennifer Robinson, Louise Burke, Jennifer Bergstrom, Jaymee Messler, Alana DeBerry, Maureen Cavanagh, and everyone at Simon & Schuster/Gallery and Jeter Publishing, thank you for your help in strengthening and promoting this book.

I am honored that Derek chose my life story to be among the first he's published. He has consistently used the gifts he was blessed with to help others, and is an excellent role model. I'm very proud to be associated with The Captain.

Thanks to my parents, Edward and Rosanna Lucas, for their love, encouragement, and for making me the man of faith that I am today. Thanks also to my wife, Allison, for her understanding, love, and support; to my sons—Eddie and Christopher (my coauthor)—for their love and encouragement throughout the years; to my daughter-in-law Sharon; my three grandsons, EJ, Adam, and Sean; my nephews, Jeffrey and Brian Hanks, and my niece, Erin Hanks Carr, her husband, Joe, and their children, Aiden and Talon; I cherish them all.

To my lifelong friends and "second parents," Phil and Cora Rizzuto, whose support and encouragement helped me to reach my dreams: I owe you a debt that I can never fully repay. Thanks for showing me how to pass your gifts along by blessing others with kind words and philanthropic deeds.

Many thanks to those who have touched my life in a meaningful way, in many areas:

My extended family: Nana Elizabeth Furey, Aunt Jean and Uncle Arthur Fitzhenry, Aunt Rosemary and Uncle Bill Furey, Aunt Claire and Uncle Vincent Furey, Aunt Jean and Uncle Eugene Furey, Aunt Marion and Uncle Jack Irwin, and Aunt Jerry and Uncle John Slowinsky, James and Maureen Fitzhenry, Carol

Ann Furey, Cathy Furey, Eugene Furey, Kevin Furey, Claire Furey, Timothy and Karen Furey, Timothy Furey Jr., Matthew Furey, Allie Furey, Jackie Furey, Vincent Furey Jr., Vincent and Jeannie Hartnett, John Hartnett, Cornelius Hartnett, Michael Hartnett, Thomas Hartnett, Marguerite Hartnett, Bobby Irwin, Larry Irwin, Rene Kegelman, Joanie Fitzhenry Kegelman, Jeannie Fitzhenry Morris, Geraldine Slowinski, John Slowinski, and Patty Slowinski. Uncle Joe and Aunt Ann Lucas Boni, Uncle George (Luke) and Aunt Evelyn Lucas, Uncle Chris and Aunt Mary Lucas, Uncle George and Aunt Marge Lucas Lunney, and Uncle Bill and Aunt Josephine Lucas McCarthy, Joe and Elaine Lucas Cidoni, Ralph and Janet Lucas DeFiore, Duke and Betty Lucas Johnson, Jim and Joan Lucas Keiter, Charlie Kuster, Bobby and Doris Kuster, George (Bubba) Lucas and Phyllis Lucas, Ray Lunney, Kenny and Pat Lunney, Denis and Annemarie McCarthy, Marilyn Kuster Mc-Gowan, and Jacqueline Lunney Murphy.

Members of my wife Allison's family: Aunt Marlene Greene; her twin sister, Lorrie, and husband, Brett Conner; Lorrie's son, Jason Jaeger; his wife, Moriah; and Brett's daughter, Shannon; her sister, Robin, and her husband, Ron Patane; and children, Ronald, Rebecca, and Ryan; and his wife, Sarah; her sister, Jill, and her husband, Kevin Durham, and children, Justine and Kimberly.

My friends and neighbors from Jersey City: Beverly Beechum, Joe Breslin, Marie Breslin, Theresa Breslin, Timothy Breslin, Msgr. Robert Coleman, Joan and Jim Collins, Arlene Collins, Mary Ann and Pat Conte, Benny Darvalics, Joe Darvalics, Barbara Donahue, Joe Doyle, Carol Garrett, Barbara Garrett, Rev. William Hornack, Rev. Michael Hornack, Gladys and Tom Kelly, Patricia

Kelly, Carol Kelly, Colleen Kelly, Kerry Kelly, Dennis Kelly, Tom Kelly Jr., Tommy Martin, Rich McCrystal, Billy McCrystal, Peggy McCrystal-Spina, Larry McGucken, Mary Ann McHugh, Donald Nagel, Claire Ruggiani, Joe Scarpa, Donna Smith, Tommy Timmerman, Gene Turner, and Joe Walsh.

My lifelong friends: the Dunphy Family; Eileen, Ed, Regina, Ann, and Mary.

My former classmates and teachers at PS 22: Margaret Boasci, Miss Burke, Robert Cauldren, Miss Demming, Anthony Gallo, Gene Mehl, Robert O'Brien, Tommy Scerbo, Louis Schuman, and Eileen Schwartz.

Holy Family School for the Blind Sisters, former students, and faculty: Sr. Gregory, Sr. Rose Magdalene, Sr. Anthony Marie, Sr. Redempta, Sr. Theresa Catherine Carbury, Sr. Ann Rutan, Sr. Ann Taylor, Antonio Cabrero, Martha Chojnacki, Diane Grimes, Sharon Kelly, Tommy McDoyle, Michael Moran, Margaret Mary Norton, Lois Perillo, Rafael Redding, Nancy Romer, Nancy Howes Scotto, Johnny Westerfield, Charles Wilson, Pauline Zook, Nadia Cartagena, Pat Conte, Mary Dixon, Ellen Fellicetta, Ella Frye, Donna Mejcz, Herb Miller, Zinnia Miller, Jerry Miller, Carolyn Norman, and Vincent Romano.

My neighbors and friends from the Weehawken/North Hudson County area: John Amato, Linda Peterson Connors, Peter Ellebrach, Madeline and Richard Gross, George and Frances Hanks, Buddy Hanks, George Hanks Jr., Jeannie Kelly, Rose Lamiere, David Lamiere, Donna Lamiere, Leon Malattia, Lois Kelly Marazzi, Ron Mardenly, Laura McLearmon, Donald Moeller, Richard Olsen, Stanley Olsen, Kevin Olsen, Gary Olsen, Ronald Olsen, Frank and Dorothy Pelsang, Nancy Pelsang, Charlie Richardson, Bob and Annmarie

Riley, Augie and Rita Robbiani, George and Terry Robbiani, Janet Sofield, Dominic and Maryann Vitolo, Bruce Weil, and Steve Weil.

NY Institute for the Blind faculty and former students: Barbara Crane, Jolee Crane, Fred Dalton, Dr. Merle Frampton, James Francis, Lester Freel, Howard Green, Chuck Harther, Seth Hoard, Miss Kerney, James Meyers, Paul Mitchell, Sam Page, Sandra Penn, Pat Pepe, Miss Quinn, Harold Ray, Morton Romano, Miss Rosenberg, Bob Sullivan, Ed Taylor, Mary Alice Travis, Bob Whitstock, Myrna Witzkecz, and Sam Wolfe.

My former classmates and instructors at the Seeing Eye: Marjorie Dunn, Morris Frank, Fred Kreitzer, Peter Lang, Richard McStraw, Mrs. Pendleton, Marshall Seiber, Betty Sue Smith, Robert Stewart, and Morton Wagman.

Seton Hall University clergy: Rev. James Carey, Msgr. John Davis, Msgr. Thomas Fay, Msgr. Walter Jarvais, Rev. Edward Larkin, Msgr. McNulty, Rev. Rocky Provenzano, Rev. Phil Rotuno, Rev. Joseph Russell, Rev. Shea, and Msgr. Robert Sheeran.

Seton Hall faculty and Home Study readers: Ann Arlinghaus, Al Close, Claire Durasmo Copozzi, Mr. Flood, Martha Leet, and Marilyn Dundero Violone, and all the divinity students who helped me out.

My former classmates and buddies at Seton Hall: Claudio Assini, Barry Baum, John Bauman, Drew Bauman, Ed Bonner, Tony Capone, Richard DeFonce, George Franconero, Ed Gracken, Frank Kelly, Lou LaSalle, Gene Lynch, Bob Monahan, John Olsen, Louis Pagano, Mike Palowicz, Chuck Paolino, basketball coach Richie Regan, Jim Rhatigan, William Rhatigan, Mario Rosellini, Howard Rosenberg, baseball coach Mike Shepherd, Martin Smith, and Dick Vitale.

Former and current Seton Hall administrators: Matthew Borowick, Alan Delozier, President Gabriel Estaban, Joseph Guasconi, Heather Hurd, Jennifer Loysen, Greg Tobin, and Tom White.

My colleagues at Provident Mutual Life Insurance Company: Gladys Fetch, Morris Frank, Phil Gillis, Doug Johnson, Fred Kiefner, and Bill Lindemann.

My longtime Meadowview Hospital associates: Joe Barcelona, May Barcelona, John Buffano, Doreen Busacca, Terri Colligan, Mike Cusack, Don Daley, Evelyn Ellis, Carl Holzberg, Hilda Klapperstuck, Chief Arthur Mack, Roberto Muniz, Whitey Murphy, Dusty Murphy, and Al Stamboni.

Longtime friends: Richard and Maureen DeFonce, George and Arlene Franconero, John and Nancy Koneckny, George and Annette Mancini, Ron and Barbara Mardenly, Nick and Maryann Masters, Gene and Karen Mehl, and Skip and Bunny Willard.

Fellow Lions Club members: John Bacchia, Roger Barr, George Bassett, Herb and Kathy Bodensiek, Phyllis Boscio, Victor Braun, Melvyn Bray, Dennis and Rhea Brubaker, Jamie Brum, Jerry Caputo, Winster Ceballos, Dave and Florence Chandler, Rick Chittum, Lou Corsaro, Tim Courtney, Billy Blair Cunningham, Ralph DelPiano, Lenny and Dotty Dian, Bob and Marge Diehl, George and Barbara Dolan, Emery Duell, Louis Enthrop, Ed Fedush, Bob Frank, Jeff Gans, John Garbo, Ed Garrett, Tom and Claire Gartley, Bill Gaughan, Dave Gotha, Victor Graziano, Stanley Grossman, Vic Heineman, Jim Hynes, Elie Katz, Arthur Keyes, Marshall Klein, Al Knaub, Richard Kubik, Robert LaHullier, Charles Landesman, Jerry LaRosa, Gene Leperiore, George Lesnik, Joe and Helga Liccardo, Don and Rita MacAteer, Bob

May, Doug McClure, George Meglio, Chris Metcalf, Paul and Sandy Meyer, Bob and Pat Millea, Bob and Elspeth Moore, Jim Murphy, Jack and Denise Nagel, Jose Nieto, Fred and Wilma Nolting, Mary Devon O'Brien, Alberto Perez, Bernie and Dottie Pryor, Chris Reichert, Manny Reyes, Nat Rogoff, Mike Roman, Al Rottini, Phil Rottini, Bud Rottini, Carl Rubenacker, Al Ruffini, Paul Sarlo, Doug Schembs, Dick and Helen Schneider, Chris Snyder, Joe Solda, Dan Stenchever, Phil Stern, Bob Talamini, Tim Trossman, Ken Turtoro, and Bob Warsak.

Political friends and associates: Gov. Brendan Byrne, Maureen Corcoran, Gov. Richard Cody, Gov. Jon Corzine, Richard Cullen, Mayor Glen Cunningham, Congressman Dominick Daniels, Tom DeGeise, Ann Dudsak, John Dudsak, Mayor Frank Eggers, Freeholder Maurice Fitzgibbons, Mayor Steven Fulop, Councilman Bill Gaughan, Eileen Gaughan, Mayor Frank Hague, Bernie Hartnett, Mayor Jeremiah Healy, John Higgins, Gov. Richard Hughes, Gov. Thomas Kean, Democratic leader J. V. Kenny, Mayor Charles Krause, Bill LaRosa, Senator Frank Lautenberg, Steve Lipsky, Michael Luggiero, Nick Mastorelli, Mayor Jerry McCann, Senator Robert Menendez, Freeholder Bill O'Dea, Judge Tom Oliveri, Chief of Staff Regina O'Neill, Councilman Charles Pruscetta, Assemblyman David Russo, Mayor Brett Schundler, Judge Richard Simeone, State Senator Loretta Weinberg, Gov. Christie Todd Whitman, Willie Wolf, Judge John Yengo, and Jeannie Zampaglione.

Directors and staff of New York Yankees Media Relations: Marty Appel, Rick Cerrone, Jackie Farrell, Bob Fishel, Harvey Greene, Irv Kaze, Mickey Morabito, Ken Nigro, Arthur Richman, Joe Safety, David Szen, Larry Wahl, Jason Zillo, Dolores Hernandez, Kenny

Leandry, Justin Long, Michael Margolis, Lauren Moran, Connie Schwab, Alex Trochinowski, and Ben Tuliebitz.

The Steinbrenner family: George M. Steinbrenner III, Joan Steinbrenner, Hal Steinbrenner, Jennifer Steinbrenner Swindal, Steve Swindal, Jessica Steinbrenner Lopez, Felix Lopez, and Hank Steinbrenner.

New York Yankee executives and staff: Randy Levine, Lonn Trost, Brian Cashman, Clyde King, Gene Michael, Sonny Haight, Al Rosen, Gabe Paul, Debbie Tymon, David Bernstein, Michael Bonner, Theresa Buonomo, Gina Chindemi, Rob Cucuzza, Lou Cucuzza Sr., Lou Cucuzza Jr., Steve Donahue, Mary Durante, John Esposito, Eddie Fasthook, Samantha Giraud, Betsy Leesman, Chris Granazio, Annette Guardabascio, Rocky Halsey, Eddie Layton, Ann Mileo, Gene Monahan, Tony Morante, Debbie Nicolisi, Bob Sheppard, Frank Swain, Joe Violone, and Monica Yurman.

New York Mets executives and staff: Fred and Jeff Wilpon, Jay Horowitz, Shannon Forde, Ethan Wilson, Stella Fiore, Sandy Alderson, Frank Cashen, Jim Duquette, Al Harazin, Joe McIlvaine, and Omar Minaya.

Broadcasters and writers: Al Albert, Kenny Albert, Marv Albert, Steve Albert, Mel Allen, Joe Angel, Richie Ashburn, Red Barber, Jack Buck, Joe Buck, Harry Caray, Skip Caray, Joe Castiglione, Tom Cheek, Gary Cohen, Jerry Coleman, David Cone, Ron Darling, Bill Daughtry, Bob Delaney, Dick Enberg, John Flaherty, Ray Fosse, George Frazier, Joe Garagiola, Marty Glickman, John Gordon, Don Gould, Doug Gould, Curt Gowdy, George Grande, Wayne Hagin, Ken (Hawk) Harrelson, Ernie Harwell, Fran Healy, Keith Hernandez, Russ Hodges, Jerry Howarth, Rex Hudler, Jim Hunter,

Tommy Hutton, Jay Johnstone, Jim Kaat, Harry Kalas, Michael Kay, Gene Kelly, Ralph Kiner, Al Leiter, Josh Lewin, Ann Ligouri, Dick Lynch, Tom McCarthy, Tim McCarver, Frank Messer, Jon Miller, Rick Monday, Joe Morgan, Bobby Murcer, Bob Murphy, Richard Neer, Lindsey Nelson, Paul O'Neill, Bob Papa, Ed Randall, Phil Rizzuto, John Rooney, Howie Rose, Spencer Ross, Chris Russo, Byron Saam, Vin Scully, Mike Shannon, Lonn Simmons, Dave Sims, Chris Singleton, Ken Singleton, Charlie Steiner, John Sterling, Gary Thorne, Jeff Torborg, Al Trautwig, Bob Uecker, Pete Van Wieren, Suzyn Waldman, Chris Wheeler, Bill White, Bob Wolfe, Jim Woods, Maury Allen, Joe Auriemma, Andrew Baumgarten, Bruce Beck, Juan Benet, Joe Benigno, Dave Buscema, Pete Caldera, Dan Castellano, Duke Castiglone, Scott Clark, Ed Coleman, Jack Curry, Bill Daughtry, Joe Donnelly, Maurice DuBois, Charlie Einstein, Mark Feinsand, David Fenster, Mike Francesa, Bill Gallo, Dan Graziano, Jim Hague, John Harper, Jon Heyman, Kim Jones, Raquel Julich, Harry Jupiter, Howie Karpin, Tyler Kepner, Kevin Kernan, Bob Klapisch, Moss Klein, Arnie Leshin, Otis Livingston, Bob Lorenz, Matt Loughlin, Mike Lupica, Bill Madden, Steve Malzberg, Mike Mancuso, Rich Marazzi, Andrew Marchand, Sal Marchiano, Bill Mazer, Mike McCann, Bud Mishken, John Montone, Sweeney Murti, Hideo Nakamura, Ian O'Connor, Paul Post, Evan Roberts, Ken Rosenthal, Chris Russo, Art Rust Jr., Russ Salzberg, Dick Schaap, Jeremy Schaap, Dan Schlossberg, Bill Shannon, Joel Sherman, Claire Smith, Steve Somers, Bobby Trainor, George Vescey, Joey Wahler, Willie Weinbaum, Kevin Williams, Warner Wolf, Bob Wolfe, and Harvey Zucker.

Major League Baseball officials: John Blundell, Dr. Bobby Brown, Tony Clark, Leonard Coleman, Blake Cullen, Charles (Chub) Feeney, Katie Feeney, Donald Fehr, Bart Giamatti, Bowie Kuhn, Bob Laurie, Lee McPhail, Phyllis Merhige, Peter O'Malley, Bud Selig, Horace Stoneham, Faye Vincent, Michael Weiner, Bill White, and Bob Wirz.

National Baseball Hall of Fame President Jeff Idelson and Vice President of Communications Brad Horn.

Ed Lucas Foundation Gene Michael Golf Classic Committee members: Herb Bodensiek, Tom Bragen, Ray Bulin, Tim Courtney, Rich Cutter, Donna DelMauro, Joe DiDio, Ed Dunphy, Mary Dunphy, James Fiorentino, Eileen Fitzpatrick, Jack Grew, Michael Grew, Brian Hirschberg, Howie Horowitz, Joanne Ippolito, George Kolodinsky, Dan Leonardi, Frank Luca, Michael Mortorano, Jim Murphy, Charlie O'Neill, Regina O'Neill, Ronald Patane, John Pennisi, Giovanna Psolka, Gene Rear, Harold Reeves, Rick Reeves, Dan Replogle, Andy Richter, Tom Rushforth, Al Russo, Christopher Russo, David Russo, Lydia Russo, Matthew Russo, Rhoda Russo, Robert Russo, John Sasso, Diane Tagliabue, Diane Thomas, Vince Thomas, Cathy Werner, Jay Zaslower, and Harvey Zucker.

Special friends: Elliot and Lynn Abbott, Gracie Abbott, Liza Abbott, Danny Barrett, David Berkowitz, Yogi and Carmen Berra, Larry Berra, Lou Biancone, Jay Boyle, Ann Brindisi, the Staff at Brooklake Country Club, Larry Brown, Ken and Jennifer Browne, Jimmy Brozzetti, Ed Byrnes, Fred Cambria, Gary Cardiello, MD, Frank Cardiello, MD, Donald Cinnotti, MD, Shaun Clancy, Patsy Ann Connor, Kevin Connors, Pat and Mary Ann Conte, Dominic and Carmella Conte, Gerry Cooney, Gene Coppola, Mike Costa,

Ed Crouse, Al Cruz, Howard Danzig, Ken Dashow, Bill Daughtry, John and Theresa Dillon, Bob Dixon, Jim Donovan, Al Durrell, John Filone, Paul Finnazo, Greg Floyd, Steve Fortunato, Pete Francisco, Mary Gallagher, Lowell Ganz and Babaloo Mandel, Barbara and Lefty George, Bonnie George, Ron and Lynn Goltsch, Bob Greenhut, Richie Gutch, Joseph Hakim, Barry Halper, Randy Hamlette, Al Hamrah, Bruce Harper, Paul Holden, Steve Jezek, Tommy John, Steve Kalafer, Alan Kalter, Jeannie Kelly, Robert Klein, Chris Kotsopolous, Norma Kreitzer, Bob Lang, Lou LaSalle, Tommy Leach, Jerry Lioi, Lorna Mack, Paul Magda, Bob Mannetta, Mark Markowitz, Tommy Martin, Ryan Millea, Paul Mirabella, John Mooney, Ross Moschitto, Mike Murphy, Eamon Nally, Karl Nelson, Randy Neumann, Kevin O'Connor, Tom and Tracy O'Neill, Lucille Pennisi, Joe Pennisi, John Pennisi, Tom Pennisi, Paul and Elaine Piscitelli, Sue Ragas, Joe Ressler, Scott Ring, Cindy Rizzuto, Patty Rizzuto, Penny Rizzuto, Phil Rizzuto, Jr., Dennis Rizzuto, Lee Rizzuto, Sr., Lee Rizzuto, Jr., Mitchell Ross, Tom Sabellica, Chuck Sales, Patrick Sales, Al Santorini, Barbara Ann Reilly Schick, Stan Schick, John Setzer, Tommy Shine, Luke Stahl, Alice Steller, Steve Stone, Penny Taylor, Jim and Terri Wentz, Robert Willard, Tom Witt, Mark Yusko, Bill and Heidi Ziff, and Dominick Zurzulo.

Extra special thanks to: Diane and Vince Thomas for their help in compiling this list.

Major League Baseball Players: Hank Aaron, Jim Abbott, Tommie Agee, Neil Allen, Richie Allen, Felipe Alou, Jesus Alou, Matty Alou, Walter Alston. Joey Amalfitano, Sparky Anderson, Luis Aparacio, Luis Arroyo, Richie Ashburn, Wally Backman, Ed Bailey, Dusty Baker, Steve (Bye Bye) Balboni, Ernie Banks,

Willie Banks, Jesse Barfield, Hank Bauer, Don Baylor, Jim Beattie, Buddy Bell, David Bell, Gus Bell, Johnny Bench, Yogi Berra, Craig Biggio, Joe Black, Paul Blair, Johnny Blanchard, Ron Blomberg, Vida Blue, Bert Blyleven, Bruce Bochy, Wade Boggs, Barry Bonds, Bobby Bonds, Aaron Boone, Bob Boone, Bret Boone, Ken Boswell, Lou Boudreau, Jim Bouton, Larry Bowa, Clete Boyer, Ken Boyer, Ralph Branca, Craig Breslow, George Brett, Lou Brock, Scott Brosius, Jay Buhner, Lew Burdette, Tommy Byrne, Matt Cain, Fred Cambria, Roy Campanella, Robinson Cano, Jose Canseco, Rod Carew, Gary Carter, Orlando Cepeda, Rick Cerrone, Bob Cerv, Ron Cey, Joba Chamberlain, Chris Chambliss, Ed Charles, Jack Clark, Will Clark, Horace Clarke, Roger Clemens, Phil Coke, Jerry Coleman, Joe Collins, David Cone, Mark Connor,Billy Connors, Joe Cowley, Billy Cox, Bobby Cox, Frank Crosetti, Johnny Damon, Alvin Dark, Ron Darling, Jim Davenport, Chili Davis, Tommy Davis, Willie Davis, Andre Dawson, Dizzy Dean, Rick Dempsey, Bucky Dent, Bill Dickey, Dom DiMaggio, Joe DiMaggio, Larry Doby, Bobby Doerr, Al Downing, Brian Doyle, Don Drysdale, Dave Duncan, Shelley Duncan, Ryne Duren, Leo Durocher, Duffy Dyer, Dennis Eckersley, Carl Erskine, Darrell Evans, Dwight Evans, Bob Feller, Tony Ferrara, Mark Fidrych, Cecil Fielder, Ed Figueroa, Rollie Fingers, Jack Fisher, Carlton Fisk, Curt Flood, Whitey Ford, Frankie Frisch, Carl Furillo, Oscar Gamble, Brett Gardner, Steve Garvey, Chad Gaudin, Gary Gentry, Bob Gerin, Jason Giambi, Bob Gibson, Kirk Gibson, Joe Girardi, Tom Glavine, Lefty Gomez, Doc Gooden, Goose Gossage, Curtis Granderson, Jim "Mudcat" Grant, Dallas Green, Ken Griffey

Sr., Ken Griffey Jr., Ron Guidry, Tony Gwynn, Steve Hamilton, Bud Harrelson, Fran Healy, Ed Hearn, Jim Hearn, Todd Helton, Rickey Henderson, Tommy Henrich. Gene Hermanski, Keith Hernandez, Orlando (El Duque) Hernandez, Tommy Herr, Orel Hersheiser, Whitey Herzog, Chuck Hiller, Gil Hodges, Rogers Hornsby, Ralph Houk, Elston Howard, Frank Howard, Steve Howe, Dick Howser, Phil Hughes, Randy Hundley, Todd Hundley, Ron Hunt, Catfish Hunter, Torii Hunter, Clint Hurdle, Fred Hutchinson, Raul Ibanez, Monte Irvin, Al Jackson, Reggie Jackson, Larry Jansen, Ferguson Jenkins, Derek Jeter, Davey Johnson, Howard Johnson, Randy Johnson, Chipper Jones, David Justice, Al Kaline, Johnny Keane, Roberto Kelley, Pat Kelly, Jimmy Key, Harmon Killebrew, Dave Kingman, Jerry Koosman, Sandy Koufax, Ed Kranepool, John Kruk, Tony Kubek, Hobie Landrith, Hal Lanier, Max Lanier, Dave Lapoint, Adam LaRoche, Dave LaRoche, Don Larsen, Tony LaRussa, Tommy Lasorda, Al Leiter, Mark Leiter, Bob Lemon, Jim Leyritz, Tim Lincecum, Phil Linz, Graeme Lloyd, Whitey Lockman, Dale Long, Kevin Long, Ed Lopat, Al Lopez, Hector Lopez, Sparky Lyle, Gil MacDougald, Greg Maddux, Dave Magadan, Sal Maglie, Bobby Malkmus, Mickey Mantle, Charlie Manuel, Juan Marichal, Roger Maris, Billy Martin, Pedro Martinez, Tino Martinez, Jon Matlack, Hideki Matsui, Eddie Matthews, Don Mattingly, Rudy May, Willie Mays, Bill Mazeroski, Tim McCarver, Mike McCormick, Willie McCovey, Lindy McDaniel, Von McDaniel, Roger McDowell, Sam McDowell, Tug McGraw, Mark McGwire, Dave McNally, Bobby Meacham, Doug Melvin, Ramiro Mendoza,

Stump Merrill, Hensley (Bam Bam) Meulens, Gene Michael, Felix Millan, Paul Mirabella, Johnny Mize, Bengie Molina, Jose Molina, Yadier Molina, Paul Molitor, John (The Count) Montefusco, Rich Monteleone, Wally Moon, Joe Morgan, Jack Morris, Ross Moschitto, Don Mueller, Thurman Munson, Bobby Murcer, Dale Murphy, Stan Musial, Mike Mussina, Jeff Nelson, Graig Nettles, Don Newcomb, Phil Niekro, Joe Niekro, Matt Noakes, Tony Oliva, Buck O'Neil, Jose Oquendo, Jesse Orosco, David Ortiz, Joe Page, Mike Pagliarulo, Jim Palmer, Mel Parnell, Dustin Pedroia, Tony Pena, Tony Perez, Gaylord Perry, Jim Perry, Johnny Pesky, Fritz Peterson, Andy Pettitte, Jimmy Piersall, Joe Pignatano, Lou Piniella, Johnny Podres, Jorge Posada, Boog Powell, Kirby Puckett, Tim Raines, Manny Ramirez, Willie Randolph, Vic Raschi, Dennis Rasmussen, Jeff Reardon, Pee Wee Reese, Hal Reniff, Jose Reyes, Allie Reynolds, Bobby Richardson, Dave Righetti, Bill Rigney, Jose Rijo, Cal Ripken, Jr., Mariano Rivera, Mickey Rivers, Robin Roberts, David Robertson, Bill Robinson, Brooks Robinson, Frank Robinson, Jackie Robinson, Ivan "Pudge" Rodriguez, Pete Rose, John Roseboro, Al Rosen, Nolan Ryan, CC Sabathia, Ray Sadecki, Johnny Sain, Billy Sample, Ryne Sandberg, Dion Sanders, Pablo Sandoval, Al Santorini, Mike Schmidt, Red Schoendienst, Tom Seaver, Art Shamsky, Bobby Shantz, Gary Sheffield, Buck Showalter, Charlie Silvera, Chris Singleton, Ken Singleton, Bill (Moose) Skowron, Enos Slaughter, Aaron Small, Ozzie Smith, John Smoltz, Duke Snider, Luis Sojo, Sammy Sosa, Warren Spahn, Shane Spencer, Chris Spier, Andy Stankiewicz, Fred Stanley, Mike Stanley,

Mike Stanton, Willie Stargell, Rusty Staub, Casey Stengel, Mel Stottlemyre, Darryl Strawberry, Tom Sturdivant, Don Sutton, Nick Swisher, Ron Swoboda, Mark Teixeira, Frank Tepedino, Ralph Terry, Tim Teufel, Frank Thomas, Jim Thome, Bobby Thomson, Luis Tiant, Jeff Torborg, Mike Torrez, Tom Tresh, Bob Turley, Jim Turner, Bobby Valentine, Johnny VanderMeer, Randy Velarde, Adam Wainwright, Harry (The Hat) Walker, Rube Walker, Earl Weaver, David Wells, Wes Westrum, Bill White, Roy White, Bob Wickman, Hoyt Wilhelm, Bernie Williams, Billy Williams, Dick Williams, Gerald Williams, Matt Williams, Ted Williams, Mookie Wilson, Dave Winfield, Gene Woodling, David Wright, Butch Wynegar, Carl Yastrzemski, Robin Yount, Sal Yvars, and Don Zimmer.

To all the other ballplayers, coaches, managers, family, friends, and supporters not mentioned in this list, I thank you all. God has truly blessed my life in abundance with your presence. I am forever grateful to Him for it.

—ED LUCAS